Royalty Restored
or, London under Charles II.

J. Fitzgerald Molloy

Contents

PREFACE TO FIRST EDITION. 7
CHAPTER I. 11
CHAPTER II. 24
CHAPTER III. 39
CHAPTER IV. 49
CHAPTER V. 60
CHAPTER VI. 73
CHAPTER VII. 89
CHAPTER VIII. 102
CHAPTER IX. 112
CHAPTER X. 119
CHAPTER XI. 139
CHAPTER XII. 150
CHAPTER XIII. 163
CHAPTER XIV. 172
CHAPTER XV. 185
CHAPTER XVI. 196
CHAPTER XVII. 209
CHAPTER XVIII. 224
CHAPTER XIX. 236
CHAPTER XX. 251
CHAPTER XXI. 266
CHAPTER XXII. 284

ROYALTY RESTORED OR, LONDON UNDER CHARLES II.

BY

J. Fitzgerald Molloy

TO THOMAS HARDY, ESQ.

DEAR MR. HARDY,

In common with all readers of the English language, I owe you a debt of gratitude, the which I rejoice to acknowledge, even in so poor a manner as by dedicating this work to you.

Believe me,
Faithfully yours always,

                        J. FITZGERALD MOLLOY.

PREFACE TO FIRST EDITION.

No social history of the court of Charles II. has heretofore been written. The Grammont Memoirs, devoid of date and detail, and addressed "to those who read only for amusement," present but brief imperfect sketches of the wits and beauties who thronged the court of the merry monarch whilst the brilliant Frenchman sojourned in England. Pepys, during the first nine years of the Restoration, narrates such gossip as reached him regarding Whitehall and the practices that obtained there. Evelyn records some trifling actions of the king and his courtiers, with a view of pointing a moral, rather than from a desire of adorning a tale.

To supply this want in our literature, I have endeavoured to present a picture of the domestic life of a king, whose name recalls pages of the brightest romance and strangest gallantry in our chronicles. To this I have added a study of London during his reign, taken as far as possible from rare, and invariably from authentic sources. It will readily be seen this work, embracing such subjects, could alone have resulted from careful study and untiring consultation of diaries, records, memoirs, letters, pamphlets, tracts, and papers left by contemporaries familiar with the court and capital. The accomplishment of such a task necessitated an expenditure of time, and devotion to labour, such as in these fretful and impatient days is seldom bestowed on work.

As in previous volumes I have writ no fact is set down without authority, so likewise the same rule is pursued in these; and for such as desire to test the accuracy thereof, or follow at further length statements necessarily abbreviated, a list is appended of the principal literature consulted. And inasmuch as I have found pleasure in this work, so may my gentle readers derive profit therefrom; and as I have laboured, so may they enjoy. Expressing which fair wishes, and moreover commending myself unto their love and service, I humbly take my leave.

J. FITZGERALD MOLLOY.

LIST OF THE PRINCIPAL BOOKS, PAMPHLETS, TRACTS, AND NEWSPAPERS, CONSULTED IN WRITING THIS VOLUME.

"Elenchus Motuum Nuperorum." Heath's "Flagellum; or, the Life and Death of Oliver Cromwell." Banks' "Life of Cromwell." "Review of the Political Life of Cromwell." "A Modest Vindication of Oliver Cromwell." "The Machivilian Cromwellist." Kimber's "Life of Cromwell." "The World Mistaken in Oliver Cromwell"(1668). "A Letter of Comfort to Richard Cromwell." "Letters from Fairfax to Cromwell." "Cromwell's Letters and Speeches." "A Collection of Several Passages concerning Cromwell in his Sickness." "The Protector's Declaration against the Royal Family of the Stuarts." "Memoirs of Cromwell and his Children, supposed to be written by himself." "Narrative of the Proceedings of the English Army in Scotland." "An Account of the Last Houres of the late renowned Oliver, Lord Protector" (1659). "Sedition Scourged." Heath's "Chronicles of the late Intestine War." Welwood's "Memoirs of Transactions in England." "Memoirs of Edmund Ludlow, M.P., in the year 1640." Forster's "Statesmen of the Commonwealth." "Killing No Murther."

Thurloe's "State Papers." Lord Clarendon's "State Papers." Tatham's "Aqua Triumphalis." "The Public Intelligencer." "Mercurius Politicus." "The Parliamentary Intelligencer." Lyon's "Personal History of Charles II." "The Boscobel Tracts, relating to the Escape of Charles II." "An Exact Narrative of his Majesty's Escape from Worcester." Several Passages relating to the "Declared King of Scots both by Sea and Land." "Charles II.'s Declaration to his Loving Subjects in the Kingdom of England." "England's Joy; or, a Relation of the most Remarkable Passages from his Majesty's Arrival at Dover to his Entrance at Whitehall." "Copies of Two Papers written by the King." "His Majesty's Gracious Message to General Monk." "King Charles, His Starre." "A Speech spoken by a Blew-Coat of Christ's Hospital to his Sacred Majesty." "Monarchy Revived." "The History of Charles II., by a Person of Quality." Lady Fanshawe's "Memoirs." "The Character of Charles II., written by an Impartial Hand and exposed to Public View." "Sports and Pastimes of the English People." "A History of Domestic Manners and Sentiments in England." Wright's "Homes of Other Days." Idalcomb's "Anecdotes of Manners and Customs of London." Pepys' "Diary." Evelyn's "Diary." Grammont's "Memoirs." Lord Romney's "Diary of the Times of Charles II." "The Life and Adventures of Colonel Blood." "Diary of Dr. Edward Lake, Court Chaplain." Bishop Burnet's "History of His Own Times." Oldmixon's "Court Tales." Madame Dunois' "Memoirs of the English Court." Heath's "Glories and Triumphs of Charles II." "Continuation of the Life of Edward, Earl of Clarendon." "Original Correspondence of Lord Clarendon." "The Memoirs of Sir John Reresby." Lister's "Life of Clarendon. Brain Fairfax's "Memoirs of the Duke of Buckingham." "Letters of Philip, Second Earl of Chesterfield." Aubrey's "Memoirs." "The Life of Mr. Anthony a Wood, written by Himself." Elias Ashmole's "Memoirs of his Life." Luttrell's "Diary." "The Althorp Memoirs" (privately printed). Lord Broghill's "Memoirs." "Memoir of Barbara, Duchess of Cleveland" (privately printed). Aubrey's "Lives of Eminent Men." Count Magalotti's "Travels in England." "The Secret History of Whitehall: consisting of Secret Memoirs which have hitherto lain conceal'd as not being discoverable by any other hand." "Athenae Oxonienses." Lord Rochester's Works. Brown's "Miscellanea Aulica." The Works of Andrew Marvell. "State Tracts, relating to the Government from the year 1660 to 1689." "Antiquities of the Crown and State of Old England." "Narrative of the Families exposed to the Great Plague of London." "Loimologia; or, an Historical Account of the Plague in

1665." "A Collection of very Valuable and Scarce Pieces relating to the Last Plague in 1665." "London's Dreadful Visitation." "Letter of Dr, Hedges to a Person of Quality." "God's Terrible Voice in the City: a Narrative of the late Dreadful Judgments by Plague and Fire." "Pestis; a Collection of Scarce Papers relating to the Plague." "An Account of the Fire of London, published by authority." Lord Clarendon's "Account of the Great Fire." "A Voyage into England, containing many things relating to the State of Learning, Religion, and other Curiosities of that Kingdom," by Mons. Sorbiere. Carte's "Life of James, Duke of Ormond." Carte's "History of England." Lord Somers' "Collection of Scarce and Valuable Tracts." "Memoirs of the Duchess of Mazarine." "Secret History of the Duchess of Portsmouth." St. Evremond's "Memoirs." "Curialia; or, an Historical Account of some Branches of the Royal Household." "Parliamentary History." Oldmixon's "History of the Stuarts." Ellis's "Original Letters." Charles James Fox's "History of James II." Sir George L'Estrange's "Brief History of the Times." Lord Romney's "Diary of the Times of Charles II." Clarke's "Life of James II." "Vindication of the English Catholics." "The Tryals, Conviction and Sentence of Titus Oates." "A Modest Vindication of Oates." "Tracts on the Popish Plot." Macpherson's "Original Papers." A. Marvell's "Account of Popery." "An Exact Discovery of the Mystery of Iniquity as Practised among the Jesuits." Smith's "Streets of London." "London Cries." Seymour's "Survey of the Cities of London and Westminster." Stow's "Survey of London and Westminster." "Angliae Metropolis." Dr. Laune's "Present State of London, 1681." Sir Roger North's "Examn." "The Character of a Coffee House." Stow's "Chronicles of Fashion." Fairholt's "Costume in England." "A Just and Seasonable Reprehension of Naked Breasts and Shoulders." Sir William Petty's "Observations of the City of London." John Ogilvy's "London Surveyed." R. Burton's "Historical Remarks." Dr. Birch's "History of the Royal Society of London." "A Century of Inventions." Wild's "History of the Royal Society." "The Philosophical Transactions of the Royal Society." Richardson's "Life of Milton." Philip's "Life of Milton." Johnson's "Lives of the Poets." Aubrey's "Collections for the Life of Milton." Langbaine's "Lives and Characters of the English Dramatic Poets." "Some Remarkable Passages in the Life of Mr. Wycherley." "Some Account of what Occurred at the King's Death," by Richard Huddlestone, O.S.B. "A True Narrative of the late King's Death."

CHAPTER I.

Cromwell is sick unto death.--Fears and suspicions.--Killing no Murder.--A memorable storm.--The end of all.--Richard Cromwell made Protector.--He refuses to shed blood.--Disturbance and dissatisfaction.--Downfall of Richard.--Charles Stuart proclaimed king.--Rejoicement of the nation.--The king comes into his own.--Entry into London.--Public joy and satisfaction.

On the 30th of January, 1649, Charles I. was beheaded. In the last days of August in the year of grace 1658, Oliver Cromwell lay sick unto death at the Palace of Whitehall. On the 27th day of June in the previous year, he had, in the Presence of the Judges of the land, the Lord Mayor and Aldermen of the City, and Members of Parliament assembled at Westminster Hall, seated himself on the coronation chair of the Stuarts, assumed the title of Lord Protector, donned a robe of violet velvet, girt his loins with a sword of state, and grasped the sceptre, symbolic of kingly power. From that hour distrust beset his days, his nights were fraught with fear. All his keen and subtle foresight, his strong and restless energies, had since then been exerted in suppressing plots against his power, and detecting schemes against his life, concocted by the Republicans whose liberty he had betrayed, and by the Royalists whose king he had beheaded.

Soon after he had assumed the title of Lord High Protector, a most daring pamphlet, openly advocating his assassination, was circulated in vast numbers throughout the kingdom. It was entitled "Killing no Murder," and was dedicated in language outrageously bold to His Highness Oliver Cromwell. "To your Highness justly belongs the honour of dying for the people," it stated, "and it cannot but be an unspeakable consolation to you, in the last moments of your life, to consider with how much benefit to the world you are likely to leave it. It is then only, my lord, the titles you now usurp will be truly yours; you will then be, indeed, the deliverer of your country, and free it from a bondage little inferior to that from which Moses delivered his, you will then be that true reformer which you would now be thought; religion shall then be restored, liberty asserted, and Parliaments have those privileges they have sought for. All this we hope from your Highness's happy expiration. To hasten this great good is the chief end of my writing this paper; and if it have the effects I hope it will, your Highness will quickly be out of the reach of men's malice, and your enemies will only be able to wound you in your memory, which strokes you will not feel."

The possession of life becomes dearest when its forfeiture is threatened, and therefore Cromwell took all possible means to guard against treachery--the only foe he feared, and feared exceedingly. "His sleeps were disturbed with the apprehensions of those dangers the day presented unto him in the approaches of any strange face, whose motion he would most fixedly attend," writes James Heath, gentleman, in his "Chronicles," published in 1675. "Above all, he very carefully observed such whose mind or aspect were featured with any chearful and debonair lineaments; for such he boded were they that would despatch him; to that purpose he always went secretly armed, both offensive and defensive; and never stirred without a great guard. In his usual journey between Whitehall and Hampton Court, by several roads, he drove full speed in the summer time, making such a dust with his lifeguard, part before and part behinde, at a convenient distance, for fear of choking him with it, that one could hardly see for a quarter of an hour together, and always came in some private way or other." The same authority, in his "Life of Cromwell," states of him, "It was his constant custom to shift and change his lodging, to which he passed through twenty several locks, and out of which he had four or five ways to avoid pursuit." Welwood, in his "Memoirs," adds the Protector wore a coat of mail beneath his dress, and carried a poniard under his cloak.

Nor was this all. According to the "Chronicle of the late Intestine War," Cromwell "would sometimes pretend to be merry, and invite persons, of whom he had some suspicion, to his cups, and then drill out of their open hearts such secrets as he wisht for. He had freaks also to divert the vexations of his misgiving thoughts, calling on by the beat of drum his footguards, like a kennel of hounds to snatch away the scraps and reliques of his table. He said every man's hand was against him, and that he ran daily into further perplexities, out of which it was impossible to extricate, or secure himself therein, without running into further danger; so that he began to alter much in the tenour of his former converse, and to run and transform into the manners of the ancient tyrants, thinking to please and mitigate his own tortures with the sufferings of others."

But now the fate his vigilance had hitherto combated at last overtook him in a manner impossible to evade. He was attacked by divers infirmities, but for some time made no outward sign of his suffering, until one day five physicians came and waited on him, as Dr. George Bate states in his ELENCHUS MOTUUM NUPERORUM. And one of them, feeling his pulse, declared his Highness suffered from an intermittent fever; hearing which "he looked pale, fell into a cold sweat, almost fainted away, and orders himself to be carried to bed." His fright, however, was but momentary. He was resolved to live. He had succeeded in raising himself to a position of vast power, but had failed in attaining the great object of his ambition--the crowned sovereignty of the nation he had stirred to its centre, and conquered to its furthest limits. Brought face to face with death, his indomitable will, which had shaped untoward circumstances to his accord with a force like unto fate itself, now determined to conquer his shadowy enemy which alone intercepted his path to the throne. Therefore as he lay in bed he said to those around him with that sanctity of speech which had cloaked his cruellest deeds and dissembled his most ambitious designs, "I would be willing to live to be further serviceable to God and his people."

As desires of waking hours are answered in sleep, so in response to his nervous craving for life he had delusive assurances of health through the special bounty of Providence. He was therefore presently able to announce he "had very great discoveries of the Lord to him in his sickness, and hath some certainty of being restored;" as Fleetwood, his son-in-law, wrote on the 24th of August in this same year.

Accordingly, when one of the physicians came to him next morning, the High Protector said, "Why do you look sad?" To which the man of lore replied evasively, "So it becomes anyone who had the weighty care of his life and health upon him." Then Cromwell to this purpose spoke: "You think I shall die; I tell you I shall not die this bout; I am sure on't. Don't think I am mad. I speak the words of truth upon surer grounds than Galen or your Hippocrates furnish you with. God Almighty himself hath given that answer, not to my prayers alone, but also to the prayers of those who entertain a stricter commerce and greater intimacy with him. Ye may have skill in the nature of things, yet nature can do more than all physicians put together, and God is far above nature." The doctor besought him to rest, and left the room. Outside he met one of his colleagues, to whom he gave it as his opinion their patient had grown light-headed, and he repeated the words which Cromwell had spoken. "Then," said his brother-physician, "you are certainly a stranger in this house; don't you know what was done last night? The chaplain and all their friends being dispersed into several parts of the palace have prayed to God for his health, and they all heard the voice of God saying, 'He will recover,' and so they are all certain of it."

"Never, indeed, was there a greater stock of prayers going on for any man," as Thurlow, his secretary, writes. So sure were those around him that Providence must hearken to and grant the fulfilment of such desires as they thought well to express, that, as Thomas Goodwin, one of Cromwell's chaplains, said, "We asked not for the Protector's life, for we were assured He had too great things for this man to do, to remove him yet; but we prayed for his speedy recovery, because his life and presence were so necessary to divers things then of great moment to be despatched." When this Puritanical fanatic was presently disappointed, Bishop Burnet narrates "he had the impudence to say to God, 'Thou hast deceived us.'"

Meanwhile the Protector lay writhing in pain and terror. His mind was sorely troubled at remembrance of the last words spoken by his daughter Elizabeth, who had threatened judgments upon him because of his refusal to save the King; whilst his body was grievously racked with a tertian fever, and a foul humour which, beginning in his foot, worked its way steadily to his heart. Moreover, some insight regarding his future seemed given to him in his last days, for he appeared, as Ludlow, his contemporary, states, "above all concerned for the reproaches he saw men would cast upon his name, in tramping upon his ashes when dead."

On the 30th of August his danger became evident even to himself, and all hope of life left him. For hours after the certain approach of death became undeniably certain, he remained quiet and speechless, seemingly heedless of the exhortation and prayers of his chaplains, till suddenly turning to one of them, he whispered,

"Tell me, is it possible to fall from grace?" The preacher had a soothing reply ready: "It is not," he answered. "Then," exclaimed this unhappy man, whose soul was red with the blood of thousands of his countrymen, "I am safe, for I know I was once in grace." Anon he cries out, whilst tossing wildly on his bed, "Lord, although I am a miserable and a wretched creature, I am in covenant with Thee through grace, and I may and will come to Thee for Thy people. Pardon such as desire to trample upon the dust of a poor worm. And give us a good night if it be Thy pleasure. Amen."

It was now the 2nd of September. As the evening of that day approached he fell into a stupor, and those who watched him thought the end had come.

Within the darkened chamber in Whitehall all was silence and gloom; without all was tumult and fear. Before the gates of the palace a turbulent crowd of soldiers and citizens had gathered in impatient anxiety. Those he had raised to power, those whose fortunes depended on his life, were steeped in gloom; those whose principles he had outraged by his usurpation, those whose position he had crushed by his sway, rejoiced at heart. Not only the capital, but the whole nation, was divided into factions which one strong hand alone had been able to control; and terror, begotten by dire remembrances of civil war and bloodshed, abode with all lovers of peace.

As evening closed in, the elements appeared in unison with the distracted condition of the kingdom. Dark clouds, seeming of ominous import to men's minds, gathered in the heavens, to be presently torn asunder and hurried in wild flight by tempestuous winds across the troubled sky. As night deepened, the gale steadily increased, until it raged in boundless fury above the whole island and the seas that rolled around its shores. In town houses rocked on their foundations, turrets and steeples were flung from their places; in the country great trees were uprooted, corn-stacks levelled to the ground, and winter fruits destroyed; whilst at sea ships sank to rise no more. This memorable storm lasted all night, and continued until three o'clock next afternoon, when Cromwell expired.

His body was immediately embalmed, but was of necessity interred in great haste. Westminster Abbey, the last home of kings and princes, was selected as the fittest resting-place for the regicide. Though it was impossible to honour his remains by stately ceremonials, his followers were not content to let the occasion of his death pass with-out commemoration. They therefore had a waxen image of him made, which they resolved to surround with all the pomp and circumstances of royalty. For this purpose they carried it to Somerset House--one of the late King's palaces--and placed it on a couch of crimson velvet beneath a canopy of state. Upon its shoulders they hung a purple mantle, in its right hand they placed a golden sceptre, and by its side they laid an imperial crown, probably the same which, according to Welwood, the Protector had secretly caused to be made and conveyed to Whitehall with a view to his coronation. The walls and ceiling of the room in which the effigy lay were covered by sable velvet; the passages leading to it crowded with soldiery. After a few weeks the town grew tired of this sight, when the waxen image was taken to another apartment, hung with rich velvets and golden tissue, and otherwise adorned to symbolize heaven, when it was placed upon a throne, clad "in a shirt of fine Holland lace, doublet and breeches of Spanish fashion with great skirts, silk stockings, shoe-strings and gaiters suitable, and black Spanish leather shoes." Over this attire was flung a cloak of purple velvet, and on his head was placed a crown with many precious stones. The room was then lit, as Ludlow narrates, "by four or five hundred candles set in flat shining candlesticks, so placed round near the roof that the light they gave seemed like the rays of the sun, by all which he was represented to be now in a state of glory." Lest, indeed, there should be any doubt as to the place where his soul abode, Sterry, the Puritan preacher, imparted the information to all, that the Protector "now sat with Christ at the right hand of the Father."

But this pomp and state in no may overawed the people, who, by pelting with mire Cromwell's escutcheon placed above the great gate of Somerset House gave evidence of the contempt in which they held his memory. After a lapse of over two months from the day of his death, the effigy was carried to Westminster Abbey with more than regal ceremony, the expenses of his lying-in-state and of his funeral procession amounting, as stated by Walker and Noble, to upwards of L29,000. "It was the joyfullest funeral I ever saw," writes Evelyn, "for there were none that cried but dogs, which the soldiers hooted away with a barbarous noise, drinking and taking tobacco as they went."

A little while before his death Cromwell had named his eldest surviving son, Richard, as his successor, and he was accordingly declared Protector, with the apparent consent of the council, soldiers, and citizens. Nor did the declaration cause any excitement, "There is not a dog who wags his tongue, so profound is the calm which we are in," writes Thurlow to Oliver's second son, Henry, then Lord Lieutenant of Ireland. But if the nation in its dejection made no signs of resistance, neither did it give any indications of satisfaction, and Richard was proclaimed "with as few expressions of joy as had ever been observed on a like occasion." For a brief while a stupor seemed to lull the factious party spirit which was shortly to plunge the country into fresh difficulties. The Cromwellians and Republicans foresaw resistless strife, and the Royalists quietly and hopefully abided results.

Nor had they long to wait. In the new Parliament assembled in January, 1659, the Republicans showed themselves numerous and bold beyond measure, and hesitated to recognise Richard Cromwell as successor to the Protectorate. However, on the 14th of the following month the Cromwellians gained the upper hand, when Richard was confirmed in his title of "Lord Protector, and First Magistrate of England, Scotland, and Ireland, with all the territories depending thereon." Further discussion quickly followed. "One party thinks the Protectorate cannot last; the other that the Republican cannot raise itself again; the indifferent hope that both will be right. It is easy to foretell the upshot," writes Hyde. The disunion spread rapidly and widely; not only was the Parliament divided against itself, but so likewise was the army; and the new Protector had neither the courage nor the ability to put down strife with a strong hand. Richard Cromwell was a man of peaceful disposition, gentle manners and unambitious mind, whom fate had forced into a position for which he was in no way fitted. By one of those strange contradictions which nature sometimes produces, he differed in all things from his father; for not only was he pleasure-loving, joyous, and humane, but he was, moreover, a Royalist at heart, and continued in friendship with the Cavaliers up to the period of his proclamation as Protector. It has been stated that, falling on his knees, he entreated his father to spare the life of Charles I.; it is certain he remained inactive whilst the civil wars devastated the land; and there is evidence to show that, during the seven months and twenty-eight days of his Protectorship, he shrank from the perpetration of cruelty and crime. Accordingly, when those who had at first supported his authority eventually conspired against him, he refrained from using his power to crush them. At this his friends were wrath. "It is time to look about you," said Lord Howard, speaking with the bluntness of a friend. "Empire and command are not now the question. Your person, your life are in peril. You are the son of Cromwell;

show yourself worthy to be his son. This business requires a bold stroke, and must be supported by a good head. Do not suffer yourself to be daunted. I will rid you of your enemies: do you stand by me, and only back my zeal for your honour with your name; my head shall answer for the consequences."

Colonel Ingoldsby seconded the advice Lord Howard gave, but Richard Cromwell hearkened to neither. "I have never done anybody any harm, and never will," said he, "will not have a drop of blood spilt for the preservation of my greatness, which is a burden to me." At this Lord Howard was indignant. "Do you think," he asked, "this moderation of yours will repair the wrong your family has committed by its elevation? Everybody knows that by violence your father procured the death of the late king, and kept his sons in banishment: mercy in the present state of affairs is unreasonable. Lay aside this pussillanimity; every moment is precious; your enemies spend the time in acting which we waste in consulting." "Talk no more of it," answered the Protector. "I am thankful for your friendship, but violent counsels suit not with me."

The climax was at hand; his fall was but a question of time. "A wonderfull and suddaine change in ye face of ye publiq," writes Evelyn, on the 25th of April, 1659. "Ye new Protector Richard slighted; several pretenders and parties strove for the Government; all anarchy and confusion. Lord have mercy on us!"

Before the month of May had expired, the House of Commons commissioned two of its members to bid Richard Cromwell leave the palace of Whitehall, and obtain his signature to a deed wherein he acknowledged complete submission to Parliament. His brief inglorious reign was therefore at an end. "As with other men," he wrote to the House of Commons, "I expect protection from the present Government: I do hold myself obliged to demean myself with all the peaceableness under it, and to procure, to the utmost of my power, that all in whom I have any interest to do the same." He retired into Hampshire, where he dwelt as a private gentleman. His brother Henry resigned his position as Lord Lieutenant of Ireland and settled in Cambridgeshire. From this time the name of Cromwell was no longer a power in the land.

During two years subsequent to the death of Oliver the government of England underwent various changes, and the kingdom suffered many disorders; until, being heartily sick of anarchy, the people desired a king might once more reign over them accordingly, they turned their eyes towards the son of him whom "the boldest villany that ever any nation saw" had sent to the block. And the time being ripe, Charles Stuart, then an exile in Breda, despatched Sir John Grenville with royal letters to both Houses of Parliament, likewise to the Lord Mayor of London and members of the Common Council, to Monk, commander of the forces, and Montagu, admiral of the fleet. These letters were received with so universal a joy and applause, that Parliament forthwith ordained Charles Stuart should be proclaimed "the most potent, mighty, and undoubted King of England, Scotland and Ireland." Moreover, both Houses agreed that an honourable body of Commissioners, all men of great quality and birth, should be sent to the king with letters, humbly begging his majesty would be pleased to hasten his long-desired return into England. And because they knew full well the royal exchequer was empty, Parliament ordered these noble gentlemen to carry with them a present of fifty thousand pieces of gold to the king, together with ten thousand to his brother of York, and five thousand to his brother of Gloucester. Nor was the City of London backwards in sending expressions of loyalty and tokens of homage and devotion; to evince which twenty valiant men and worthy citizens were despatched with messages of goodwill towards him, and presents in gold to the amount of twelve thousand pounds.

And presently Admiral Montagu arriving with his fleet upon the coast of Holland, awaited his majesty near Scheveling; and all things being in readiness the king with his royal brothers and a most noble train set sail for England.

It came to pass that on the 25th day of May, 1660, a vast concourse of nobility, gentry, and citizens had assembled at Dover to meet and greet their sovereign king, Charles II., on his landing. On the fair morning of that day a sound of cannon thundering from the castle announced that the fleet, consisting of "near forty sail of great men-of-war," which conveyed his majesty to his own, was in sight; whereon an innumerable crowd betook its joyful way to the shore. The sun was most gloriously bright, the sky cloudless, the sea calm. Far out upon the blue horizon white-winged ships could be clearly discerned. By three o'clock in the afternoon they had reached the harbour, when the king, embarking in a galley most richly adorned, was rowed to shore. Then cannon roared once more from the castle, and were answered from the beach; bells rang from church towers, and a mighty shout went up from the hearts of the people.

In the midst of these rejoicings Charles II. landed, and the gallant General Monk, who had been mainly instrumental in bringing his royal master to the throne without loss of blood, now fell upon his knees to greet his majesty. The king raised the general from the ground, embraced and kissed him. Then the nobility hastened to pay their duty likewise, and the Mayor and Aldermen of Dover presented him with a most loyal address. And presently, with the roar of cannon, the clangour of bells, the sound of music, and the shouts of a great multitude ringing in his ears, the king advanced on his way towards Canterbury. At the gates of this ancient city he was met by the mayor and aldermen, and was presented by them with a golden tankard, Here he spent the following day, which being Sunday, he went with a great train to the cathedral, where service according to the Church of England, long disused by the Puritans, was restored, to the satisfaction of many.

Setting out from Canterbury on Monday, the 29th of May--which was, moreover, the anniversary of his birth--he journeyed to Blackheath, where he reviewed the forces drawn up with great pomp and military splendour to greet him, and bestowed many gracious expressions on them. Then, having received assurances of their loyal homage through their commander, Colonel Knight, he turned towards London town. And the nearer he approached, the more dense became crowds thronging to meet him; the fields on either side the long white road being filled with persons of all conditions, who cheered him lustily. As he passed they flung leaves of trees and sweet May flowers beneath his horse's feet, and waved green boughs on high, And when he came to St. George's Fields, there was my lord mayor in his robes of new velvet, wearing his collar of wrought gold, and attended by his aldermen in brave apparel likewise. Going down on his knees my lord mayor presented the king with the city sword, which his majesty with some happy expressions of confidence gave back into his good keeping, having first struck him with it upon the shoulder and bade him rise up Sir Thomas Allen. Whereon that worthy man rose to his feet and conducted the king to a large and richly adorned pavilion, and entertained him at a splendid collation, it being then one of the clock. And being refreshed his majesty set forth again, and entered the city, which had never before shown so brave and goodly an appearance as on this May day, when all the world seemed mad with joy.

From London Bridge even to Whitehall Palace the way was lined on one side by the train-bands of the city, and on the other by the city companies in their rich livery gowns; to which were added a number of gentlemen volunteers, all in white doublets, commanded by Sir John Stanel. Across the streets hung garlands of spring flowers that made the air most sweet, and at the corners thereof were arches of white hawthorn in full bloom, bedecked with streamers of gay colours. From wooden railed balconies, jutting windows, and quaint gables hung fair tapestries, rich silks, and stuffs of brilliant hues; and from the high red chimneys, grey turrets, and lofty spires, floated flags bearing the royal arms of England, and banners inscribed with such mottoes as loyalty and affection could suggest. The windows and galleries were filled with ladies of quality in bright dresses; the roofs and scaffolding, with citizens of all classes, who awaited with eager and joyous faces to salute their lord and king.

And presently, far down the line of streets, a sound was heard of innumerable voices cheering most lustily, which every minute became nearer and louder, till at last a blare of trumpets was distinguished, followed by martial music, and the tramp and confusion of a rushing crowd which suddenly parted on all sides. Then there burst on view the first sight of that brave and glorious cavalcade to the number of twenty thousand, which ushered the king back unto his own. First came a troop of young and comely gentlemen, three hundred in all, representing the pride and valour of the kingdom, wearing cloth of silver doublets and brandishing naked swords which flashed in the sunlight. Then another company, less by a hundred in number, habited in rich velvet coats, their footmen clad in purple liveries; and next a goodly troop under the command of Sir John Robinson, all dressed in buff coats with cloth of silver sleeves, and green scarves most handsome to behold. These were followed by a brave troop in blue doublets adorned with silver lace, carrying banners of red silk fringed with gold. Then came trumpets, and seven footmen in sea-green and silver liveries, bearing banners of blue silk, followed by a troop in grey and blue to the number of two hundred and twenty, and led by the most noble the Earl of Northampton. After various other companies, all brave in apparel, came two trumpets bearing his majesty's arms, followed by the sheriffs' men in red cloaks and silver lace, and by a great body of gentlemen in black velvet coats with gold chains. Next rode six hundred brave citizens, twelve ministers, the king's life guards, led by Sir Gilbert Gerrard, the city marshals with eight footmen, the city waits and officers, the sheriffs and aldermen in scarlet gowns, the maces and heralds in great splendour, the lord mayor carrying a naked sword in his strong right hand, the Duke of Buckingham, and General Monk, soon to be created Duke of Albermarle.

Now other heralds sound their trumpets with blasts that make all hearts beat quicker; church bells ring far louder than before; voices are raised to their highest pitch, excitement reaches its zenith, for here, mounted on a stately horse caparisoned in royal purple and adorned with gold, rides King Charles himself; on his right hand his brother of York, on his left his brother of Gloucester. Handkerchiefs are waved, flowers are flung before his way, words of welcome fall upon his ear, in answer to which he bows with stately grace, smiles most pleasantly, and gives such signs of delight as "cheared the hearts of all loyal subjects even to extasie and transportation." Last of all came five regiments of cavalry, with back, breast, and head piece, which "diversified the show with delight and terrour." John Evelyn stood in the Strand and watched the procession pass, when that worthy man thanked God the king had been restored without bloodshed, and by the very army that had rebelled against him. "For such a restauration was never mention'd in any history ancient or modern, since the returne of the Jews from the Babylonish captivity; nor so joyfull a day and so bright ever seene in this nation, this hapning when to expect or effect it was past all human policy."

For full seven hours this "most pompous show that ever was" wound its way through the city, until at nine of the clock in the evening it brought his majesty to the palace of Whitehall, where the late king had "laid down his sacred head to be struck off upon a block," almost twelve years before. Then the lord mayor and his aldermen took their goodly leave, and the king entered into the banquet hall, where the lords and commons awaited him, and where an address was made to him by the Earl of Manchester, Speaker to the House of Peers, congratulating him on his miraculous preservation and happy restoration to his crown and dignity after so long and so severe a suppression of his just right and title. Likewise his lordship besought his majesty to be the upright assertor of the laws and maintainer of the liberties of his subjects. "So," said the noble earl, "shall judgment run down like a river, and justice like a mighty stream, and God, the God of your mercy, who hath so miraculously preserved you, will establish your throne in righteousness and peace." Then the king made a just and brief reply, and retired to supper and to rest.

The worthy citizens, however, were not satisfied that their rejoicements should end here, and "as soon as night came," says Dr. Bate, "an artificial day was begun again, the whole city seeming to be one great light, as, indeed, properly it was a luminary of loyalty, the bonfires continuing till daybreak, fed by a constant supply of wood, and maintained with an equal excess of gladness and fewel." Wine flowed from public fountains, volleys of shot were discharged from houses of the nobility, drums and other musical instruments played in the streets, citizens danced most joyfully in open places, and the effigy of Cromwell was burned, together with the arms of the Commonwealth with expressions of great delight.

CHAPTER II.

The story of the king's escape.--He accepts the Covenant and lands in Scotland.--Crowned at Scone.--Proclaimed king at Carlisle.--The battle of Worcester.--Bravery of Charles.--Disloyalty of the Scottish cavalry.--The Royalists defeated.--The King's flight.--Seeks refuge in Boscobel Wood.--The faithful Pendrells.--Striving to cross the Severn.--Hiding in an oak tree.--Sheltered by Master Lane.--Sets out with Mistress Lane.--Perilous escapes.--On the road.--The king is recognised.--Strange adventures.--His last night in England.

That King Charles had been miraculously preserved, as my Lord Manchester set forth, there can be no doubt. His courageous efforts to regain the Crown at the battle of Worcester and his subsequent escapes from the vigilant pursuits of the Cromwellian soldiers, would, if set down in justice and with detail, present a story more entertaining than any romance ever written. Here they must of necessity be mentioned with brevity.

In the year 1645, Charles I., having suffered the loss of many great battles, became fearful of the danger which threatened his family and himself. He therefore ordered his son Charles, who had already retired into the west, to seek refuge in the Scilly Isles. The prince complied with his desires, and went from thence to Paris, where his mother, Henrietta Maria, had already taken shelter, and, after a short stay with her, travelled to the Hague. Soon after the king was beheaded, the Scots, who regarded that foul act with great abhorrence, invited Charles to come into their kingdom, provided he accepted certain hard conditions, which left the government of all civil business in the hands of Parliament, and the regulation of all religious matters in charge of the Presbyterians. No other prospect of regaining his rights, and of enabling him to fight for his throne presenting itself, he accepted what was known as the Covenant, and landed in Scotland in 1650. He was received with the respect due to a monarch, but placed under the surveillance forced on a prisoner. The fanatical Presbyterians, jealous of that potent influence which his blithe ways exercised over all with whom he associated, neither permitted him to attend the council nor command the army; they, however, preached to him incessantly, admonished him of his sins and those of his parents, guarded him as a captive, and treated him as a puppet. Meanwhile Cromwell, being made aware of his presence in the kingdom, advanced at the head of a powerful body into Scotland, fought and won the battle of Dunbar, stormed and captured Leith, and took his triumphal way towards Edinburgh town. Charles was at this time in Perth, and being impatient at his enforced inaction whilst battles were fought in his name, and lives lost in his cause, made his escape from the Covenanters, with the determination of arousing the Royalists who lay in the north. But the Scots soon overtook and recaptured him. However, this decisive action awoke them to a better understanding of the deference due to his position, and therefore they crowned him at Scone on the first day of the year 1651, with much solemnity, and subsequently made him commander of the army.

After spending some months in reorganizing the troops, he boldly declared his intention of marching into England, and fighting the rebel force. Accordingly, on the 31st of July, 1651, he set out from Sterling with an army of between eleven and twelve thousand men. At Carlisle he was proclaimed king, and a declaration was published in his name, granting free grace and pardon to all his subjects in England, of whatever nature or cause their offences, saving Cromwell, Bradshaw and Cooke. He then marched to Lancashire, and on the 23rd of August unfurled the Royal standard at Worcester, amidst the enthusiastic acclamations of his troops and the loyal demonstrations of the citizens. Weary of civil strife, depressed with fear of Cromwell's severities, and distrustful of the Presbyterians, who chiefly composed the young king's army, the Royalists had not gathered to his standard in such numbers as he had anticipated. His troops, since leaving Scotland, had been reinforced merely by two thousand men; but Charles had hopes that fresh recruits would join him when news of the rising got noised abroad.

The Republicans were filled with dismay at the king's determined action, but were prompt to make a counter-move, Accordingly, additional troops were levied,

London was left to be defended by volunteers, and Cromwell, heading an army of thirty-four thousand men, marched against the Royalists. On the 28th of August, they drew near Worcester, and on the 3rd of September the battle was fought which will remain for ever famous in the annals of civil war. On the morning of that day, the king, ascending the cathedral tower, saw the enemy's forces advancing towards Worcester: before reaching the city, it was necessary they should cross the Severn, and, in order to prevent this if possible, Charles hurried down and directed that some of his troops, under the command of Montgomery, should defend Powick Bridge; whilst he stationed others under Colonel Pitscottie lower down, at a point of the river towards which the Republicans were marching with pontoons, by means of which they intended to cross. The young king, hopeful of victory and full of enthusiasm, rode speedily out at the head of his troops and placed them at their various stations. Scarcely had he done so, when he became aware that the main body of the enemy had opened an artillery fire on Fort Royal, which guarded the city on the south-east side. He therefore galloped back in hot haste to headquarters, and reconnoitred the advanced posts eastward of the city, in full front of the enemy's fire. Meanwhile Montgomery, having exhausted his ammunition, was obliged to retreat in disorder from Powick Bridge, followed by the Cromwellians. The king now courageously resolved to attack the enemy's camp at Perry Wood, which lay south-east of Worcester. Accordingly he marched out with the flower of his Highland infantry and the English cavaliers, led by the Dukes of Hamilton and Buckingham. Cromwell, seeing this, hastened to intercept the king's march, whereon a fierce battle was bravely fought on either side. Nothing could be more valiant than the conduct of the young king, who showed himself wholly regardless of his life in the fierce struggle for his rights. Twice was his horse shot under him; but increasing danger seemed but to animate him to greater daring. So bravely did his army fight likewise, that the Republicans at first gave way before them. For upwards of four hours the engagement raged with great fierceness. Cromwell subsequently declared it was "as stiff a contest as he had ever seen," and his experience was great. Success seemed now to crown the Royalists, anon to favour the Roundheads. The great crisis of the day at length arrived: the Cromwellians began to waver and give way just as the Royalist cavalry had expended their ammunition; the king had still three thousand Scotch cavalry in the rear under the command of Leslie, who had not yet been called into action. He therefore ordered them to advance; but, to his horror, not one of these men, who had looked on as passive spectators, made a movement. In this hour, when victory or defeat hung upon a thread the Scots ignominiously failed their king. Charles instantly saw he was undone. The English cavalry continued to fight bravely, in their desperation using the butt ends of their muskets; but they were gradually compelled to give way before the enemy, who, seeing their condition, had renewed the attack. The Royalists therefore fell back into the city. When the king re-entered Worcester he saw before him a scene of the most disastrous confusion. Royalists and Republicans encountered and fought each other in every thoroughfare; the air was filled with the report of muskets, the imprecations of soldiers, the groans of wounded men, and the shrieks of women. The streets ran red with blood. At such a sight his heart sank within him, but, manning himself for fresh efforts, he called his troops together and sought to incite them with courage to make a final charge. "I would rather," he cried out, "you would shoot me than keep me alive to see the sad consequences of this fatal day." Those who heard him were disheartened: it was too late to retrieve their heavy losses: most of them refused to heed him; many sought safety in flight. Then the young king's friends, gathering round, besought him to make good his escape; and accordingly, with a sad heart, he rode out of St. Martin's Gate humbled and defeated. In order to cover his retreat from the enemy now advancing, my Lord Cleveland, Sir James Hamilton, Colonel Careless, and some other worthy gentlemen defended Sudbury Gate, towards which the main body of the Republicans approached. They held this position a sufficient time to gain the end for which it was undertaken. But at length the Republicans, forcing open the gate, marched upon the fort, defended by fifteen hundred soldiers under Colonel Drummond. This loyal man refusing to surrender, the fort was speedily stormed; and he and those of his men who survived the attack were mercilessly put to the sword.

    Dr. George Bate gives a quaint and striking picture of what followed. "Deplorable and sad was the countenance of the town after that," writes he; "the victorious soldiers on the one hand killing, breaking into houses, plundering, sacking, roaring, and threatening; on the other hand, the subdued flying, turning their backs to be cut and slashed, and with outstretched hands begging quarter; some, in vain resisting, sold their lives as dear as they could, whilst the citizens to no purpose prayed, lamented, and bewailed. All the streets are strewed with dead and mangled bodies. Here were to be seen some that begged relief, and then again others weltering in their own gore, who desired that at once an end might be put to their lives and miseries. The dead bodies lay unburied for the space of three days or more, which was a loathsome spectacle that increased the horror of the action."

Concerning his subsequent dangers and narrow escapes, the king, in his days of peace and prosperity, was wont to discourse at length, for they had left impressions on his mind which lasted through life. Edward Hyde, Lord Clarendon, his Lord High Chancellor, Dr. George Bate, his learned physician, and Samuel Pepys, Esquire, sometime Surveyor-General to the Victualling Office, have preserved the records of that time of peril, as told by his majesty. True, their various stories differ in minor details, but they agree in principal facts. The king had not ridden many miles from Worcester when he found himself surrounded by about four thousand of his army, including the Scots under the command of Leslie. Though they would not fight for him, they were ready enough to fly with him. At first he thought of betaking himself to Scotland; but having had sad proof of the untrustworthy character of those with whom he travelled, he feared they would further betray him if pursued by the enemy. He therefore resolved to reach London before the news of his defeat arrived thither, and make his escape from thence; but this scheme presented many difficulties. Amongst the persons of quality who accompanied him were my Lord Duke of Buckingham, the Earls of Derby and Lauderdale, and the Lords Wilmot and Talbot. During their journey it fell from my Lord Derby's lips, that when he had been defeated at Wigan, one Pendrell, an honest labourer and a Papist, had sheltered him in Boscobel House, not far distant from where they then rode. Hearing this, the king resolved to trust this same faithful fellow, and for the present seek such refuge as Pendrell could afford. It was not easy, however, for his majesty to escape the Scots; but when night came, he and his gentlemen slipped away from the high road, which the others continued to pursue, and made for Boscobel Wood, led by Charles Giffard, a loyal gentleman and true. The house they sought was situated between Tong Castle and Brewood, in a woody place most fitting for retreat; it was, moreover, six and twenty miles from Worcester, and stood in Shropshire, on the borders of Staffordshire.

In order to gain this haven of rest, it was necessary for them to pass through

Stourbridge, where a troop of the Republican army lay quartered. Midnight had fallen ere they reached the town, which was now wrapt in darkness, and was, moreover, perfectly still. The king and his friends, dismounting, led their horses through the echoing streets as softly as possible, being filled the while with dire apprehensions. Safely leaving it, they rode into the wood until they came to the old convent of Whiteladies, once the home of Cistercian nuns, who had long since been driven from their peaceful retreat. The house was now the habitation of the Giffard family, with whom George Pendrell lived as servant. On being aroused, he came forth with a lantern, and admitted them, when Charles Giffard made known to him in whose presence he stood, and acquainted him with their situation. Thereupon the honest fellow promised to serve the king faithfully, and sent immediately for his brothers four: William, who took charge of Boscobel House, not far removed; Humphrey, who was miller at Whiteladies; Richard, who lived at Hobbal Grange; and John, who was a woodman, and dwelt hard by. When they had all arrived, Lord Derby showed them the king's majesty, and besought them for God's sake, for their loyalty's sake, and as they valued all that was high and sacred, to keep him safe, and forthwith seek some place of decent shelter where he might securely lurk. This they readily swore to compass, though they risked their lives in the attempt.

It being considered that greater safety lay in the king being unattended, his loyal friends departed from him with many prayers and hopes for a joyful reunion: all of them save my Lords Wilmot and Buckingham set out to join Leslie's company, that they might proceed together towards Scotland; but they had not marched six miles in company with the Scots when these three thousand men and more were overtaken and were routed by a single troop of the enemy's horse, and my Lord Derby, being taken, was condemned and executed. Lords Wilmot and Buckingham set out for London, to which place it was agreed the king should follow them.

When his majesty's friends had departed, the Pendrells undertook to disguise him; towards which end one of them cut the long locks reaching his shoulders, another rubbed his hands and face with dust, and a third brought him a suit of clothes. "The habit of the king," says Pepys, "was a very greasy old grey steeple-crowned hat, with the brims turned up, without lining or hatband, the sweat appearing two inches deep through it round the band place; a green cloth jump-coat, threadbare, even to the threads being worn white, and breeches of the same, with long knees down to the garter; with an old sweaty leathern doublet, a pair of white flannel stockings next to his legs, and upon them a pair of old green yarn stockings, all worn and darned at the knees, with their feet cut off: his shoes were old, all slashed for the ease of his feet, with little rolls of paper between his toes to keep them from galling; and an old coarse shirt, patched both at the neck and hands, of that very coarse sort which go by the name of nogging shirts."

When Charles was attired in this fashion, Richard Pendrell opened a back door and led him out into the wood; not a moment too soon, for within half an hour Colonel Ashenhurst, with a company of Cromwell's soldiers, rode up to Whiteladies, rushed into the house, searched every chamber and secret place, pulled down the wainscoting, and otherwise devastated the mansion in the search for the king. A damp cold September morning now lengthened to a day of gloom and depression. Rain fell in heavy torrents, dripped from the leafless branches of trees, and saturated the thick undergrowth and shrubs where his majesty lay hidden. Owing to the condition of the weather, the soldiers neglected to search Boscobel Wood; and, after uttering many threats and imprecations, withdrew from Whiteladies. When he considered himself quite alone, Richard Pendrell ventured forth, taking with him a billhook, that if observed he might seem engaged in trimming hedges; and drawing near the spot where his majesty lay, assured him of his safety. Later on he besought an old woman, his neighbour, to take victuals into the wood to a labourer she would find there. Without hesitation the good woman carried some eggs, bread, butter, and milk towards the spot indicated to her. On seeing her the king was much alarmed fearing recognition and dreading her garrulity; wherefore he said to her: "Can you be true to anyone who hath served the king?" Upon which she readily made answer: "Yes, sir; I'd die sooner than betray you." Being reassured at this, he ate heartily.

When night fell, Richard brought him into the house again, and the king, now abandoning his intention of proceeding to London, expressed his anxiety to reach Wales where he had many friends, and which afforded him ready opportunities of escaping from the kingdom. Pendrell expressed himself willing to conduct him thither. Accordingly, about nine of the clock, they set out with the determination of crossing the Severn, intending to pass over a ferry between Bridgenorth and Shrewsbury. When they had walked some hours they drew near a water-mill. "We could see the miller," said the king in relating the story, "as I believe, sitting at the mill-door, he being in white clothes, it being a very dark night. He called out sturdily, 'Who goes there?' Upon which Richard Pendrell answered, 'Neighbours going home,' or suchlike words. Whereupon the miller cried out: 'If you be neighbours, stand, or I will knock you down.' Upon which, we believing there was company in the house, Richard bade me follow him close, and he ran to a gate that went up a dirty lane up a hill. The miller cried out: 'Rogues--rogues!' And thereupon some men came out of the mill after us, which I believe were soldiers; so we fell a-running, both of us up the lane as long as we could run, it being very deep and very dirty, till at last I bade him leap over a hedge, and lie still to hear if anybody followed us--which we did, and continued lying down upon the ground about half an hour, when, hearing nobody come, we continued our way."

This led to the house of an honest gentleman named Woolfe, living at Madeley, who was a Catholic, and loyal to his king, and as such was known to the Pendrells. When they drew near to his house, Richard, leaving his majesty in a field, went forward and asked this worthy man if he would shelter one who had taken part in the battle of Worcester; whereon he made answer he would not venture his neck for any man unless it were the king himself, upon which Pendrell made known to him it was his majesty who sought refuge from him. Mr. Woolfe came out immediately and carried the king by a back way into a barn, where he hid him for the day, it being considered unsafe for him to stay a longer period there, as two companies of militia were at that time stationed in the town, and were very likely to search the house at any minute. Moreover he advised his majesty by no means to adventure crossing the Severn, as the strictest guard was then kept at the ferries to prevent any Royalist fugitives from escaping into Wales. The king was therefore obliged to retrace his steps, and now sought Boscobel House, not far distant from his first resting-place of Whiteladies. Arriving there, he remained secreted in the wood, whilst Richard went to see if soldiers were in occupation of the dwelling. There was no one there, however, but Colonel Careless, the same good man and true who had helped to keep Sudbury Gate whilst Charles made his escape.

The Colonel had been hiding in the forest, and, being sore pressed by hunger, had come to beg a little bread. Being informed where the king was, he came forth with great joy, and, the house not being considered a safe refuge, they both climbed into the branches of a leafy oak, situated in an open part of the wood, from whence they could see all round them. They carried with them some bread and cheese and small beer, and stayed there that day. "While we were in the tree," says the king, "we saw soldiers going up and down in the thicket of the wood, searching for persons escaped, we seeing them now and then peeping out of the wood." When this danger had passed away, the king, worn out by his sore fatigues, laid his head on his friend's breast and slept in his arms. At night they descended, and going to Boscobel House, were shown a secret hiding-place, such as were then to be found in the mansions of all Catholic families, called the priests' hole a little confined closet built between two walls, in the principal stack of chimneys, and having a couple of exits for the better escape of those compelled to seek its shelter. Here the king rested in peace for a day and a night.

Meanwhile Humphrey Pendrell went into Shifnal to pay his taxes; and it being known he had come from Whiteladies, he was questioned closely as to whether he knew aught of Charles Stuart. On stoutly denying all knowledge of him, he was told that any man who discovered him would gain a thousand pounds, but he that sheltered him would suffer death without mercy; these being the terms of a proclamation just issued. This the honest miller on his return narrated to the king, swearing roundly he would run all risks for his sake. It chanced at this time one of the Pendrells heard that my Lord Wilmot who had not been able to make his way to London, was hiding in a very secure place, at the house of a gentleman named Whitegrave, above seven miles distant. This coming to the king's knowledge, he became anxious to see his faithful friend and hold communication with him. Accordingly one of the Pendrells was despatched to request Lord Wilmot to meet his majesty that night, in a field close by Mr. Whitegrave's house. And the time of night being come, the king was impatient of delay; but his feet were sore from the rough shoes he had worn on his journey, so that he was scarce able to walk; therefore he was mounted on Humphrey's mill-horse, and, the four loyal brothers forming a guard, they directed their way towards Moseley. The king's eagerness to see Wilmot being great, he complained of the horse's slow pace. "Can you blame him, my liege," said Humphrey, who loved a jest, "that he goes heavily, having the weight of three kingdoms on his back?"

When they had travelled with him a great part of the journey it was thought safer three of them should withdraw themselves. They therefore turned away; but scarcely had they gone when the king, who, being lost in thought, had remained unconscious of their departure, suddenly stopped, and caused John, who remained, to speedily summon them back. When they returned he gave them his hand to kiss, and, with that charm of manner which never failed in winning friends, said to them sadly, "My sorrows make me forget myself. I earnestly thank you all."

They kissed his hand heartily, and prayed God to save him. In the days of his prosperity he remembered their kindness and rewarded their loyalty.

Arriving at the trysting place the king found Mr. Whitegrave, a Benedictine monk named Father Huddlestone, Sir John Preston, and his brother awaiting him. It may be mentioned here this monk was destined, many years later, to play an important part in the closing scene of his majesty's life. Mr. Whitegrave conducted Charles with great show of respect to his house, where the king spoke with my Lord Wilmot, feasted well, and rested safe that night. Next morning the worthy host had private notice given that a company of soldiers were on their way to arrest him as one who had served in the king's army. He, being innocent of this charge, did not avoid them, but received them boldly at his door, spoke confidently in his own defence, and referred them to the testimony of his neighbours, whereon they departed quietly.

It was feared, however, the house was no longer safe, and that another refuge had best be sought for his majesty. Therefore, Father Huddlestone informed the king of an honest gentleman, the owner of a fair estate some six miles removed, who was generous and exceedingly beloved, and the eldest justice of peace in the county of Stafford. This gentleman was named Lane, "a very zealous Protestant, yet he lived with so much civility and candour towards the Catholics, that they would all trust him as much as they would any of their own profession." The king, however, not being willing to surprise this worthy man, immediately despatched the Benedictine to make certain of his welcome; receiving due assurances of which he and Lord Willmot set out by night for Master Lane's mansion, where they were heartily received, and where Charles rested some days in blessed security. Knowing, however, in what risk he placed those who sheltered him, and how vigilant the pursuit after him, he became most anxious for his safe delivery out of the kingdom. To this end it was desirable he should draw near the west coast, and await an opportunity of sailing from thence for France.

The members of Master Lane's family then living with him consisted of a son and a daughter: the former a man of fearless courage and integrity, the latter a gentlewoman of good wit and discretion, as will be seen hereafter. Consulting, amongst themselves as to the best means of compassing the king's escape, it was resolved Mistress Lane should visit a kinswoman of hers with whom she had been bred, that had married one Norton, and was now residing within five miles of Bristol. It was likewise decided she should ride on her journey thence behind the king, he being habited in her father's livery, and acting as her servant; and for greater safety her sister and her sister's husband were to accompany them on the road. Mistress Jane Lane then procured from a colonel of the rebel army a passport for herself and her servant, her sister and her brother-in-law, to travel without molestation to her cousin Mistress Norton, who was ready to lie in. With this security Jane set out, her brother bearing them company part of the way, with a hawk upon his fist and two or three spaniels at his heels, which warranted him keeping the king and his friends in sight without seeming to be of their company.

The first day's journey was not accomplished without an exciting incident. The horse ridden by Mistress Lane and the king--now bearing the name of William Jackson--lost a shoe; and being come to Bromsgrove, he must dismount and lead the animal to the village blacksmith.

"As I was holding my horse's foot," said his majesty, when narrating the story to Mr. Pepys, "I asked the smith what news. He told me that there was no news that he knew of, since the good news of the beating the rogues of the Scots. I asked him whether there was none of the English taken that joined with the Scots, He answered he did not hear if that rogue, Charles Stuart, were taken; but some of the others, he said, were taken. I told him that if that rogue were taken, he deserved to be hanged more than all the rest, for bringing in the Scots. Upon which he said I spoke like an honest man; and so we parted."

At the end of the first day's journey they were met by Lord Wilmot at the inn; and he continued to join them wherever they rested at night, without appearing to travel with them by day. Mistress Lane took all possible care to guard the king against recognition, stating at every house of accommodation where they tarried he was "a neighbour's son whom her father had lent her to ride before her in hope that he would the sooner recover from a quartan ague with which he had been miserably afflicted, and was not yet free." Which story served as sufficient excuse for his going to bed betimes, and so avoiding the company of servants. At the end of three days they arrived at their destination. Jane Lane was warmly received by her cousin, and the whole party made heartily welcome. Jane, however, did not entrust her secret to Mistress Norton's keeping, but repeated her tale of the good youth being newly recovered from ague, and desired a chamber might be provided for him, and a good fire made that he might retire early to bed. Her desires being obeyed, the king withdrew, and was served with an excellent good supper by the butler, a worthy fellow named Pope, who had been a trooper in the army of Charles I., of blessed memory.

"The next morning" said the king continuing his strange story, "I arose pretty early, having a very good stomach, and went to the buttery-hatch to get my breakfast, where I found Pope and two or three other men in the room, and we all fell to eating bread and butter, to which he gave us very good ale and sack. And as I was sitting there, there was one that looked like a country fellow sat just by me, who, talking, gave so particular an account of the battle of Worcester to the rest of the company that I concluded he must be one of Cromwell's soldiers. But I, asking how he came to give so good an account of that battle, he told me he was in the King's regiment, by which I thought he meant one Colonel King's regiment. But questioning him further, I perceived he had been in my regiment of Guards, in Major Broughton's company--that was my Major in the battle. I asked him what kind of man I was; to which he answered by describing exactly both my clothes and my horse, and then, looking upon me, he told me that the king was at least three fingers taller than I. Upon which I made what haste I could out of the buttery, for fear he should indeed know me, as being more afraid when I knew he was one of our own soldiers than when I took him for one of the enemy's. So Pope and I went into the hall, and just as we came into it Mistress Norton was coming by through it; upon which I, plucking off my hat and standing with it in my hand as she passed by, Pope looked very earnestly in my face. But I took no notice of it, but put on my hat again and went away, walking out of the house into the field."

When he returned, however, the butler followed him into a private room, and going down on his stiff knees, said, with tears in his old eyes, he was rejoiced to see his majesty in safety. The king affected to laugh at him, and asked him what he meant; but Pope told him he knew him well, for before he was a trooper in his father's service he had been falconer to Sir Thomas Jermyn, groom of the bedchamber to the king when he was a boy. Charles saw it was useless longer to deny himself, and therefore said he believed him to be a very honest man, and besought he would not reveal what he knew to anyone. This the old man readily promised, and faithfully kept his word. Having spent a couple of days at Norton's, the king, by advice of Lord Wilmot, went to the house of a true friend and loyal man, one Colonel Windham, who lived at Trent. This town was notable as a very hotbed of republicanism; a proof of which was afforded his majesty on the very day of his entrance. As he rode into the principal street, still disguised as a waiting man to Mistress Lane, he heard a great ringing of bells, and the tumult of many voices, and saw a vast concourse of people gathered in the churchyard close by. On asking the cause he was informed one of Cromwell's troopers was telling the people he had killed Charles Stuart, whose buff coat he then wore; whereon the rebels rang the church bells, and were about to make a great bonfire for joy.

Having brought him to Trent, Mistress Lane returned home, carrying with her the king's friendship and gratitude, of which he gave her ample proof when he came unto the throne. Charles stayed at Colonel Windham's over a week, whilst that gallant man was secretly striving to hire a ship for his majesty's safe transportation into France. Presently succeeding in this object, the king, yet wearing his livery, and now riding before Mistress Judith Coningsby, cousin of Colonel Windham, started with high hopes for Lyme; but at the last moment the captain of the vessel failed him, and he was again left in a state of painful uncertainty and danger. Lord Wilmot was sent to ascertain the cause of this disappointment, and for greater safety the king rode on to Burport with his friends. Being come to the outskirts of the town, they were alarmed at finding the streets in a state of confusion, and full of Cromwell's soldiers, fifteen hundred of whom were about to embark for Jersey. His majesty's coolness and presence of mind did not fail him; he resolved to ride boldly into the town, and hire a chamber at the best inn. The yard of the hostelry was likewise crowded with troopers; but this did not dismay his majesty.

"I alighted," said he, "and taking the horses, thought it the best way to go blundering in among them, and lead them through the middle of the soldiers into the stable; which I did, and they were very angry with me for my rudeness. As soon as I came into the stable I took the bridle off the horses, and called the ostler to me to help me, and to give the horses some oats. And as the hostler was helping me to feed the horses, 'Sure, sir,' says he, 'I know your face?' which was no very pleasant question to me. But I thought the best way was to ask him where he had lived, or whether he had always lived there or no. He told me that he was but newly come thither; that he was born in Exeter, and had been ostler in an inn there, hard by one Mr. Potter's, a merchant in whose house I had lain in the time of the war. So I thought it best to give the fellow no further occasion of thinking where he had seen me, for fear he should guess right at last; therefore I told him, 'Friend, certainly you have seen me then at Mr. Potter's, for I served him a good while above a year.' 'Oh,' says he, 'then I remember you a boy there;' and with that was put off from thinking any more on it, but desired that we might drink a pot of beer together, which I excused by saying that I must go wait on my master, and get his dinner ready for him; but told him that my master was going to London, and would return about three weeks hence, when he would be there, and I would not fail to drink a pot with him."

The king and his friends, having dined at the inn, got word that the master of the ship, suspecting that it was some dangerous employment he had been hired for, absolutely refused to fulfil his contract. Therefore they, being sad at heart and fearful, retraced their steps to Trent, and presently his majesty went further into Sussex, and abode with a staunch Royalist, one Colonel Gunter, who resided within four miles of Salisbury. This excellent man at last succeeded in hiring a ship to carry away the king, and so Charles made another journey to Brighthelmstone, where he met the captain of the vessel and the merchant that had hired her on behalf of Colonel Gunter, both of whom had been kept in ignorance of their future passenger's identity. Arriving at Brighthelmstone, they entered an inn and ordered supper, during which the captain more than once looked hard at the king. And the meal being ended, the captain called the merchant aside and said he was not dealt with fairly, inasmuch as he had not been told the king was the person to be conveyed from thence. The merchant, not being so wise as the master, denied such was the case; but the honest fellow told him not to be troubled. "For I think," said he, "I do God and my country good service in preserving the king: and by the grace of God I will venture my life and all for him, and set him safely on shore, if I can, in France."

Nor was this the last of his majesty's numerous risks, for being presently left alone, he stood thoughtful and somewhat melancholy by the fire, resting one hand on a chair; and the landlord, coming in and seeing him engaged in this manner, softly advanced, suddenly kissed the king's hand, and said, "God bless you, wherever you go." Charles started, and would have denied himself; but the landlord cried out, "'Fore God, your majesty may trust me; and," he added, "I have no doubt, before I die, to be a lord, and my wife a lady."

That night, the last his majesty was to spend in England for many years, he was sad and depressed. The scenes of bloodshed he had witnessed, the imminent dangers he had escaped, were vividly present to his mind. The past was fraught with horror; the future held no hope. Though a king, he was about to become an outcast from his realm. Surmising his thoughts, his companions sought to cheer him. Now the long-desired moment of escape was at hand, no one thought of repose. The little vessel in which he intended sailing lay dry upon the shore, the tide being at low water. The king and his friends, the merchant, the captain, and the landlord, sat in the well-lighted cosy parlour of the seaport inn, smoking, playing cards, telling stories and drinking good ale.

With all such diversions the hours wore heavily away. Their noisy joviality had an undercurrent of sadness; jokes failed to amuse; laughter seemed forced; words, mirthful in leaving the lips, sounded ominous on reaching the ear. At four o'clock the captain rose to survey his ship, and presently returned saying the tide had risen. Thereon the king and his friends prepared to depart. A damp, chilly November fog hung over the sea, hiding its wide expanse without deadening its monotonous moan. A procession of black figures leaving the inn sped noiselessly through darkness. Arriving at the shore, those who were not to accompany his majesty, knelt and kissed his hand. Then he, with Lord Wilmot and the captain, climbed on board the vessel and entered the cabin. The fog had turned to rain. Four hours later, the tide being favourable, the ship sailed out of port, and in due time the king was safely landed in France.

CHAPTER III.

Celebration of the Kings return.--Those who flocked to Whitehall My Lord Cleveland's gentlemen.--Sir Thomas Allen's supper.--Touching for King's evil.--That none might lose their labour.--The man with the fungus nose.--The memory of the regicides.--Cromwell's effigy.--Ghastly scene at Tyburn.--The King's clemency.--The Coronation procession.--Sights and scenes by the way.--His Majesty is crowned.

The return of the king and his court was a signal for universal joy throughout the nation in general and the capital in particular. For weeks and months subsequent to his majesty's triumphal entry, the town did not subside from its condition of excitement and revelry to its customary quietude and sobriety. Feasts by day were succeeded by entertainments at night; "and under colour of drinking the king's health," says Bishop Burnet, "there were great disorder and much riot."

It seemed as if the people could not sufficiently express their delight at the presence of the young king amongst them, or satisfy their desire of seeing him. When clad in rich velvets and costly lace, adorned with many jewels and waving feathers, he walked in Hyde Park attended by an "abundance of gallantry," or went to Whitehall Chapel, where "the organs and singing-men in surplices" were first heard by Mr. Pepys, a vast crowd of loyal subjects attended him on his way. Likewise, when, preceded by heralds, he journeyed by water in his barge to open Parliament, the river was crowded with innumerable boats, and the banks lined with a great concourse anxious for sight of him. Nor were his subjects satisfied by the glimpses obtained of him on such occasions; they must needs behold their king surrounded by the insignia of royalty in the palace of his ancestors, and flocked thither in numbers. "The eagerness of men, women, and children to see his majesty, and kisse his hands was so greate," says Evelyn, "that he had scarce leisure to eate for some dayes, coming as they did from all parts of the nation: and the king being as willing to give them that satisfaction, would have none kept out, but gave free access to all sorts of people." Indeed his loyal subjects were no less pleased with him than he with them; and in faith he was sorry, he declared, in that delicate strain of irony that ran like a bright thread throughout the whole pattern of his speech, he had not come over before, for every man he encountered was glad to see him.

Day after day, week after week, the Palace of Whitehall presented a scene of ceaseless bustle. Courtiers, ambassadors, politicians, soldiers, and citizens crowded the antechambers, flocked through the galleries, and tarried in the courtyards. Deputations from all the shires and chief towns in the three kingdoms, bearing messages of congratulation and loyalty, were presented to the king. First of all came the worshipful lord mayor, aldermen and council of the city of London, in great pomp and state; when the common-sergeant made a speech to his majesty respecting the affection of the city towards him, and the lord mayor, on hospitable thoughts intent, besought the honour of his company to dinner, the which Charles promised him most readily. And the same day the commissioners from Ireland presented themselves, headed by Sir James Barry, who delivered himself of a fine address regarding the love his majesty's Irish subjects bore him; as proof of which he presented the monarch with a bill for twenty thousand pounds, that had been duly accepted by Alderman Thomas Viner, a right wealthy man and true. Likewise came the deputy steward and burgesses of the city of Westminster, arrayed in the glory of new scarlet gowns; and the French, Italian, and Dutch ministers, when Monsieur Stoope pronounced an harangue with great eloquence. Also the vice-chancellor of the University of Oxford, with divers doctors, bachelors of divinity, proctors, and masters of arts of the same learned university, who, having first met at the Temple Church, went by two and two, according to their seniority, to Essex House, that they might wait on the most noble the Marquis of Hertford, then chancellor. Accompanied by him, and preceded by eight esquires and yeomen beadles, having their staves, and three of them wearing gold chains, they presented themselves before the king, and spoke him words of loyalty and greeting. The heads of the colleges and halls of Cambridge, with some masters of arts, in like manner journeyed to Whitehall, when Dr. Love delivered a learned Latin oration, expressive of their devotion to royalty in the person of their most illustrious monarch.

Amongst others came, one day, my Lord Cleveland at the head of a hundred gentlemen, many of them being officers who had formerly served under him, and other gentlemen who had ridden to meet the king when coming unto his own; and having arrived at Whitehall, they knelt down in the matted gallery, when his majesty "was pleased to walk along," says MERCURIUS PUBLICUS, "and give everyone of them the honour to kiss his hand, which favour was so highly received by them, that they could no longer stifle their joy, but as his majesty was walking out (a thing thought unusual at court) they brake out into a loud shouting."

Then the nobility entertained the king and his royal brothers with much magnificence, his Excellency Lord General Monk first giving at his residence in the Cockpit, a great supper, after which "he entertained his majesty with several sorts of musick;" Next Earl Pembroke gave a rare banquet; also the Duke of Buckingham, my Lord Lumley, and many others. Nor was my lord mayor, Sir Thomas Allen, behindhand in extending hospitality to the king, whom he invited to sup with him. This feast, having no connection with the civic entertainments, was held at good Sir Thomas's house. The royal brothers of York and Gloucester were likewise bidden, together with several of the nobility and gentry of high degree. Previous to supper being served, the lord mayor brought his majesty a napkin dipped in rose-water, and offered it kneeling; when his majesty had wiped his hands, he sat down at a table raised by an ascent, the Duke of York on his right hand, and the Duke of Gloucester on his left. They were served with three several courses, at each of which the tablecloth was shifted, and at every dish which his majesty or the dukes tasted, the napkins were moreover changed. At another table in the same room sat his Excellency the Lord General, the Duke of Buckingham, the Marquis of Ormond, the Earl of Oxford, Earl of Norwich, Earl of St. Albans, Lords De la Ware, Sands, Berkeley, and several other of the nobility, with knights and gentlemen of great quality. Sir John Robinson, alderman of London, proposed his majesty's health, which was pledged standing by all present. His majesty was the while entertained with a variety of rare music. This supper was given on the 16th of June; and a couple of weeks later, on the 5th of July, the king went "with as much pompe and splendour as any earthly prince could do to the greate City feast, the first they had invited him to since his returne."

But whilst entertainments were given, and diversions occupied the town, Charles was called upon to touch for the evil, an affliction then most prevalent throughout the kingdom. According to a time-honoured belief which obtained until the coming of George I., when faith in the divinity of kings was no longer possible to the most ignorant, the monarch's touch was credited with healing this most grievous disease. Majesty in those days was sacred, and superstition rife. Accordingly we read in MERCURIUS PUBLICUS that, "The kingdom having for a long time, by reason of his majesty's absence, been troubled with the evil, great numbers flocked for cure. Saturday being appointed by his majesty to touch such as were so troubled, a great company of poor afflicted creatures were met together, many brought in chairs and baskets; and being appointed by his majesty to repair to the banqueting house, the king sat in a chair of state, where he stroked all that were brought to him, and then put about each of their necks a white ribbon with an angel of gold on it. In this manner his majesty stroked above six hundred; and such was his princely patience and tenderness to the poor afflicted creatures, that though it took up a long time, the king, being never weary of well doing, was pleased to make inquiry whether there were any more that had not been touched. After prayers were ended the Duke of Buckingham brought a towel, and the Earl of Pembroke a basin and ewer, who, after they had made their obeysance to his majesty, kneeled down till his majesty had washed."

This was on the 23rd of June, a few days earlier than the date fixed by Evelyn as that on which the king first began "touch for ye evil." A week later we find he stroked as many as two hundred and fifty persons. Friday was then appointed as the day for those suffering from this disease to come before the king; it was moreover decided that only two hundred persons should be presented each week and these were first to repair to Mr. Knight, his majesty's surgeon, living at the Cross Guns, in Russell Street, Covent Garden, over against the Rose tavern, for tickets of admission. "That none might lose their labour." the same Mr. Knight made it known to the public he would be at home on Wednesdays and Thursdays, from two till six of the clock; and if any person of quality should send for him he would wait upon them at their lodgings. The disease must indeed have been rife: week after week those afflicted continued to present themselves, and we read that, towards the end of July, "notwithstanding all discouragements by the hot weather and the multitude of sick and infirm people, his majesty abated not one of his accustomed number, but touched full two hundred: an high conviction of all such physicians, surgeons, and apothecaries that pretend self-preservation when the languishing patient requires their assistance." Indeed, there were some who placed boundless faith in the king's power of healing by touch; amongst whom was one Avis Evans, whom Aubrey, in his "Miscellanies," records "had a fungus nose, and said it was revealed to him that the king's hand would cure him. And at the first coming of King Charles II. into St. James's Park, he kissed the king's hand, and rubbed his nose with it, which disturbed the king, but cured him."

The universal joy which filled the nation at the restoration of his majesty was accompanied, as might be expected, by bitter hatred towards the leaders of Republicanism, especially towards such as had condemned the late king to death. The chief objects of popular horror now, however, lay in their graves; but the sanctity of death was neither permitted to save their memories from vituperation nor their remains from moltestation. Accordingly, through many days in June the effigy of Cromwell, which had been crowned with a royal diadem, draped with a purple mantle, in Somerset House, and afterwards borne with all imaginable pomp to Westminster Abbey, was now exposed at one of the windows at Whitehall with a rope fixed round its neck, by way of hinting at the death which the original deserved. But this mark of execration was not sufficient to satisfy the public mind, and seven months later, on the 30th of January, 1661, the anniversary of the murder of Charles I., the bodies of Oliver Cromwell, Henry Ireton, and John Bradshaw were taken from their resting places in Westminster Abbey, and drawn on hurdles to Tyburn, the well-known site of public executions. "All the way the universal outcry and curses of the people went along with them," says MERCURIUS PUBLICUS. "When these three carcasses arrived at Tyburn, they were pulled out of their coffins, and hanged at the several angles of that triple tree, where they hung till the sun was set; after which they were taken down, their heads cut off; and their loathsome trunks thrown into a deep hole under the gallows. The heads of those three notorious regicides, Oliver Cromwell, John Bradshaw, and Ireton are set upon poles on the top of Westminster Hall by the common hangman. Bradshaw placed in the middle (over that part where the monstrous high court of justice sat), Cromwell and his son-in-law Ireton on either side of Bradshaw."

Before this ghastly execution took place, Parliament had brought to justice such offenders against the late king's government and life as were in its power. According to the declaration made by the king at Breda, a full and general pardon was extended to all rebellious subjects, excepting such persons as should be hereafter excepted by Parliament. By reason of this clause, some who had been most violent in their persecution of royalty were committed to the Tower before the arrival of his majesty, others fled from the country, but had, on another proclamation summoning them to surrender themselves, returned in hope of obtaining pardon. Thirty in all were tried at the Old Bailey before the Commissioners of Oyer and Terminer and a special jury of knights and gentlemen of quality in the county of Middlesex. Twenty-nine of these were condemned to death. The king was singularly free from desires of revenge; but many of his council were strangers to clemency, and, under the guise of loyalty to the crown, sought satisfaction for private wrongs by urging severest measures. The monarch, however, shrank from staining the commencement of his reign with bloodshed and advocated mercy. In a speech delivered to the House of Lords he insisted that, as a point of honour, he was bound to make good the assurances given in his proclamation of Breda, "which if I had not made," he continued, "I am persuaded that neither I nor you had now been here. I pray, therefore, let us not deceive those who brought or permitted us to come together; and I earnestly desire you to depart from all particular animosities and revenge or memory of past provocations." Accordingly, but ten of those on whom sentence of death had been passed were executed, the remainder being committed to the Tower. That they were not also hung was, according to the mild and merciful Dr. Reeves, Dean of Westminster, "a main cause of God's punishing the land" in the future time. For those destined to suffer, a gibbet was erected at Charing Cross, that the traitors might in their last moments see the spot where the late king had been executed. Having been half hung, they were taken down, when their heads were severed from their trunks and set up on poles at the south-east end of Westminster Hall, whilst their bodies were quartered and exposed upon the city gates.

Burnet tells us that "the regicides being odious beyond all expression, the trials and executions of the first who suffered were run to by crowds, and all the people seemed pleased with the sight;" yet by degrees these cruel and ghastly spectacles became distasteful and disgusting. "I saw not their executions," says Evelyn, speaking of four of the traitors who had suffered death on the 17th of October, "but met their quarters mangled and cutt and reeking as they were brought from the gallows in baskets on the hurdle. Oh the miraculous providence of God!"

Seven months later, the people were diverted by the more cheerful pageant of the king's coronation, which was conducted with great magnificence. "Two days," as Heath narrates, "were allotted to the consummation of this great and most celebrated action, the wonder, admiration and delight of all persons, both foreign and domestick." Early on the morning of the 22nd of May, the day being Monday, the king left Whitehall, by water, for the Tower, in order that he might, according to ancient custom, proceed through the city to Westminster Abbey. It was noticed that it had previously rained for a month together, but on this and the next day "it pleased God that not one drop fell on the king's triumph." At ten o'clock the roaring of cannon announced the procession had left the Tower on its way to Whitehall, where his majesty was to rest the night. The splendour of the pageant was such as had never before been witnessed. The procession was headed by the king's council at law, the masters of chancery and judges, who were followed by the lords according to their rank, so numerous in all, that those who rode first reached Fleet Street, whilst the king was yet in the Tower.

No expense was spared by those who formed part of that wonderful cavalcade, towards rendering their appearance magnificent. Heath tells us it was incredible to think "what costly cloathes were worn that day. The cloaks could hardly be seen what silk or satin they were made of, for the gold and silver laces and embroidery that was laid upon them; the like also was seen on their foot-cloathes. Besides the inestimable value and treasures of diamonds, pearls, and other jewels worn upon their backs and in their hats, not to mention the sumptuous and rich liveries of their pages and footmen, some suits of liveries amounting to fifteen hundred pounds." Nor had the city hesitated in lavishing vast sums towards decorating the streets through which the king was to pass. Four triumphal arches were erected, that were left standing for a year in memory of this joyful day. These were "composed" by John Ogilby, Esquire; and were respectively erected in Leadenhall Street, the Exchange on Cornhill, Wood Street, and Fleet Street.

The thoroughfares were newly gravelled, railed all the way on both sides, and lined with the city companies and trained bands. The "relation of his majesty's entertainment passing through the City of London," as narrated by John Ogilby, and by the papers of the day, is extremely quaint and interesting, but too long for detailed description. During the monarch's progress through "Crouched Friers," he was diverted with music discoursed by a band of eight waits, placed upon a stage. At Aldgate, and at several other stages of his journey, he was received in like manner. Arriving at the great arch in Leadenhall Street, his ears were greeted by sounds of trumpets and drums playing marches; when they had finishes, a short scene was enacted on a balcony of the arch, by figures representing Monarchy, Rebellion, and Loyalty. Then the great procession wended its way to the East India House, situate in the same street, when the East India Company took occasion to express their dutiful affections, in a manner "wholly designed by person of quality." As the king advanced, a youth in an Indian habit, attended by two blackamoors, knelt down before his majesty's horse, and delivered himself of some execrable verse, which he had no sooner ended than another youth in an Indian vest, mounted on a camel, was led forwards and delivered some lines praying his majesty's subjects might never see the sun set on his crown or dignity. The camel, it my be noticed, bore panniers filled with pearls, spices, and silks, destined to be scattered among the spectators. At Cornhill was a conduit, surmounted by eight wenches representing nymphs--a sight which must have rejoiced the king's heart; and on the tower of this same fountain sounded "a noise of seven trumpets." Another fountain flowed with wine and water; and on his way the king heard several speeches delivered by various symbolic figures. One of these, who made a particularly fine harangue, represented the River Thames, as a gentleman whose "garment loose and flowing, coloured blue and white, waved like water, flags and ozier-like long hair falling o'er his shoulders; his beard long, sea-green, and white." And so by slow degrees the king came to Temple Bar, where he was entertained by "a view of a delightful boscage, full of several beasts, both tame and savage, as also several living figures and music of eight waits." And having passed through Temple Bar into his ancient and native city of Westminster, the head bailiff in a scarlet robe and the high constable, likewise in scarlet, on behalf of the dean, chapter, city, and liberty, received his majesty with great expressions of joy.

Never had there been so goodly a show so grand a procession; the citizens, still delighted with their young king, had certainly excelled in doing him honour, and some foreigners, Heaton says, "acknowledged themselves never to have seen among all the great magnificences of the world any to come near or equal this: even the vaunting French confessed their pomps of the late marriage with the Infanta of Spain, at their majesties' entrance into Paris, to be inferior in its state, gallantry, and riches unto this most illustrious cavalcade." Amongst those who witnessed the procession was Mr. Pepys, who has left us a realistic description, without which this picture would be incomplete. He tells us he arose early on this day; and the vain fellow says he made himself as fine as could be, putting on his velvet coat for the first time, though he had it made half a year before. "And being ready," he continues, "Sir W. Batten, my lady, and his two daughters, and his son and wife, and Sir W. Pen and his son and I, went to Mr. Young's, the flag-maker, in Corne-hill; and there we had a good room to ourselves, with wine and good cake, and saw the show very well. In which it is impossible to relate the glory of this day, expressed in the clothes of them that rid, and their horses and horses' clothes; among others, my Lord Sandwich's embroidery and diamonds were ordinary among them. The Knights of the Bath was a brave sight of itself. Remarquable were the two men that represent the two Dukes of Normandy and Aquitane. My Lord Monk rode bare after the king, and led in his hand a spare horse, as being Master of the Horse. The king, in a most rich embroidered suit and cloak, looked most noble. Wadlow, the vintner, at the Devil, in Fleet Street, did lead a fine company of soldiers, all young comely men in white doublets. There followed the Vice-Chamberlain, Sir G. Carteret, and a company of men all like Turkes. The streets all gravelled, and the houses hung with carpets before them, made brave show; and the ladies out of the windows, one of which over against us, I took much notice of, and spoke of her, which made good sport among us. So glorious was the show with gold and silver, that we were not able to look at it, our eyes at last being so much overcome with it. Both the king and the Duke of York took notice of us as they saw us at the window. The show being ended, Mr. Young did give us a dinner, at which we were very merry and pleased above imagination at what we have seen."

The next day, being the feast of St. George, patron of England, the king went in procession from Whitehall to Westminster Abbey, where he was solemnly crowned in the presence of a vast number of peers and bishops. After which, surrounded by the same brilliant company, he passed from the Abbey to Westminster Hall, the way being covered with blue cloth, and lined with spectators to the number of ten thousand. Here his majesty and the lords, spiritual and temporal, dined sumptuously, whilst many fine ceremonies were observed, music of all sorts was played, and a great crowd of pretty ladies looked down from the galleries. And when the banquet was over, and a general pardon had been read by the lord chancellor, and the champion had drank out of the king's gold cup, Charles betook himself to Whitehall. Then, after two days of fair weather, it suddenly "fell a-raining, and thundering and lightning," says Pepys, "as I have not seen it do for some years; which people did take great notice of."

CHAPTER IV.

The King's character.--His proverbial grace.--He tells a story well.--"A warmth and sweetness of the blood."--Beautiful Barbara Palmer.--Her intrigue with my Lord Chesterfield.--James, Duke of York.--His early days.--Escape from St. James's.--Fights in the service of France.--Marriage with Anne Hyde.--Sensation at Court.--The Duke of Gloucester's death.--The Princess of Orange.--Schemes against the Duke of York's peace.--The "lewd informer."--Anne Hyde is acknowledged Duchess of York.

Whilst the kingdom was absorbed by movements consequent on its change of government, the court was no less engrossed by incidents relative to the career it had begun. In the annals of court life there are no pages more interesting than those dealing with Charles II, and his friends; in the history of kings there is no more remarkable figure than that of the merry monarch himself.

Returning to rule over a nation which, during his absence, had been distracted by civil strife, King Charles, young in years, brave in deeds, and surrounded by that halo of romance which misfortune lends its victims, entirely gained the hearts of his subjects. Nature had endowed him with gifts adapted to display qualities that fascinated, and fitted to hide blemishes which repelled. On the one hand his expressive features and shapely figure went far towards creating a charm which his personal grace and courtesy of manner completed; on the other, his delicate tact screened the heartlessness of his sensualism, whilst his surface sympathies hid the barrenness of his cynicism.

With the coolness and courage he had shown in danger, the shrewdness and wit he continually evinced, and the varied capacities he certainly possessed, Charles II. might have made his reign illustrious, had not his love of ease and detestation of business rendered him indifferent to all things so long as he was free to follow his desires. But these faults, which became grievous in the eyes of his subjects, commended him to the hearts of his courtiers, the common purpose of whose lives was pursuit of pleasure. Never was sovereign more gracious to those who came in contact with him, or less ceremonious with his friends; whilst abroad he had lived with his little band of courtiers more as a companion than a king. The bond of exile had drawn them close together; an equal fortune had gone far towards obliterating distinctions of royalty; and custom had so fitted the monarch and his friends to familiarity, that on his return to England neither he nor they laid aside a mutual freedom of treatment which by degrees extended itself throughout the court. For all that, "he was master," as Welwood says, "of something in his person and aspect that commanded both love and admiration at once."

Among his many gifts was that of telling a story well--a rare one 'tis true in all ages. Never was he better pleased than when, surrounded by a group of gossips, he narrated some anecdote of which he was the hero; and, though his tales were more than twice told, they were far from tedious; inasmuch as, being set forth with brighter flashes of wit and keener touches of irony, they were ever pleasant to hear. His conversation was of a like complexion to his tales, pointed, shrewd, and humorous; frequently--as became the manner of the times--straying far afield of propriety, and taking liberties of expression of which nice judgments could not approve. But indeed his majesty's speech was not more free than his conduct was licentious. He could not think, he gravely told Bishop Burnet, "God would make a man miserable for taking a little pleasure out of the way." Accordingly he followed the free bent of his desires, and his whole life was soon devoted to voluptuousness; a vice which an ingenious courtier obligingly describes as a "warmth and sweetness of the blood that would not be confined in the communicating itself--an overflowing of good nature, of which he had such a stream that it would not be restrained within the banks of a crabbed and unsociable virtue."

The ease and freedom of his continental life had no doubt fostered this lamentable depravity; for his misfortunes as an exiled king by no means prevented him following his inclinations as an ardent lover. Accordingly, his intrigues at that time were numerous, as may be judged from the fact of Lady Byron being described as "his seventeenth mistress abroad." The offspring of one of his continental mistresses was destined to plunge the English nation into civil warfare, and to suffer a traitor's death on Tower Hill in the succeeding reign.

"The profligacy which Charles practised abroad not being discontinued at home, he resumed in England an intrigue commenced at Brussels a short time before the restoration. The object of this amour was the beautiful Barbara Palmer, afterwards, by reason of her lack of virtue, raised to the peerage under the titles of Countess of Castlemaine, and Duchess of Cleveland. This lady, who became a most prominent figure in the court of the merry monarch, was daughter of William, second Viscount Grandison, a brave gentleman and a loyal, who had early in life fallen in the civil war whilst fighting for his king. He is described as having, among other gifts, "a faultless person," a boon, which descended to his only child, the bewitching Barbara. In the earliest dawn of her womanhood she encountered her first lover in the person of Philip Stanhope, second Earl of Chesterfield. My lord was at this time a youthful widower, and is described as having "a very agreeable face, a fine head of hair, an indifferent shape, and a pleasant wit. He was, moreover, an elegant beau and a dissolute man--testimony of which latter fact may be gathered from a letter written to him in 1658, by his sister-in-law, Lady Essex, to prevent the "ruin of his soule." Writes her ladyship: "You treate all the mad drinking lords, you sweare, you game, and commit all the extravagances that are insident to untamed youths, to such a degree that you make yourselfe the talke of all places, and the wonder of those who thought otherwise of you, and of all sober people."

When Barbara was sixteen, my lord, then in his twenty-third year, inherited the title and estates of his grandfather: he therefore became master of his own fortune and could bestow his hand where he pleased. That he was in love with Barbara is, indeed, most true; but that his passion was dishonourable is likewise certain: for though he wrote her letters full of tenderness, and kept assignations with her at Butler's shop, on Ludgate Hill, he was the while negotiating a marriage with one Mrs. Fairfax, to whom he was not, however, united. His intrigue with Barbara continued for upwards of three years, when it was temporarily suspended by her marriage to one Roger Palmer, a student of the Inner Temple, the son of a Middlesex knight, and, moreover, a man of the most obliging temper, as will hereafter be seen. Barbara's loyalty to her husband was but of short duration. Before she had been nine months a wife, we find her writing to her old lover she is "ready and willing to goe all over the world" with him--a sacrifice he declined to accept! though eager to take advantage of the affection which prompted it. A little while later he was obliged to quit England; for it happened in the first month of the year 1660 he quarrelled with and killed one Francis Woolley, a student at law, to avoid the consequences of which act he speedily fled the country.

Arriving at Calais, he wrote to King Charles, who was then preparing to return, throwing himself on his mercy, and beseeching his pardon; which the king granting, Lord Chesterfield sought his majesty at Brussels. Soon afterwards Barbara Palmer and her complaisant husband, a right loyal man, joined the king's court abroad, when the intrigue begun which was continued on the night of the monarch's arrival in London. True the loyal PARLIAMENTARY INTELLIGENCER stated "his majesty was diverted from his pious intention of going to Westminster to offer up his devotions of prayer and praise in publick according to the appointment of his Majesty, and made his oblations unto God in the presence-chamber;" but it is, alas, equally certain, according to Oldmixon, Lord Dartmouth, and other reliable authorities, he spent the first night of his return in the company of Barbara Palmer. From that time this abandoned woman exercised an influence over the king which wholly disgraced his court, and almost ruined his kingdom.

Another prominent figure, whose history is inseparable from the king's, was that of his majesty's brother, James, Duke of York--a man of greater ambition and lesser talents than the merry monarch, but one whose amorous disposition equalled the monarch's withal. At an early period of his life the Duke of York was witness of the strife which divided his unhappy father's kingdom. When only eight years old he was sent for by Charles I. to York, but was forbidden by the Parliament to leave St. James's Palace. Despite its commands he was, however, carried to the king by the gallant Marquis of Hereford. That same year the boy witnessed the refusal of Sir John Hotham, Governor of Hull, to admit his majesty within the gates; and James was subsequently present at the siege of Bristol, and the famous battle of Edgehill, when his life at one period of the engagement was in imminent peril.

Until 1646 he continued under the guardianship of his father, when, on the entrance of Fairfax into Oxford, the young duke was found among the prisoners, and by Cromwell's orders committed to the charge of Sir George Ratcliffe. A few months later he was removed to St. James's Palace, when in company with his brother, the

Duke of Gloucester, and his sister, the Princess Elizabeth, he was placed under the care of Lord Northumberland, who had joined the Republican cause.

Though by no means treated with unkindness, the young duke, unhappy at the surveillance placed upon his actions and fearful of the troubles quickly gathering over the kingdom, twice sought escape. This was a serious offence in the eyes of Cromwell's Parliament; a committee was accordingly sent to examine him, and he was threatened with imprisonment in the Tower. Though only in his fourteenth year he already possessed both determination and courage, by reason of which he resolved to risk all danger, and make a third effort for freedom. Accordingly he laid his plans with much ingenuity, selecting two men from those around him to aid his undertaking. These were George Howard and Colonel Bamfield. The latter had once served in the king's army, but when the fortunes of war had gone against his royal master, had professed himself friendly to the Republicans. No doubt the young duke saw the gallant colonel was still true at heart to the Royalist cause, and therefore trusted him at this critical juncture.

Now for a fortnight previous to the night on which he designed to escape, James made it his habit to play at hide-and-seek every evening after supper with his brother and sister, and the children of the officers then located in the palace; and in such secure places did he secrete himself that his companions frequently searched for over half an hour without discovering him. This of course accustomed the household to miss him, and was cunningly practised for the purpose of gaining time on his pursuers when he came to be sought for in good earnest.

At last the eventful night fixed for his escape arrived; and after supper a pleasant group of merry children prepared to divert themselves in the long dark halls and narrow winding passages of the grim old palace. James, as usual, proposed concealing himself, and leaving his companions for the purpose, disappeared behind some arras; but, instead of hiding, he hastened to his sister's chamber, where he locked up a favourite dog that was in the habit of following his footsteps wherever he went, and then noiselessly slipped down a back stairs which led to an inner garden. Having taken care to provide himself with a key fitting the garden door, he quickly slipped into the park. Here he found Colonel Bamfield waiting, who, giving him a cloak and a wig for his better disguise, hurried him into a hackney coach, which drove them as far as Salisbury House in the Strand. From thence they went through Spring Garden, and down Ivy Lane, when, taking boat, they landed close by London Bridge. Here entering the house of a surgeon friendly to their adventure, they found a woman named Murray awaiting them, who immediately provided a suit of woman's wearing apparel for the young duke, in which she helped to attire him. Dressed in this costume he, attended by the faithful Bamfield, hastened to Lion Quay, where they entered a barge hired for their conveyance to a Dutch frigate stationed beyond Gravesend.

Meanwhile, the children not being able to discover their playfellow in the palace, their elders became suspicious of the duke's escape, and began to aid the search. Before an hour elapsed they were convinced he had fled, and St. James's was thrown into a state of the utmost excitement and confusion. Notice of his flight was at once despatched to General Fairfax at Whitehall, who immediately gave orders have all the roads from London guarded, especially those leading to the north; for it was surmised he would in the first instance seek to escape into Wales. The duke, however, had taken a safer course, but one which was not unattended by danger. He had not sailed far in the barge when its master became suspicious that he was aiding the escape of some persons of consequence, and became frightened lest he should get into trouble by rendering them his services. And presently his surmise was converted into certainty; for looking through a cranny of the barge-room door, he saw the young woman fling her leg on the table and pull up her stocking in a most unmaidenly manner. He therefore at once peremptorily declared to Colonel Bamfield they must land at Gravesend, and procure another boat to carry them to the ship; for it would be impossible for the barge to pass the block-house lower down without being observed, and consequently inspected, as was the custom at this troubled time. On hearing which Colonel Bamfield was filled with dismay; but, knowing that at heart the people were loyal towards the Stuarts, he confided the identity of his passenger, and begged him not to betray them in this hour of peril. To give his appeal further weight, he promised the fellow a considerable sum if they safely reached the frigate; for human nature is weak, and greed of gold is strong. On this, the bargee, who was a loyal man, promised he would help them to the best of his powers; the lights were therefore extinguished, the oars drawn in, and, the tide fortunately answering, the barge glided noiselessly down under cover of night, and passed the block-house unobserved. In good time they reached the frigate, which, the duke and Colonel Bamfield boarding, at once set sail, and in a few days landed them at Middleburgh. James proceeded to the court of his sister, the Princess of Orange, and later on joined his mother in France.

At the age of twenty he served in the French army, under Turenne, against the Spanish forces in Flanders, and subsequently in several campaigns, where he invariably showed himself so brave and valiant that the Prince de Conde declared that if ever there was a man without fear, it was James, Duke of York. Now it happened that in 1658 the Princess of Orange went to Paris in order to visit the queen mother, as the widow of Charles I. was called. The Duke of York was in the gay capital at this time, and it soon became noticed that he fixed his attention overmuch on one of his sister's maids of honour, Anne Hyde. This gentlewoman, then in her twenty-first year, was the possessor of a comely countenance, excellent shape, and much wit. Anne was daughter of Edward Hyde, a worthy man, who had been bred to the law, and proved himself so faithful a servant to Charles I., that his majesty had made him Privy Councillor and Chancellor of the Exchequer. After the king's execution, in 1649, the chancellor thought it wise for himself and his family to seek refuge in exile, and accordingly joined Charles II., with whom he lived in the closest friendship, and for whose return he subsequently negotiated with General Monk.

Now James, after his fashion, made love to Mistress Hyde, who encouraged his advances until they reached a certain stage, beyond which the judicious maiden forbade them to proceed unless blessed by the sanction of holy church. The Duke, impatient to secure his happiness, was therefore secretly united to Mistress Hyde in the bonds of matrimony on the 24th of November, in the year of grace 1659, at Breda, to which place the Princess of Orange had returned. In a little while, the restoration being effected, the duke returned to England with the king, leaving his bride behind. And Chancellor Hyde being presently re-established in his offices, and settled in his residence at Worcester House in the Strand, sent for his wife and children; the more speedily as he had received an overture from a noble family, on behalf of "a hopeful, well-bred young gentleman," who expressed himself anxious to wed with Mistress Anne.

The same young lady had not long returned, when she informed her husband she was about to become a mother; whereon the duke, seeking the king, fell upon his knees before him, laid bare his secret, and besought him to sanction his union, "that he might publicly marry in such a manner as his majesty thought necessary for the consequence thereof;" adding that, if consent were refused, he would "immediately take leave of the kingdom and spend his life in foreign parts." King Charles was astonished and perplexed by this confession. James was heir, and as such it behoved him to wed with one suited, by reason of her lineage, to support the dignity of the crown, and calculated by her relation towards foreign powers to strengthen the influence of the throne. The duke was fully aware of this, and, moreover, knew he could without much difficulty have his marriage annulled; but that he did not adopt this course was an honourable trait in his character; and, indeed, his conduct and that of the king was most creditable throughout the transactions which followed; an account of which is set forth with great minuteness in the "Continuation of Edward Hyde, Lord Clarendon's Life."

Without the advice of his council, the king could give no satisfactory reply to his brother. He therefore summoned two of his trusty friends, the Marquis of Ormond and the Earl of Southampton, whom he informed of the duke's marriage, requesting them to communicate the same to the chancellor, and return with him for private consultation. The good man's surprise at this news concerning his daughter was, according to his own account, exceeding great, and was only equalled by his vast indignation. His loyalty towards the royal family was so fervent that it overlooked his affection to his child. He therefore fell into a violent passion, protested against her wicked presumption, and advised that the king "should immediately cause the woman to be sent to the Tower, and to be cast into a dungeon, under so strict a guard that no person should be admitted to come to her; and then that an act of parliament should be immediately passed for the cutting off her head, to which he would not only give his consent, but would very willingly be the first man that should propose it." All this he presently repeated to the king, and moreover, assured him an example of the highest severity, in a case so nearly concerning himself, would serve as a warning that others might take heed of offences committed against his regal dignity.

News of this marriage spread throughout the court with rapidity, and caused the utmost excitement; which in a little while was somewhat abated by the announcement that the king's youngest brother, Henry, Duke of Gloucester, was taken ill of small-pox. This young prince, who is described as "a pretty boy," possessed parts which bade fair to surpass his brothers. He was indeed associated by his family with their tenderest memories, inasmuch as he had been with his father on the sad day previous to his execution. On that melancholy occasion, Charles I. had taken him upon his knee, and said to him very tenderly, "Sweetheart, they will cut off thy father's head," at which the boy shuddered and turned pale. "Mark, child, what I say," continued the unhappy king, "they will cut off my head, and, perhaps, make thee a king; but mark what I say, you must not be made king as long as your brothers Charles and James are alive, for they will cut off thy brothers' heads when they catch them, and cut off thy head at last; and therefore I charge you not to be made a king by them." To which the lad replied very earnestly, "I will be torn in pieces first." Sometime after the death of his father he was allowed to join his family in France, and, like his brother James, entered the army of that country. On the restoration, he had returned with the king, and, three months later, this "prince of very extraordinary hopes" died, grievously lamented by the court, and especially by his majesty, who declared he felt this loss more than any other which had previously fallen upon him.

Scarcely had he been laid to rest in the vault containing the dust of Mary Queen of Scots and Lady Arabella Stuart, when the Princess of Orange arrived in England to pay the king a visit of ceremony. No sooner was she settled at court, than rumour of her brother's marriage reached her; on which she became outrageous; but her wrath was far exceeded by that of the queen mother, who, on hearing the news, wrote to the duke expressing her indignation "that he should have such low thoughts as to marry such a woman." The epistle containing this sentence was at once shown by James to his wife, whom he continually saw and spent much time with, unknown to her father, who had given orders she should keep her chamber. Parliament now sat, but no mention was made of the duke's marriage by either House; and, inasmuch as the union so nearly concerned the nation, this silence caused considerable surprise. It was surmised the delay was made in deference to the feelings of the queen mother, who at this juncture set out for England, to prevent what she was pleased to term "so great a stain and dishonour to the crown." The king regarded his brother's alliance in a lenient spirit, and not only spoke of it frequently before the court, but expressed his desire of bringing the indiscretion to a happy conclusion by a public acknowledgment.

The queen mother, being an ambitious woman, had cherished certain schemes for extending the power of her family by the respective marriages of her sons, which the duke's union was, of course, calculated to curtail. She therefore regarded his wife with the bitterest disdain. Whenever that woman should be brought into Whitehall by one door, her majesty declared she would leave it by another and never enter it again. The marriage was rendered all the more disagreeable to the queen, because the object of her son's choice was daughter of the lord chancellor, whose influence over Charles II. had frequently opposed her plans in the past, and threatened to prevent their realization in the future. The monarch, however, paid little attention to his mother's indignation. He was resolved no disgrace which he could hinder should fall upon the family of one who had served him with disinterested loyalty; and, by way of proving his friendship towards the chancellor on the present occasion, he, before setting out to meet his mother on her arrival at Dover, presented him with twenty thousand pounds, and left a signed warrant for creating him a baron, which he desired the attorney-general to have ready to pass the seals at his return.

In the meantime a wicked plot, for the purpose of lessening James's affection for his wife, and ultimately preventing the acknowledgment of his marriage, was promoted by the chancellor's enemies and the duke's friends, principal amongst whom were the Princess of Orange and Sir Charles Berkley, "a fellow of great wickedness," Sir Charles was his royal highness's most trusted friend, and was, moreover, devoted to the service of the princess and her mother. He therefore determined to hinder the duke from taking a step which he was of opinion would injure him irretrievably. Accordingly, when James spoke in confidence concerning his marriage, Sir Charles told him it was wholly invalid, inasmuch as it had taken place without the king's consent; and that a union with the daughter of an insignificant lawyer was not to be thought of by the heir to the crown. Moreover, he hinted he could a tale unfold regarding her behaviour. At this the duke became impatient to hear what his good friend had to say; whereon that valiant gentleman boasted, with an air of bravery and truth, of certain gallantries which had passed between him and the lady. On hearing this, James, being credulous was sorely depressed. He ceased to visit his wife, withdrew from general company; and so well did Sir Charles's scheme succeed, that before the queen's arrival, the duke had decided on denying his marriage with one who had brought him dishonour. The king, however, put no faith in these aspersions; he felt sure "there was a wicked conspiracy set on foot by villains."

It therefore happened the queen was spared the trouble she had anticipated with her son; indeed, he humbly begged her pardon for "having placed his affections so unequally, of which he was sure there was now an end"--a confession most gratifying to her majesty. The duke's bitter depression continued, and was soon increased by the death of his sister, the Princess of Orange, which was occasioned by smallpox on the 23rd of December, 1660. In her last agonies Lord Clarendon says "she expressed a dislike of the proceedings in that affair, to which she had contributed too much." This fact, together with his royal highness's unhappiness, had due weight on Sir Charles Berkley, who began to repent of the calumnies he had spoken. Accordingly, the "lewd informer" went to the duke, and sought to repair the evil he had wrought. Believing, he said, such a marriage would be the absolute ruin of his royal highness, he had made the accusation which he now confessed to be false, and without the least ground; for he was very confident of the lady's honour and virtue. He then begged pardon on his knees for a fault committed out of pure devotion, and trusted the duke would "not suffer him to be ruined by the power of those whom he had so unworthily provoked, and of which he had so much shame that he had not confidence to look upon them."

James was so much relieved by what he heard that he not only forgave Sir Charles, but embraced him, and promised him protection. Nor did his royal highness longer withhold the reparation due to his wife, who, with the approval of the king and the reluctant consent of the queen, was received at court as Duchess of York. Such was the romance connected with the marriage of her who became mother of two English queens--Mary, wife of William of Orange, and Anne, of pious memory.

CHAPTER V.

Morality of the Restoration.--Puritan piety.--Conduct of women under the Republic.--Some notable courtiers.--The Duke of Ormond and his family.--Lord St. Albans and Henry Jermyn.--His Grace of Buckingham and Mistress Fairfax.--Lord Rochester.--Beautiful Barbara Palmer.--The King's Projected marriage.--Catherine of Braganza.--His Majesty's speech.--A Royal love-letter.--The new Queen sets sail.

A general idea obtains that the libertine example set forth by Charles II. and his courtiers is wholly to blame for the spirit of depravity which marked his reign. That it was in part answerable for the spread of immorality is true, inasmuch as the royalists, considering sufficient aversion could not be shown to the loathsome hypocrisy of the puritans, therefore fell into an opposite extreme of ostentatious profligacy. But that the court was entirely responsible for the vice tainting all classes of society whilst the merry monarch occupied the throne, is false.

Other causes had long been tending to produce this unhappy effect. The reign of the Commonwealth had not been, remarkable for its virtue, though it had been notable for its pharisaism. With the puritan, words of piety took place of deeds of grace; the basest passions were often hidden under sanctimonious exteriors. Even Cromwell, "a man of long and dark discourses, sermons, and prayers," was not above reproach. Bishop Burnet, who has no harsh words for him, and few gentle ones for Charles, states the Protector's intrigue with Lady Dysart was "not a little taken notice of;" on which, the godly man "broke it off." He therefore, Heath records, began an amour with a lady of lesser note--Mrs. Lambert, the wife of a puritan, herself a lady devoted to psalm singing and audible prayer when, not otherwise pleasantly engaged.

The general character of many news-sheets of the day proves that morality under the Republic was at a low ebb. Anarchy in a kingdom invariably favours dissoluteness in a people, inasmuch as the disturbance of civil order tends to unsettle moral law. Homes being divided amongst themselves by political strife, paternal care was suspended, and filial respect ignored. In the general confusion which obtained, the distinction of social codes was overlooked. Lord Clarendon states that; during this unhappy period, young people of either sex were "educated in all the liberty of vice, without reprehension or restraint." He adds, "The young women conversed without any circumspection or modesty, and frequently met at taverns and common eating-houses." An additional description of the ways and manners of young maidens under the Republic is given in a rare and curious pamphlet entitled "A Character of England as it was lately presented in a Letter to a Nobleman of France"; printed in the year 1659, for Jo. Crooke, and sold at the Ship in St. Paul's Yard. Having spoken of taverns where "fury and intemperance" reign, and where, "that nothing may be wanting to the height of luxury and impiety, organs have been translated out of the churches for the purpose of chanting their dithyrambics and bestiall bacchanalias to the tune of those instruments which were wont to assist them in the celebration of God's praises," the writer continues: "Your lordship will scarce believe me that the ladies of greatest quality suffer themselves to be treated in one of those taverns, where a curtezan in other cities would scarcely vouchsafe to be entertained; but you will be more astonish't when I shall assure you that they drink their crowned cups roundly, strain healths through their smocks, daunce after the fiddle, kiss freely, and tearm it an honourable treat." He furthermore says they were to be found until midnight in company with their lovers at Spring Garden, which seemed to be "contrived to all the advantages of gallantry." From which evidences it may be gathered, that London under the Commonwealth was little less vicious than under the merry monarch.

The court Charles speedily gathered round him on his restoration was the most brilliant the nation had ever witnessed. Those of birth and distinction who had sought refuge abroad during the late troubles, now joyfully returned: whilst the juvenile branches of noble families living in retirement in England, to whom royalty had been a stranger, no less eagerly flocked to the presence of the gay young king. The wit and politeness of the men, the grace and beauty of the women, who surrounded Charles II. have become proverbial; whilst the gallantries of the one, and the frailties of the other, savour more of romance than reality.

That the condition of the court on its establishment may be realized, it is necessary, at this stage of its history, to introduce briefly some of the chief personages who surrounded his majesty, and occupied prominent attention in the annals of his reign. Notably amongst them were the gallant Duke of Ormond and his family. His grace, now in his fiftieth year, was distinguished for his commanding appearance, gracious manner, and excellent wit. During the troubles of the civil war, he had proved himself a most loyal subject, inasmuch as he had vested his fortune and ventured his person in service of the late king. Subsequently refusing liberal offers made him by Cromwell, on condition of living in peaceful retirement, he, after the execution of Charles I., betook himself to France, and shared exile with the young king until the restoration. In consequence of his proven fealty, honours were then deservingly showered upon him: he was made grand steward of the household, first lord of the bedchamber, and subsequently lord lieutenant of Ireland. The duchess, who had participated in her husband's misfortunes with a courage equal to his own, was a high-minded and most virtuous lady, who had brought up her family with great care. Scarcely less distinguished in mien and manner than the duke, were his two sons, Thomas, Earl of Ossory, and Lord Richard Butler, afterwards Earl of Arran. My lord of Ossory was no less remarkable for his beauty than famous for his accomplishments: he rode and played tennis to perfection, performed upon the lute to entrancement, and danced to the admiration of the court; he was moreover a good historian, and well versed in chronicles of romance. No less was the Earl of Arran proficient in qualifications befitting his birth, and gifted with attributes aiding his gallantry.

A third member of this noble family played a more remarkable part in the history of the court during her brief career than either of her brothers. This was the Lady Elizabeth Butler, eldest daughter of the duke, who, unfortunately for her own happiness, married my Lord Chesterfield at the Hague, when, a few months before the restoration, that nobleman fled to the continent to escape the consequences of Francis Woolley's murder. In Lely's picture of the young Countess of Chesterfield, her piquancy attracts at a glance, whilst her beauty charms on examination. Her cousin, Anthony Hamilton, describes her as having large blue eyes, very tempting and alluring, a complexion extremely fair, and a heart "ever open to tender sentiments," by reason of which her troubles arose, as shall be set down in proper sequence.

Henry Jermyn, Earl of St. Albans, and his nephew, "the little Jermyn," were also notable as figuring in court intrigues. The earl was member of the privy council to his majesty, and moreover held a still closer connection to the queen mother; for, according to Sir John Reresby, Madame Buviere, and others, her majesty had privately married his lordship abroad--an act of condescension he repaid with inhumanity. Madame Buviere says he never gave the queen a good word; and when she spoke to him he used to say, "Que me veut cette femme?" The same authority adds, he treated her majesty in an extremely ill manner, "so that whilst she had not a faggot to warm herself, he had in his apartments a good fire and a sumptuous table." [This testimony concerning the queen's poverty is borne out by Cardinal de Retz. In his interesting Memoirs he tells of a visit he paid the queen mother, then an exile in Paris. He found her with her youngest daughter, Henrietta, in the chamber of the latter. "At my coming in," says the Cardinal, "she (the queen) said, 'You see, I am come to keep Henrietta company; the poor child could not rise to-day for want of a fire.' The truth is, that the Cardinal (Mazarin) for six months together had not ordered her any money towards her pension; that no tradespeople would trust her for anything and there was not at her lodgings a single billet. You will do me the justice to think that the princess of England did not keep her bed the next day for want of a faggot... Posterity will hardly believe that a princess of England, granddaughter to Henry the Great, hath wanted a faggot in the month of January, in the Louvre, and in the eyes of the French court."] Pepys records that the marriage of her majesty to the earl was commonly talked of at the restoration; and he likewise mentions it was rumoured "that they had a daughter between them in France. How true," says this gossip, "God knows."

The earl's nephew, Henry Jermyn, is described as having a big head and little legs, an affected carriage, and a wit consisting "in expressions learned by rote, which he occasionally employed either in raillery or love." For all that, he being a man of amorous disposition, the number of his intrigues was no less remarkable than the rank of those who shared them. Most notable amongst his conquests was the king's eldest sister, widow of the Prince of Orange--a lady possessing in no small degree natural affections for which her illustrious family were notorious. During the exile of Charles II., Henry Jermyn had made a considerable figure at her court in Holland by reason of the splendour of his equipage, entirely supported by his uncle's wealth; he had likewise made a forcible impression on her heart by virtue of the ardour of his addresses, wholly sustained by his own effrontery. The effect of his presence on the princess soon became visible to the court. Rumour whispered that as Lord St. Albans had already made an alliance with royalty, his nephew had likewise followed his example; but scandal declared that young Jermyn and the princess had omitted the ceremony which should have sanctioned their happiness. The reputation of such an amour gained him the immediate attention of many women, whose interest in his character increased with the knowledge of his abilities, and helped to associate him in their memories with tenderest emotions.

Another figure prominent in this gay and goodly assembly was George Villiers, second Duke of Buckingham. The faultless beauty of his face, and graceful symmetry of his figure, would have rendered him distinguished in a court less sensuously impressionable to physical perfection, even if his talents had not dazzled, and his wit amused. On the death of the first Duke of Buckingham, "styled the handsomest bodied man in England," the late king of pious memory undertook the charge of the young duke, and had him educated with his own sons. Subsequently he was sent to Cambridge, and then travelled into France, the better to acquire that polish of manner and grace of bearing for which he became distinguished. But, whilst abroad, word was brought him of the distress of his master, the king; on which the young duke hastened back into England, became a cavalier, and fought his majesty's battles with great gallantry. Soon after Charles I. had been beheaded, his faithful servitor went abroad; but being loyal to the Stuart cause, he journeyed with Charles II. to Scotland, and afterwards fought beside him in the bloody battle of Worcester. Whilst the monarch was hiding in Boscobel Wood, the duke betook himself to London, where, donning a wizard's mask, a jack-pudding coat, a hat adorned with a fox's tail and cock's feathers, he masqueraded as a mountebank, and discoursed diverting nonsense from a stage erected at Charing Cross. After running several risks, he escaped to France. But alas for the duke, who was born as Madame Dunois avows, doubtless from experience--"for gallantry and magnificence," he was now penniless, his great estates being confiscated by Cromwell. However, conceiving a scheme that might secure him part of his fortune, he hastened to put it into execution.

It happened that my Lord Fairfax, one of Cromwell's great generals, had allotted to him by the Protector a portion of the Buckingham estates that returned five thousand pounds a year. The general was, moreover, placed in possession of York House, which had likewise belonged to his grace.

Now it happened Lord Fairfax, a generous-tempered man and brave soldier, had an only child, a daughter destined to become his heiress; aware of which the duke resolved to marry her, that he might in this manner recover portion of his estate. The fact of the lady never having seen him did not interfere with his plans; that she would reject his suit seemed an impossibility; that she would succumb to the fascination he invariably exercised over woman was a certainty. Nor did it matter that Mistress Fairfax was no beauty; for the duke, being grateful for past favours liberally bestowed by the opposite sex, had no intention of becoming under any circumstances churlish enough to limit his devotion to one lady, though she were his wife.

Carefully disguising himself, he journeyed to London, where he was met by a faithful friend, who promised he would aid him in winning Mistress Fairfax, towards which end he promptly introduced the duke to that estimable gentlewoman. Having once obtained speech of her, the remainder of his scheme was comparatively easy of accomplishment. She loved the gay and graceful gallant at first sight, and through years of bitter wrong and cruel neglect continued his faithful and devoted slave.

Though she had become clandestinely acquainted with him, she was too good a daughter to wed without her father's consent. But this she had not much difficulty in obtaining. Though Lord Fairfax had fought against his king, he was not sufficiently republican to scorn alliance with nobility, nor so thoroughly puritan as to disdain connection with the ungodly. Accordingly he gave his sanction to the union, which was celebrated at his mansion at Nun Appleton, within six miles of York. Now, my Lord Fairfax had not consulted Cromwell's goodwill concerning this alliance, the news of which reaching the Protector in due time, made him exceedingly wroth. For he had daughters to marry, and, that he might strengthen his power, was desirous of wedding them to scions of nobility; Buckingham being one of those whom he had mentally selected to become a member of his family. His anger was therefore at once directed against Fairfax and his grace. The former he could not molest, but the latter he committed to the Tower; and if the great Protector had not been soon after seized by fatal illness, the duke would have made his last journey from thence to Tower Hill. As it fell out he remained a prisoner until within a year of the coming of Charles, whom he welcomed with exceeding joy. Being bred with the merry monarch, he had from boyhood been a favourite of his majesty, with whom he shared a common love for diversion. He was, therefore, from the first a prominent figure at Whitehall; his handsome person and extravagant dress adorned the court; his brilliant wit and poignant satire amused the royal circle.

His grace, however, had a rival, the vivacity of whose temper and piquancy of whose humour went far to eclipse Buckingham's talent in these directions. This was the young Earl of Rochester, son of my Lord Wilmot, who had so successfully aided the king's escape after the battle of Worcester, for which service he had been created Earl of Rochester by Charles in Paris. That worthy man dying just a year previous to the restoration, his son succeeded to his titles, and likewise to an estate which had been preserved for him by the prudence of his mother. Even in his young days Lord Rochester gave evidence of possessing a lively wit and remarkable genius, which were cultivated by his studies at Oxford and his travels abroad. So that at the age of eighteen, when he returned to England and presented himself at Whitehall, his sprightly parts won him the admiration of courtiers and secured him the favour of royalty. Nor was the young earl less distinguished by his wit and learning than by his face and figure; the delicate beauty of his features and natural grace of his person won him the love of many women, whom the tenderness of his heart and generosity of his youth did not permit him to leave unrequited.

Soon surfeited by his conquests in the drawing-room, he was anxious to extend his triumphs in another direction; and, selecting the sea as a scene of action, he volunteered to sail under my Lord Sandwich in quest of the Dutch East Indian fleet. At the engagements to which this led he exhibited a dauntless courage that earned him renown abroad, and covered him with honour on his return to court. From that time he, for many years, surrendered himself to a career of dissipation, often abandoning the paths of decency and decorum, pursuing vice in its most daring and eccentric fashion, employing his genius in the composition of lampoons which spared not even the king, and in the writing of ribald verses, the very names of which are not proper to indite. Lord Orford speaks of him as a man "whom the muses were fond to inspire, and ashamed to avow; and who practised, without the least reserve, that secret which can make verses more read for their defects than for their merits." More of my Lord Rochester and his poems anon.

Thomas Killigrew, another courtier, was a poet, dramatist, and man of excellent wit. He had been page in the service of his late majesty, and had shared exile with the present monarch, to whose pleasures abroad and at home he was ever ready to pander. At the restoration he was appointed a groom of the bedchamber, and, moreover, was made master of the revels--an office eminently suited to his tastes, and well fitted to exercise his capacities. His ready wit amused the king so much, that he was occasionally led to freedoms of speech which taxed his majesty's good-nature. His escapades diverted the court to such an extent, that he frequently took the liberty of affording it entertainment at the expense of its reputation. The "beau Sidney," a man "of sweet and caressing temper," handsome appearance, and amorous disposition; Sir George Etherege, a wit and a playwright; and Charles Sackville, Earl of Dorset, a poet and man of sprightly speech, were likewise courtiers of note.

Among such congenial companions the merry monarch abandoned himself wholly to the pursuit of pleasure, and openly carried on his intrigue with Barbara Palmer. According to the testimony of her contemporaries, she was a woman of surpassing loveliness and violent passions. Gilbert Burnet, whilst admitting her beauty, proclaims her defects. She was, he relates, "most enormously vicious and ravenous, foolish but imperious, very uneasy to the king, and always carrying on intrigues with other men, while she yet pretended she was jealous of him." Pepys testifies likewise to her physical attractions so long as she reigned paramount in the king's affections; but when another woman, no less fair, came betwixt my lady and his majesty's favour, Mr. Pepys, being a loyal man and a frail, found greater beauty in the new love, whose charms he avowed surpassed the old. To his most interesting diary posterity is indebted for glimpses of the manner in which the merry monarch and his mistress behaved themselves during the first months of the restoration. Now he tells of "great doings of musique," which were going on at Madame Palmer's house, situated in the Strand, next Earl Sandwich's, and of the king and the duke being with that lady: again, in the Chapel Royal, Whitehall, he observed, whilst Dr. Herbert Croft prayed and preached, "how the Duke of York and Mrs. Palmer did talk to one another very wantonly through the hangings that part the king's closet and the closet where the ladies sit." And later on, when he witnessed "The Humorous Lieutenant" performed before the court, he noted the royal favourite was likewise present, "with whom the king do discover a great deal of familiarity."

Presently, in February, 1661, exactly nine months after his majesty's return, Mrs. Palmer gave birth to a daughter. To the vast amusement of the court, no less than three men claimed the privilege of being considered father of this infant. One of these was my Lord Chesterfield, whom the child grew to resemble in face and person; the second was Roger Palmer, who left her his estate; the third was King Charles, who had her baptized Anne Palmer Fitzroy, adopted her as his daughter, and eventually married her to the Earl of Sussex.

Soon after the restoration the subject of his majesty's marriage was mooted by his councillors, who trusted a happy union would redeem him from vice, and, by bringing him heirs, help to establish him more firmly in the affections of his people. The king lending a willing ear to this advice, the sole difficulty in carrying it into execution rested in the selection of a bride congenial to his taste and equal to his sovereignty. King Louis of France had no sisters, and his nieces had not commended themselves to the merry monarch's favour during his stay abroad. Spain had two infantas, but one was wedded to the King of France, and the other betrothed to the heir of the royal house of Austria. Germany, of course, had princesses in vast numbers, who awaited disposal; but when they were proposed to King Charles, "he put off the discourse with raillery," as Lord Halifax narrates. "Odd's fish," he would say, shrugging his shoulders and making a grimace, "I could not marry one of them: they are all dull and foggy!"

Catherine of Braganza, daughter of Don Juan IV. of Portugal, was unwedded, and to her Charles ultimately addressed himself. Alliance with her commended itself to the nation from the fact that the late king, before the troubled times began, had entered into a negotiation with Portugal concerning the marriage of this same infanta and his present majesty; and such was the esteem in which the memory of Charles I. was now held, that compliance with his desires was regarded as a sacred obligation. The Portuguese ambassador assured the merry monarch that the princess, by reason of her beauty, person, and age, was most suited to him. To convince him of this, he showed his majesty a portrait of the lady, which the king examining, declared "that person could not be unhandsome." The ambassador, who was of a certainty most anxious for this union, then said it was true the princess was a catholic, and would never change her faith; but she was free from "meddling activity;" that she had been reared by a wise mother, and would only look to the freedom of practising her own religion without interfering with that of others. Finally, he added that the princess would have a dowry befitting her high station, of no less a sum than five hundred thousand pounds sterling in ready money.

Moreover, by way of addition to this already handsome portion, the Queen of Portugal was ready to assign over and annex to the English crown, the Island of Bombay, in the East Indies, and Tangier on the African coast--a place of strength and importance, which would be of great benefit and security to British commerce. Nor was this all. Portugal was likewise willing to grant England free trade in Brazil and the East Indies, a privilege heretofore denied all other countries. This was indeed a dower which none of the "dull and foggy" German princesses could bring the crown. The prospect of obtaining so much ready money especially commended the alliance to the extravagant taste of his majesty, who had this year complained to Parliament of his poverty, by reason of which he "was so much grieved to see many of his friends come to him at Whitehall, and to think they were obliged to go somewhere else for a dinner."

The merry monarch was therefore well pleased at the prospect of his union, as were likewise the chancellor and four or five "competent considerers of such an affair" whom he consulted. These worthy counsellors and men of sage repute, who included in their number the Duke of Ormond and Sir Edward Nicholas, Secretary of State, the Earl of Manchester, and the Earl of Southampton, after regretting it was not agreeable to his majesty to select a queen who professed the protestant religion, gave it as their opinion there was no catholic princess in Europe whom he, with so much reason and advantage, could marry as the infanta of Portugal. They, moreover, added that the sum promised as part of her portion, setting aside the places, "was much greater--almost double to what any king had ever received in money by any marriage." The council, therefore, without a dissenting voice, advised him to the marriage.

On the 8th of May, 1661, his majesty, being clad in robes of state, and wearing the crown, rode in great pomp to open Parliament, which he addressed from the throne. In the course of his speech, he announced his approaching marriage in a singularly characteristic address. "I will not conclude without telling you some news," he said, "news that I think will be very acceptable to you, and therefore I should think myself unkind, and ill-natured if I did not impart it to you. I have been put in mind by my friends that it was now time to marry, and I have thought so myself ever since I came into England. But there appeared difficulties enough in the choice, though many overtures have been made to me; and if I should never marry until I could make such a choice against which there could be no foresight of any inconvenience that may ensue, you would live to see me an old bachelor, which I think you do not desire to do. I can now tell you, not only that I am resolved to marry, but with whom I am resolved to marry. If God please, it is with the daughter of Portugal. And I will make all the haste I can to fetch you a queen hither, who, I doubt not, will bring great blessings with her to me and you."

Next day addresses of congratulation were presented to his majesty by both Houses. This gratifying news was made known to the Portuguese ambassador, Count da Ponte, by the lord high chancellor, who visited his excellency for the purpose, attended by state befitting such a great and joyful occasion; two gentlemen preceded him, bearing respectively a gilded mace and a crimson velvet purse embroidered with the arms of Great Britain, and many others following him to the ambassador's residence. A month later, the marriage articles were signed; the new queen being guaranteed the free exercise of her faith, and the sum of thirty thousand a year during life; whilst the king was assured possession of her great dowry, together with the territories already mentioned, one of which, Bombay, ultimately became of such vast importance to the crown.

Charles then despatched the Portuguese ambassador to Catherine--from this time styled queen--in order to make arrangements for her journey into England. Likewise he wrote a letter, remarkable for the fervour of its sentiments and elegance of its diction, which da Ponte was commissioned to convey her. This courtly epistle, addressed by Charles to "The Queen of Great Britain, my wife and lady, whom God preserve," is dated July 2nd, 1661, and runs as follows:

"MY LADY AND WIFE,

"Already, at my request, the good Count da Ponte has set off for Lisbon; for me the signing of the marriage act has been great happiness; and there is about to be despatched at this time after him one of my servants, charged with what would appear necessary, whereby may be declared, on my part, the inexpressible joy of this felicitous conclusion, which, when received, will hasten the coming of your majesty.

"I am going to make a short progress into some of my provinces; in the meantime, whilst I go from my most sovereign good, yet I do not complain as to whither I go, seeking in vain tranquillity in my restlessness; hoping to see the beloved person of your majesty in these kingdoms already your own, and that with the same anxiety with which, after my long banishment, I desired to see myself within them, and my subjects, desiring also to behold me amongst them, having manifested their most ardent wishes for my return, well known to the world. The presence of your serenity is only wanting to unite us, under the protection of God, in the health and content I desire. I have recommended to the queen, our lady and mother, the business of the Count da Ponte, who, I must here avow, has served me in what I regard as the greatest good in this world, which cannot be mine less than it is that of your majesty; likewise not forgetting the good Richard Russell, who laboured on his part to the same end. [Richard Russell was Bishop of Portalegre, in Portugal, and Almoner to Catherine of Braganza.]

"The very faithful husband of your majesty, whose hand he kisses,
"CHARLES REX."
London, 2nd of July, 1661.

During many succeeding months preparations were made in England to receive the young Queen. The "Royal Charles," a stately ship capable of carrying eighty cannon and six hundred men, was suitably fitted to convey her to England.

The state room and apartments destined for use of the future bride were furnished and ornamented in most luxuriant manner, being upholstered in crimson velvet, handsomely carpeted, and hung with embroideries and taffeties. Lord Sandwich was made commander of the gallant fleet which in due time accompanied the

"Royal Charles." He was likewise appointed ambassador extraordinary, and charged with safely conducting the bride unto her bridegroom.

In due time, my lord, in high spirits, set sail with his gallant fleet, and on arriving at Portugal was received with every remark of profound respect, and every sign of extravagant joy. Stately ceremonies at court and brilliant rejoicings in public made time speed with breathless rapidity. But at length there came a day when my Lord Sandwich encountered a difficulty he had not foreseen. According to instructions, he had taken possession of Tangier before proceeding for the queen; and he had likewise been directed to see her dowry put on board one of his ships, before receiving her on the "Royal Charles."

Now the Queen of Portugal, who acted as regent since the death of her husband, being strongly desirous of seeing her daughter the consort of a great sovereign, and of protecting her country from the tyranny of Spain by an alliance with England, had gathered the infanta's marriage portion with infinite trouble; which had necessitated the selling of her majesty's jewels and much of her plate, and the borrowing of both plate and jewels from churches and monasteries all over the land. The sums accumulated in this manner she had carefully stowed away in great sacks; but, alas, between the date on which the marriage treaty had been signed, and arrival of the English ambassador to claim the bride, Spain had made war upon Portugal, and the dowry had to be expended in arming the country for defence. Therefore, when my Lord Sandwich mentioned the dowry, her majesty, with keen regrets and infinite apologies, informed him so great were the straits of poverty to which her kingdom was reduced, that she could pay only half the stipulated sum at present, but promised the remaining portion should be made up the following year. Moreover, the part which she then asked him to accept was made up of jewels, sugars, spices and other commodities which she promised to have converted by arrangement into solid gold in London.

The ambassador was therefore sorely perplexed, and knew not whether he should return to England without the bride, or take her and the merchandise which represented half her dowry on board his ship. He decided on the latter course, and the queen, with her court and retinue, set sail for merry England on the 23rd of April, 1662.

CHAPTER VI.

The king's intrigue with Barbara Palmer.--The queen arrives at Portsmouth.--Visited by the Duke of York.--The king leaves town,--First interview with his bride.--His letter to the lord chancellor.--Royal marriage and festivities.--Arrival at Hampton Court Palace.--Prospects of a happy union.--Lady Castlemaine gives birth to a second child.--The king's infatuation.--Mistress and wife.--The queen's misery.--The king's cruelty.--Lord Clarendon's messages.--His majesty resolves to break the queen's spirit.--End of the domestic quarrel.

Whilst the king conducted the negotiations of his marriage with Catherine of Braganza, he likewise continued the pursuit of his intrigue with Barbara Palmer. The unhappy fascination which this vile woman exercised over his majesty increased with time; and though his ministers declared a suitable marriage would reform his ways, his courtiers concluded he had no intention of abandoning his mistress in favour of his wife. For Barbara Palmer, dreading the loss of her royal lover and the forfeiture of wealth accruing from this connection, had firmly bound him in her toils. Moreover, in order that he might continually abide under her influence, she conceived a scheme which would of necessity bring her into constant intercourse with him and the young queen. She therefore demanded he would appoint her one of the ladies of the bedchamber to her majesty, to which he, heedless of the insult this would fix upon his wife, readily consented.

In order to qualify Barbara Palmer for such a position, it was necessary she should be raised to the peerage. This could only be accomplished by ennobling her husband, unless public decency were wholly ignored, and she was created a peeress in her own right, whilst he remained a commoner. After some faint show of hesitation, Roger Palmer accepted the honours thrust upon him by reason of his wife's infamy. On the 11th of December, 1661, he was created Earl of Castlemaine, and Baron Limerick in the peerage of Ireland, when the royal favourite became a countess.

And now the merry month of May being arrived, the queen was speedily expected; and on the night of the 13th joyful tidings reached London that the "Royal Charles," accompanied by the fleet, was in sight of Portsmouth. At which news there was great rejoicing throughout the town, church bells ringing merrily, and bonfires blazing brightly; but before the Countess of Castlemaine's house, where the king, according to his custom was at supper, there was no fire, though such signs of joy burned "at all the rest of the doors almost in the streets, which was much observed."

Next day the fleet arrived in the harbour of Portsmouth, about four in the afternoon. Heath says the people gathered to receive the bride with all possible demonstrations of honour, "the nobility and gentry and multitudes of Londoners, in most rich apparel and in great numbers, waiting on the shore for her landing; and the mayor and aldermen and principal persons of that corporation being in their gowns, and with a present and a speech ready to entertain her; the cannon and small shot, both from round that town and the whole fleet echoing to one another the loud proclamations of their joy." These good people were, however, destined to disappointment; for though the bride was impatient to land, because suffering from prostration consequent on a rough voyage and severe illness, she was not, in observance of court etiquette, permitted to leave the ship until the king arrived. This did not take place until six days later, Charles being detained in town by reason of some important bills then passing in Parliament, which it was necessary for him to sign. He had, however, despatched his royal brother of York, then Lord High Admiral of England, to meet her at sea, and give her greeting in his name. Accordingly the duke had encountered the fleet at the Isle of Wight, and gone on board the queen's ship, when she received him in her cabin seated under a canopy on a chair of state. His royal highness expressed his joy at her arrival, presented "his majesty's high respects and his exceeding affection for her," and paid her many compliments. Lord Chesterfield, who had been appointed chamberlain to the queen, tells us: "Although James, in consequence of his near connection with the sovereign, might have saluted the royal bride, he did not avail himself of this privilege, out of a delicate regard to his majesty's feelings, that he might be the first man to offer that compliment to his queen; she coming out of a country where it was not the fashion." The Duke of York presented some noblemen who had accompanied him; after which she introduced the members of her suite. The queen and her brother-in-law then held a conversation in the Spanish language, when James assured her of his affection, and besought her to accept his services. To these compliments she replied in like manner, when he arose to depart. The queen advanced three paces with him, not withstanding that he protested against such courtesy, bidding her remember her rank. At this she smiled, and answered with much sweetness, "She wished to do that out of affection, which she was not obliged to do"--a reply which made a favourable impression on his mind. Whilst she continued on board, the duke and his suite visited her daily, entering freely into conversation with her, and finding her "a most agreeable lady." Probably at the desire of the king, she left the ship before his arrival, and was conveyed to his majesty's house at Portsmouth, where she was received by the Countess of Suffolk, first lady of the bedchamber, and four other ladies who had been appointed members of her household. One of her first requests to these was--as may be learned from a letter of Lord Sandwich, preserved in the Bodleian library--"that they would put her in that habit they thought would be most pleasing to the king." Before leaving the "Royal Charles" she spoke to all the officers of the ship, thanked them for their services, and permitted them to kiss her hand. She then presented a collar of gold to the captain, and gave money to be distributed among the crew.

When at length the parliamentary business was concluded, the king found himself in readiness to depart. The last words he addressed to his faithful commons before starting are worth recording: "The mention of my wife's arrival," said he, in the pleasant familiar tone it was his wont to use, "puts me in mind to desire you to put that compliment upon her, that her entrance into this town may be made with more decency than the ways will now suffer it to be; and to that purpose I pray you would quickly pass such laws as are before you, in order to the mending those ways, that she may not find Whitehall surrounded with water."

At nine o'clock on the night of the 19th of May, his majesty left London in Lord Northumberland's carriage, on his way to Portsmouth. Arriving at Kingston an hour later, he entered Lord Chesterfield's coach, which awaited him there by appointment, and drove to Guildford, at which town he slept the night. In the morning he was up betimes, and posted to Portsmouth, where he arrived at noon. The queen, being ill of a slight fever, was yet in bed: but the king, all impatient to see the bride which heaven had sent him, sought admittance to her chamber. The poor princess evidently did not look to advantage; for his majesty told Colonel Legg he thought at first glance "they had brought him a bat instead of a woman." On further acquaintance, however, she seemed to have afforded more pleasure to the king's sight, for the next day he expressed the satisfaction he felt concerning her, in a letter addressed to the lord chancellor, which is preserved in the library of the British Museum, and runs as follows:

"PORTSMOUTH, 21st May (Eight in the Morning).

"I arrived here yesterday about two in the afternoon, and, as soon as I had shifted myself, I went into, my wife's chamber, whom I found in bed, by reason of a little cough and some inclination to a fever: but I believe she will find herself very well in the morning when she wakes. I can now only give you an account of what I have seen abed, which, in short, is, her face is not so exact as to be called a beauty, though her eyes are excellent good, and not anything in her face that in the least degree can shock one: on the contrary, she hath as much agreeableness in her looks altogether as ever I saw; and if I have any skill in physiognomy, which I think I have, she must be as good a woman as ever was born. Her conversation, as much as I can perceive, is very good, for she has wit enough, and a most agreeable voice. You would wonder to see how well acquainted we are already. In a word, I think myself very happy; for I am confident our two humours will agree very well together. I have no more to say: my Lord Lieutenant will give you an account of the rest."

The king was attended by Lord Sandwich during this interview, and his lordship, in a letter addressed to the lord chancellor, informed him the meeting between his majesty and the infanta, "hath been with much contentment on both sides, and that we are like to be very happy in their conjunction." Next morning the Countess of Suffolk, and other ladies appointed to wait upon the bride, dressed her according to the English fashion, in "a habit they thought would be most pleasing to the king," in which she was married. The ceremony was first performed according to the rites of the Catholic Church, by the Rev. Lord Aubigny, brother to the Duke of Richmond, in the queen's bedchamber; that apartment being selected for the purpose, as affording a privacy necessary to be maintained, by reason of the prejudice then existing towards Catholicism. There were present the Duke of York, Philip, afterwards Cardinal Howard, and five Portuguese, all of whom were bound over to keep the strictest secrecy concerning what they witnessed. Later in the day, Dr. Sheldon, Bishop of London, married their majesties according to the form prescribed by the Church of England. The latter ceremony took place in the presence chamber. A rail divided the apartment, at the upper part of which the king and queen, the bishops, the Spanish Ambassador, and Sir Richard Fanshaw stood; the lower portion being crowded by the court. When Dr. Sheldon had declared their majesties married, the Countess of Suffolk, according to a custom of the time, detached the ribbons from the bride's dress, and, cutting them in pieces, distributed them amongst those present.

Feasting, balls, and diversions of all kinds followed the celebration of the royal nuptials, and for a time the king was delighted with his bride. Four days after the marriage he writes again to the lord chancellor in most cheerful tone:

"My brother will tell you of all that passes here, which I hope will be to your satisfaction. I am sure 'tis so much to mine that I cannot easily tell you how happy I think myself, and must be the worst man living (which I hope I am not) if I be not a good husband. I am confident never two humours were better fitted together than ours are. We cannot stir from hence till Tuesday, by reason that there is not carts to be had to-morrow to transport all our GUARDE INFANTAS, without which there is no stirring: so you are not to expect me till Thursday night at Hampton Court."

They did not reach the palace until the 29th of May, that being the king's birthday, and, moreover, the anniversary of his entrance into London; a date which the Queen's arrival now caused to be celebrated with triple magnificence and joy. When the coach that conveyed their majesties drew near, the whole palace seemed astir with happy excitement. Double lines of soldiers, both horse and foot, lined the way from the gates to the entrance. In the great hall the lord chancellor, foreign ambassadors, judges, and councillors of state awaited to pay homage to their majesties; whilst in various apartments were the nobility and men of quality, with their ladies, ranged according to their rank, being all eager to kiss the new queen's hand. Sure never was such show of gladness. Bells rang people cheered, bonfires blazed.

In the evening news was brought that the Duchess of York was being rowed to Hampton from town; hearing which, the king, with a blithe heart, betook his way to meet her through the garden, now bright with spring flowers and fragrant with sweet scents, till he arrived at the gate by which the silver streak of the pleasant Thames flowed past. And presently on this calm May eve the sound of oars splashing in the tide was heard, and anon a barge came in sight, hung with silken curtains and emblazoned with the arms of royalty. From this the Duchess of York disembarked, aided by the king. When she had offered her congratulations to him, he, taking her hand, led her to his bride, that such fair speeches might be repeated to her majesty. And coming into the queen's presence the duchess would have gone upon her knees and kissed her majesty's hand; but Catherine raised her in her arms, and kissed her on the cheek. Then amidst much joy the happy evening waned to night.

The royal palace of Hampton Court, in which Charles had decided on spending his honeymoon, had been raised by the magnificent Wolsey in the plenitude of his power as a place of recreation. Since his downfall it had been used by royalty as a summer residence, it being in truth a stately pleasure house. The great pile contained upwards of four hundred rooms. The principal apartments had cedar or gilded and frescoed ceilings, and walls hung with rare tapestries and curtains heavy with gold. Moreover, these rooms contained furniture of most skilful design and costly manufacture, and were adorned by the choice works of such masters of their art as Holbein, Bellini, Vansomer, Rubens, and Raphael; and withal enriched with Indian cabinets, such as never were seen in England before, which the queen had brought with her from Portugal.

The great hall had been the scene of many sumptuous banquets. The chapel was rich in carved designs. Her majesty's bedroom, with its curtains of crimson silk, its vast mirror and toilet of beaten and massive gold, was a splendid apartment--the more so from its state bed, which Evelyn says was "an embroidery of silver on crimson velvet, and cost L8,000, being a present made by the States of Holland, when his majesty returned, and had formerly been given by them to our king's sister, ye Princess of Orange, and being bought of her againe, was now presented to ye king." Around this noble residence, where the court was wont to tarry in summer months, stretched broad and flowerful gardens, with wide parterres, noble statues, sparkling fountains, and marble vases; and beyond lay the park, planted "with swete rows of lime-trees."

And here all day long, in the fair summer time of this year, pleasure held boundless sway. Sauntering in balmy gardens, or seeking shelter from sun-rays in green glades and leafy groves, their majesties, surrounded by their brilliant court, chased bright hours away in frolic and pleasantry from noon till night. Then revelry, gaining new life, began once more, when courtly figures danced graceful measures to sounds of mirthful strains, under the lustre of innumerable lights.

For a while it seemed as if a brave prospect of happiness was in store for the young queen. Her love for her husband, her delight in his affection, her pride in his accomplishments, together with her simplicity, innocence, and naivete, completely won his heart. These claims to his affection were, moreover, strengthened by the charms of her person. Lord Chesterfield, a man whom experience of the sex had made critical, writes that she "was exactly shaped, has lovely hands, excellent eyes, a good countenance, a pleasing voice, fine hair, and, in a word, what an understanding man would wish for in a wife." Notwithstanding the attractions of her majesty's person which he enumerates, he adds his fears that "all these will hardly make things run in the right channel; but, if it should, our court will require a new modelling." In this note of alarm he forebodes danger to come. A man of his majesty's character, witty and careless, weak and voluptuous, was not likely to reconstruct his court, or reclaim it from ways he loved. Nor was his union calculated to exercise a lasting impression on him. The affection he bore his wife in the first weeks of their married life was due to the novelty he found in her society, together with the absence of temptation in the shape of his mistress. Constancy to the marriage vow was scarcely to be expected from a man whose morals had never been shackled by restraint; yet faithlessness to a bride was scarcely to be anticipated ere the honeymoon had waned. This was, however, the unhappy fate which awaited Catherine of Braganza.

It happened early in the month of June, whilst the court was at Hampton, my Lady Castlemaine, who had remained in town through illness, gave birth to a second child. The infant was baptized Charles Palmer, adopted by the king as his own, and as such subsequently created Duke of Southampton. This event seemed to renew all his majesty's tenderness towards her. Wearied by the charm of innocence in the person of his wife, his weak nature yielded to the attraction of vice in that of his mistress. He, therefore, frequently left Hampton Court that he might ride to London, visit the countess, and fritter away some hours in her presence; being heedless alike of the insult he dealt the queen, and the scandal he gave the nation.

The while my Lord Castlemaine lived with the lady who shared his title, and whom he called his wife; but their continuance to abide in harmony and goodwill was, soon after the birth of this child, interrupted for ever. My lord was certainly a loyal subject, but he was likewise a religious man, as may be judged, not by that which has been recorded, but from the narration which follows. Having been bred a Catholic, he was anxious his wife's son should be enrolled a member of the same community. To this end he had him baptized by a priest, a proceeding of which the king wholly disapproved; not because his majesty was attached to any religion in particular, but rather that he resented interference with the infant whom he rested satisfied was his own child. Accordingly, by the king's command, Lady Castlemaine's son was rebaptized by the rector of St. Margaret's, Westminster, in the presence of his majesty, the Earl of Oxford, and the Countess of Suffolk, first lady of the bedchamber to the queen and aunt to the king's mistress.

This exasperated my Lord Castlemaine to such a degree that high words passed between him and his lady: on which he resolved to part from her for ever. However, she was more prompt to act in the matter than he; for, taking advantage of his absence one day, she packed up her jewels, plate, and household treasures, and departed to the residence of her uncle, Colonel Edward Villiers, at Richmond. This step was probably taken, if not by his majesty's suggestion, at least with his full approval; for the house she selected brought her within an easy distance of Hampton Court, into which the king designed promptly to introduce her.

Now rumour of the king's liason had spread beyond the English nation, and had been whispered even at the secluded court of Portugal, into the ears of the bride elect. And the queen regent, dreading the trouble this might draw upon her daughter, had counselled her never to admit his majesty's mistress into her presence. This advice the young queen determined to act upon; and accordingly when Charles, a couple of days after their marriage, presented her with a list of those appointed to her household--amongst whom was my Lady Castlemaine--her majesty drew a pen across the name of the dreaded favourite. The king, if surprised or indignant, made no remark at the time, but none the less held to the resolution he had taken of appointing the countess a lady of the bedchamber. No further attempt of intruding his mistress's presence upon his wife was made until Lady Castlemaine came to Richmond.

It happened on the afternoon of the day on which the favourite arrived her majesty sat in the great drawing-room, surrounded by a brilliant throng of noble and beautiful women and gay and gallant men. The windows of the apartment stood open; outside fountains splashed in the sun; music played in a distant glade: and all the world seemed glad. And as the queen listened to pleasant sounds of wit and gossip, murmuring around her, the courtiers, at sound of a well-known footstep, suddenly ceasing their discourse, fell back on either side adown the room. At that moment the king entered, leading a lady apparelled in magnificent attire, the contour of whose face and outline of whose figure distinguished her as a woman of supreme and sensuous loveliness.

His majesty, suceedingly rich in waving feathers, glittering satins, and fluttering ribbons, returned the gracious bows of his courtiers to right and left; and, unconscious of the curious and perplexed looks they interchanged, advanced to where his wife sat, and introduced my Lady Castlemaine. Her majesty bowed and extended her hand, which the countess, having first courtesyed profoundly, raised to her lips. The queen either had not caught the name, or had disassociated it from that of her husband's mistress; but in an instant the character of the woman presented, and the insult the king had inflicted, flashed upon her mind. Coming so suddenly, it was more than she could bear; all colour fled from her face, tears rushed to her eyes, blood gushed from her nostrils, and she fell senseless to the floor.

Such strong evidence of the degree in which his young wife felt the indignity forced upon her, by no means softened his majesty's heart towards her, but rather roused his indignation at what he considered public defiance of his authority. But as his nature was remote from roughness, and his disposition inclined to ease, he at first tried to gain his desire by persuasion, and therefore besought the queen she would suffer his mistress to become a lady of the bedchamber. But whenever the subject was mentioned to her majesty, she burst into tears, and would not give heed to his words. Charles therefore, incensed on his side, deserted her company, and sought the society of those ever ready to entertain him. And as the greater number of his courtiers were fully as licentious as himself, they had no desire he should become subject to his wife, or alter the evil tenor of his ways.

Therefore in their conversation they cited to him the example of his grandfather, King James I., of glorious memory, who had not dissembled his passions, nor suffered the same to become a reproach to those who returned his love; but had obliged his queen to bear with their company, and treat them with grace and favour; and had, moreover, raised his natural children to the degree of princes of the blood. They told Charles he had inherited the disposition of his grandsire, and they were sure he would treat the objects of his affection in like manner as that king had done. Lady Castlemaine, her friends moreover argued, had, by reason of her love for his majesty, parted from her husband; and now that she had been so publicly made an object of the queen's indignation, she would, if abandoned by him, meet with rude contempt from the world. To such discourses as these the king lent a willing ear, the more as they encouraged him to act according to his desires. He was therefore fully determined to support his mistress; and firmly resolved to subdue his wife.

Meanwhile, all joyousness vanished from the court; the queen seemed thoroughly dejected, the king bitterly disappointed, and the courtiers grievously disturbed. Moreover, rumours of the trouble which had risen between their majesties became noised abroad, and gave the people occasion of speaking indifferently of their lord the king. Now Charles in his unhappiness betook himself to the chancellor, who was not only his sage adviser and trusted friend, but who had already gained the esteem and confidence of the queen. My lord, by reason of his services to the late king, and his friendship towards his present majesty, took to himself the privilege of speaking with freedom and boldness whenever his advice was asked by the monarch. As Burnet tells us, the worthy chancellor would never make any application to the king's mistress, nor allow anything to pass the seal in which she was named; nor would he ever consent to visit her, which the bishop considered "was maintaining the decencies of virtue in a very solemn manner." The king knowing my lord was the only one of all the strangers surrounding the queen whom she believed devoted to her service, and to whose advice she would hearken with trust, therefore bade him represent to her the advisability of obedience.

Whereon the chancellor boldly pointed out to him "the hard-heartedness and cruelty of laying such a command upon the queen, which flesh and blood could not comply with." He also begged to remind the monarch of what he had heard him say upon the occasion of a like indignity being offered by a neighbouring king to his queen, inasmuch as he had compelled her to endure the presence of his mistress at court. On hearing which King Charles avowed it was "a piece of ill-nature that he could never be guilty of; and if ever he should be guilty of having a mistress after he had a wife, which he hoped he should never be, she should never come where his wife was; he would never add that to the vexation, of which she would have enough without it." Finally my lord added that pursuit of the course his majesty had resolved on, was a most certain way to lose the respect and affections of his people; that the excesses he had already fallen into had in some degree lost him ground in their good esteem, but that his continuance of them would "break the hearts of all his friends, and be grateful only to those who desired the destruction of monarchy."

Charles heard him with some impatience, but in his reply betrayed that graciousness of manner which, never forsaking him, went far in securing the favour of those with whom he conversed. He commenced by telling the chancellor he felt assured his words were prompted by the affection in which he held him; and then having by a pathway of courteous speeches found his way to the old man's heart, his majesty broached the subject uppermost in his mind. His conscience and his honour, he said, for he laid claim to both, led him to repair the ruin he had caused Lady Castlemaine's reputation by promoting her to the position of a lady of the bedchamber; and his gratitude prompted him to avow a friendship for her, "which he owed as well to the memory of her father as to her own person," and therefore he would not be restrained from her company and her conversation.

Moreover, he had proceeded so far in the business, that if not successful Lady Castlemaine would be subjected to all imaginable contempt, and be exposed to universal ridicule. If, he added, the queen conformed to his wishes in this regard, it would be the only hard thing he should ever require of her; and, indeed, she might make it very easy, for my lady must behave with all possible respect in her presence, otherwise she should never see his face again. Then he begged the chancellor to wait upon her majesty, lay bare his arguments, and urge her to receive the countess with some show of favour. The chancellor, though not pleased with his mission, yet in hope of healing private discord and averting public scandal, undertook to counsel the queen to obedience, and accordingly waited on her in her private apartments.

Now her majesty's education had been such as kept her in complete ignorance of the world's ways. The greater part of her life had been spent in the peaceful retirement of a convent, which she left for her mother's country palace, a home scarcely less secluded. Maynard, in a letter preserved in the State Paper Office, written from Lisbon when the royal marriage was proposed, says the infanta, "as sweete a disposition princess as everr was borne," was "bred hugely retired. She hath," he continues, "hardly been tenn tymes out of the palace in her life. In five years tyme she was not out of doores, untill she hurde of his majestie's intentions to make her queen of Ingland, since which she hath been to visit two saintes in the city; and very shortly shee intends to pay her devotion to some saintes in the country."

From a life of innocence she was brought for the first time face to face with vice, by one who should have been foremost in shielding her from its contact. All her training taught her to avoid the contamination sought to be forced upon her; all her new-born love for her husband prompted her to loathe the mistress who shared his affections. A stranger in a strange land, a slighted queen, a neglected wife, an outraged woman, her sufferings were bitter, Her wrongs were hard to bear. Therefore when my lord chancellor came and made known the object of his visit, she broke into a passion of tears, and could not speak from force of sobs that seemed to rend her heart, and wholly choked her utterance.

The chancellor then retired with some dismay, but waited on her again next day, when he found her more calm. She begged he would excuse the outburst of feeling he had witnessed, but added very pitifully that when she thought of her misfortunes "she sometimes gave vent to that passion which was ready to break her heart." The advice, or, as he terms it, "the evidence of his devotion," which the chancellor gave was worthy of a courtier and a philosopher. He told the young queen he doubted "she was little beholden to her education, that had given her no better information of the follies and iniquities of mankind; of which he presumed the climate from whence she came could have given more instances than this cold region would afford." Had she been properly instructed, he furthermore hinted, she would never have thought herself so miserable, or her condition so insupportable; and indeed he could not comprehend the reason of her loud complaint.

At this she could no longer suppress the tears which came into her dark eyes, and cried out she did not expect to find her husband in love with another woman.

Then my lord besought her submission to the king; but she remained unshaken in the resolution she had formed. She was ready to ask his majesty's pardon for tiny passion or peevishness she had been guilty of, but added, "the fire appearing in her eyes where the water was," she would never endure the presence of his mistress; and rather than submit to such insult she would "put herself on board any little vessel" and return to Lisbon.

Back went the chancellor, with a heavy heart and a troubled face, to the king. He softened the queen's words as much as possible, and assured his majesty her resistance to his will proceeded "from the great passion of love she had for him, which transported her beyond the limits of reason." But this excuse, which should have rejoiced a husband's heart, only irritated his majesty's temper. That night a violent quarrel took place between the husband and wife, yet scarce more than bride and bridegroom. When they had retired, the king--being inflamed with the words of his courtiers, who assured him the dispute had now resolved itself into a question of who should govern--reproached the queen with stubbornness and want of duty; upon which she answered by charging him with tyranny and lack of affection. One word borrowed another, till, in his anger, he used threats when she declared she would leave the kingdom. "The passion and noise of the night reached too many ears to be a secret the next day," says the chancellor, "and the whole court was full of that which ought to have been known to nobody."

When the royal pair met next morning, they neither looked at nor spoke to each other. Days passed full of depression and gloom for the young wife, who spent most of her time in seclusion, whilst the king sought distraction in the society of his courtiers. The chancellor, after his second interview with the queen, absented himself from court, not wishing to be furthermore drawn into a quarrel which he saw himself powerless to heal. During his absence the king wrote him a letter which evinced determination to carry out his design. This epistle, preserved in the library of the British Museum, runs as follows:

"HAMPTON COURT, THURSDAY MORNING.

"I forgot when you were here last to desire you to give Broderich good council not to meddle any more with what concerns my Lady Castlemaine, and to let him have a care how he is the author of any scandalous reports; for if I find him guilty of any such thing, I will make him repent it to the last moment of his life.

"And now I am entered on this matter, I think it very necessary to give you a little good council in it, lest you may think that by making a farther stir in the business you may divert me from my resolution, which all the world shall never do; and I wish I may be unhappy in this world and in the world to come, if I fail in the least degree of what I have resolved, which is of making my Lady Castlemaine of my wife's bedchamber. And whosoever I find in any endeavours to hinder this resolution of mine (except it be only to myself), I will be his enemy to the last moment of my life. You know how true a friend I have been to you; if you will oblige me eternally, make this business as easy to me as you can, of what opinion soever you are of; for I am resolved to go through with this matter, let what will come on it, which again I solemnly swear before Almighty God.

"Therefore, if you desire to have the continuance of my friendship, meddle no more with this business except it be to bear down all false and scandalous reports, and to facilitate what I am sure my honour is so much concerned in. And whosoever I find is to be my Lady Castlemaine's enemy in this matter, I do promise, upon my word, to be his enemy as long as I live. You may show this letter to my lord lieutenant, and if you have both a mind to oblige me, carry yourselves like friends to me in this matter."

The chancellor was, soon after the receipt of this letter, summoned to Hampton Court, when his majesty, with some passion, declared the quarrel was spoken of everywhere, and wholly to his disadvantage. He was therefore anxious to end it at once, and commanded my lord to wait again upon the queen, and persuade her to his wishes. The chancellor informed the king he "had much rather spend his pains in endeavouring to convert his majesty from pursuing his resolution, which he did in his conscience believe to be unjust, than in persuading her majesty to comply with it, which yet he would very heartily do." Saying which, he departed on his errand; to which the queen answered, her conscience would not allow her to consent that the king's mistress should be one of her attendants. Then the chancellor besought his royal master, saying he hoped he might be no more consulted with, nor employed concerning an affair, in which he had been so unsuccessful.

By reason of this opposition the king was now more resolved than ever to honour his mistress and humble his wife; and, with a cruelty unusual to his nature, determined to break her majesty's spirit, and force her into obedience.

On coming to England the young bride had brought in her train some Portuguese gentlewomen and nobles, whom she was anxious to employ in various offices about her person, that she might not feel quite in the midst of strangers. These his majesty believed were in some measure answerable for the queen's resistance to his desires, and therefore decided on sending them back to their own country; knowing moreover, this was an act which would sorely grieve her majesty. Therefore, without first deigning to inform, the Queen of Portugal, he named a day for them to embark. This was a sad blow to the hopes of the Portuguese, who had entertained high expectations of being placed in advantageous circumstances about the court; nor did the king by any show of liberality help to lessen their disappointment. The queen was indeed afflicted at the prospect of their loss; and her mortification was the greater because, having received no money since she came into the kingdom, it was out of her power to make them compensation for their services.

The thought of being deprived of her people in her present unhappy condition rendered her so miserable, that she besought the king to allow some of them to remain; and, likewise, she employed others to make the same petition on her behalf. Therefore one of her ladies, the Countess of Penalva, who had been her attendant since childhood, and who now, because of weakness of sight and other infirmities, scarce ever left her apartments, was allowed to stay, as were likewise "those necessary to her religion," and some servants employed in her kitchen.

But these were not the only means the king took to thwart her majesty and all connected with her. He upbraided the Portuguese ambassador for not having instructed the queen "enough to make her unconcerned in what had been before her time, and in which she could not reasonably be concerned." Moreover he reproached him with the fact of the queen regent having sent only half the marriage portion; and so harassed was the ambassador by royal wrath, that he took to his bed, "and sustained such a fever as brought him to the brink of the grave." Regarding that part of the dowry which had arrived, Charles behaved in an equally ungracious and undignified manner. He instructed the officers of the revenue to use all strictness in its valuation, and not make any allowances. And because Diego de Silva--whom the queen had designed for her treasurer, and who on that account had undertaken to see the money paid in London--did not make sufficient haste in the settlement of his accounts, he was by the king's command cast into prison.

These various affronts grievously afflicted her majesty, but the insults she had to endure before the whole court wounded her far more. For meanwhile the king lodged his mistress in the royal household, and every day she was present in the drawing-room, when his majesty entered into pleasant conversation with her, while his wife sat patiently by, as wholly unheeded as if unseen. When the queen occasionally rose and indignantly left the apartment to relieve her anguish by a storm of tears, it may be one or two of the courtiers followed her, but the vast number of the brilliant throng remained; and Lord Clarendon adds, "they, too, often said those things aloud which nobody ought to have whispered."

Charles no longer appeared with the grave and troubled expression his face had worn at the commencement of the quarrel, but seemed full of pleasantry and eager for enjoyment. Those surrounding him took their tone from the monarch, and followed his example the more because he "did shew no countenance to any that belong to the queen." Her majesty, on the contrary, took her misery to heart, and showed dejection by the sadness of her face and listlessness of her gait. There was universal diversion in all company but hers; sounds of laughter rang all day and far into the night in every apartment of the palace but those appropriated to her use. Charles steadily avoided her, and the attendants who replaced her countrywomen showed more deference to the king's mistress than to his queen. The solitary condition to which the helpless foreigner and forsaken wife was reduced increased day by day, her gloom deepened hour by hour, until, worn out by the unequal conflict, her spirit broke. "At last," says Lord Clarendon, "when it was least expected or suspected, the queen on a sudden let herself fall, first to conversation, and then to familiarity, and even, in the same instant, to a confidence with the lady; was merry with her in public, talked kindly of her, and in private used no lady more friendly."

From that hour her majesty never interfered with the king's amours, and never again did a quarrel rise between them even to the day of his death.

CHAPTER VII.

Their majesties arrive at Whitehall.--My Lady Castlemaine a spectator.--Young Mr. Crofts.--New arrivals at court.--The Hamilton family.--The Chevalier de Grammont.--Mrs. Middleton and Miss Kirke.--At the queen's ball--La belle Hamilton.--The queen mother at Somerset House.--The Duke of Monmouth's marriage.--Fair Frances Stuart.--Those who court her favour.--The king's passion.

On the 23rd of August, 1662, their majesties journeyed from Hampton Court to the palace of Whitehall by water. The gay and goodly procession formed on that occasion has been described as "the most magnificent triumph that ever floated on, the Thames." First came barges belonging to city companies, beginning with the mercers and grocers, most of them being attended with a pageant, and all of them richly adorned as became their affection and loyalty. Then followed barges of statesmen, nobility, and courtiers, with their retinues, brave in numbers, gay in colours, and attended by bands of music. And finally came the king and queen, seated side by side in a galley of antique shape, all draped with crimson damask, bearing a canopy of cloth of gold, supported by Corinthian pillars, wreathed with ribbons, and festooned with garlands of fragrant flowers.

The whole city was abroad, watchful of their approach; the Thames was covered with boats to the number of ten thousand; and the banks were crowded with spectators beyond reckoning. On this fair August day the sky had not a single cloud to mar its universal blue; the sun shone gloriously bright, turning the river to sheets of gleaming gold: whilst the air was filled with roaring of cannon, strains of music, and hearty shouts of a loyal multitude.

Mr. Samuel Pepys, though he offered as much as eight shillings for a boat to attend him that day, could not obtain one, and was therefore obliged to view this gallant procession from the roof of the royal banqueting hall, which commanded a glorious view of the Thames. But what pleased his erratic fancy best on this occasion was, not the great spectacle he had taken such trouble to survey, but a sight of my Lady Castlemaine, who stood over against him "upon a piece of Whitehall." The worthy clerk of the Admiralty "glutted" himself with looking on her; "but methought it was strange," says he, "to see her lord and her upon the same place walking up and down without taking notice of one another, only at first entry he put off his hat, and she made him a very civil salute, but afterwards took no notice of one another; but both of them now and then would take their child, which the nurse held in her arms, and dandle it. One thing more: there happened a scaffold below to fall, and we feared some hurt, but there was none; but she of all the great ladies only ran down among the common rabble to see what hurt was done, and did take care of a child that received some little hurt, which methought was so noble. Anon there came one there booted and spurred, that she talked long with. And by-and-by, she being in her haire, she put on her hat, which was but an ordinary one, to keep the wind off. But methinks it became her mightily, as everything else do."

It was notable the countess did not accompany her majesty in the procession to Whitehall, as one of her attendants; but in fact she had not obtained the position sought for, though she enjoyed all the privileges pertaining to such an appointment. "Everybody takes her to be of the bedchamber," the lord chancellor writes to the Duke of Ormond, "for she is always there, and goes abrode in the coach. But the queen tells me that the king promised her, on condition she would use her as she doth others, that she should never live in court; yet lodgings I hear she hath." Lodgings the countess certainly had provided for her in that block of the palace of Whitehall, separated from the main buildings by the old roadway running between Westminster and the city.

A few days after their majesties' arrival at Whitehall, the queen mother returned to town, and established her court at Somerset House, which had been prepared for her future abode. She had arrived in England before the king and queen left Hampton Court, and had taken up her residence at Greenwich Palace. The avowed object of her visit was to congratulate them upon their marriage. Charles and his bride therefore took barge to Greenwich, one bright July day, followed by a brilliant and illustrious train, that they might wait upon her majesty. And she, being made aware of their approach, met them at the portal of the palace. There Catherine would have gone down upon her knees to this gracious lady--the survivor of great sorrows--but she took the young queen in her arms, and calling her beloved daughter, kissed her many times. Then she greeted her sons Charles and James, likewise the Duchess of York, and led them to the presence-chamber, followed by the whole court. And presently when Catherine would, through her interpreter, have expressed her gratitude and affection, the elder queen besought her to lay aside all ceremony, for she "should never have come to England again except for the pleasure of seeing her, to love her as her daughter, and serve her as her queen." At these sweet words the young wife, now in the first days of her grief, was almost overcome by a sense of thankfulness, and could scarce restrain her tears; but she answered bravely, "Believe me, madam, that in love and obedience neither the king nor any of your children shall exceed me."

The court of the merry monarch and that of the queen mother being now settled in town, a period of vast brilliancy ensued, during which great festivity and much scandal obtained, by reason of intrigues in which the king and his friends indulged. Whitehall, the scene of so much gaiety and gallantry, was a palace by no means befitting the luxurious Charles. It consisted of a series of irregular houses built for different purposes at various periods; these contained upwards of two thousand rooms, most of which were small, and many of which were without doors. The buildings were intersected by grassy squares, where fountains played, statues were grouped, and dials shadowed the passing hour. At hand stood St. James's Park, with its fair meadows and leafy trees; close by flowed the placid Thames, bearing heavily laden lighters and innumerable barges. Attached to these dwellings, and forming part of the palace, stood the great banquet hall, erected from designs by Inigo Jones for James I. Here audiences to ambassadors, state balls, and great banquets were held. The ceiling was painted by Rubens, and was, moreover, handsomely moulded and richly gilt. Above the entrance-door stood a statue of Charles I., "whose majestic mien delighted the spectator;" Whilst close by one of the windows were the ineradicable stains of blood, marking the spot near which he had been beheaded.

Now in the train of the queen mother there had travelled from France "a most pretty sparke of about fourteen years," whom Mr. Pepys plainly terms "the king's bastard," but who was known to the court as young Mr. Crofts. This little gentleman was son of Lucy Walters, "a brown, beautiful, bold creature," who had the distinction of being first mistress to the merry monarch. That he was his offspring the king entertained no doubt, though others did; inasmuch as young Mr. Crofts grew to resemble, "even to the wart on his face," Colonel Robert Sidney, whose paramour Lucy Walters had been a brief while before his majesty began an intrigue with her. Soon after the boy's birth that beautiful woman abandoned herself to pleasures, in which the king had no participation. He therefore parted from her; had her son placed under the guardianship of Lord Crofts, whose name he bore, and educated by the Peres de l'Oratoire at Paris. The while he was continually at the court of the queen mother, who regarded him as her grandson, and who, by the king's command, now brought him into England. The beauty of his face and grace of his figure could not be exceeded, whilst his manner was as winning as his air was noble. Moreover, his accomplishments were numerous; he danced to perfection, sang with sweetness, rode with skill; and so gallant was his nature that he became at this early age, as Hamilton affirms, "the universal terror of husbands and lovers."

The king betrayed the greatest affection for him, and took exceeding pride in being father of such a brave and comely youth, at which my Lady Castlemaine was both wrathful and jealous, fearing he would avert the royal favour from her own offspring; but these feelings she afterwards overcame, as will be duly shown. His majesty speedily showered honours upon him, allotted him a suite of apartments in the royal palace of Whitehall, appointed him a retinue befitting the heir apparent, created him Duke of Orkney and of Monmouth, and installed him a knight of the garter.

But, before this had been accomplished, there arrived in town some personages whose names it will be necessary to mention here, the figure they made at court being considerable. These were Sir George Hamilton and his family, and Philibert, Chevalier de Grammont. Sir George was fourth son of James, Earl of Abercorn, and of Mary, sister to James, first Duke of Ormond. Sir George had proved himself a loyal man and a brave during the late civil war, and had on the murder of his royal master sought safety in France, from which country he, in the second year of the restoration, returned, accompanied by a large family; the women of which were fair, the men fearless. The Hamiltons being close kin to the Ormond great intimacy existed between them; to facilitate which they lived not far apart--the duke residing in Ormond Yard, St. James's Square, and the Hamiltons occupying a spacious residence in King Street. James Hamilton, Sir George's eldest son, was remarkable for the symmetry of his figure, elegance of his manner, and costliness of his dress. Moreover, he possessed a taste shaped to pleasure, and a disposition inclined to gallantry, which commended him so strongly to the king's favour, that he was made groom of the bedchamber and colonel of a regiment.

His brother George was scarcely less handsome in appearance or less agreeable in manner. Another brother, Anthony, best remembered as the writer of Grammont's memoirs, was likewise liberally endowed by nature. Elizabeth, commonly called "la belle Hamilton," shared in the largest degree the hereditary gifts of grace and beauty pertaining to this distinguished family. At her introduction to the court of Charles II. she was in the bloom of youth and zenith of loveliness. The portrait of her which her brother Anthony has set before the world for its admiration is delicate in its colours, and finished in its details. "Her forehead," he writes, "was open, white, and smooth; her hair was well set, and fell with ease into that natural order which it is so difficult to imitate. Her complexion was possessed of a certain freshness, not to be equalled by borrowed colours; her eyes were not large, but they were lovely, and capable of expressing whatever she pleased; her mouth was full of graces, and her contour uncommonly perfect; nor was her nose, which was small, delicate, and turned up, the least ornament of so lovely a face. She had the finest shape, the loveliest neck, and most beautiful arms in the world; she was majestic and graceful in all her movements; and she was the original after which all the ladies copied in their taste and air of dress."

Now, about the same time the Hamiltons arrived at court, there likewise appeared at Whitehall one whose fame as a wit, and whose reputation as a gallant, had preceded him. This was the celebrated Chevalier de Grammont, whose father was supposed to be son of Henry the Great of France. The chevalier had been destined by his mother for the church, the good soul being anxious he should lead the life of a saint; but the youth was desirous of joining the army, and following the career of a soldier. Being remarkable for ingenuity, he conceived a plan by which he might gratify his mother's wishes and satisfy his own desires at the same time. He therefore accepted the abbacy his brother procured for him; but on appearing at court to return thanks for his preferment, comported himself with a military air.

Furthermore, his dress was combined of the habit and bands pertaining to an ecclesiastic, and the buskins and spurs belonging to a soldier. Such an amalgamation had never before been witnessed, and caused general attention; the court was amazed at his daring, but Richelieu was amused by his boldness. His brother regarded his appearance in the dual character of priest and soldier as a freak, and on his return home asked him gravely to which profession he meant to attach himself. The youth answered he was resolved "to renounce the church for the salvation of his soul," upon condition that he retained his beneficed abbacy. It may be added, he kept this resolution.

A soldier he therefore became, and subsequently a courtier. His valour in war and luck in gambling won him the admiration of the camp; whilst his ardour in love and genius for intrigue gained him the esteem of the court, but finally lost him the favour of his king. For attaching himself to one of the maids of honour, Mademoiselle La Motte Houdancourt, whom his most Christian Majesty Louis XIV. had already honoured with his regard, Grammont was banished from the French court.

Accordingly, in the second year of the merry monarch's reign he presented himself at Whitehall, and was received by Charles with a graciousness that served to obliterate the memory of his late misfortune. Nor were the courtiers less warm in their greetings than his majesty. The men hailed him as an agreeable companion; the ladies intimated he need not wholly abandon those tender diversions for which he had shown such natural talent and received such high reputation at the court of Louis XIV. He therefore promptly attached himself to the king, whose parties he invariably attended, and whose pleasures he continually devised; made friends with the most distinguished nobles, whom he charmed by the grace of his manner and extravagance of his entertainments; and took early opportunities of proving to the satisfaction of many of the fairer sex that his character as a gallant had by no means been exaggerated by report.

Amongst those to whom he paid especial attention were Mrs. Middleton, a woman of fashion, and Miss Kirk, a maid of honour, to whom Hamilton, in his memoirs of Grammont, gives the fictitious name of Warmestre. The former was at this time in her seventeenth summer, and had been two years a wife. Her exquisitely fair complexion, light auburn hair, and dark hazel eyes constituted her a remarkably beautiful woman. Miss Kirk was of a different type of loveliness, inasmuch as her skin was brown, her eyes dark, and her complexion brilliant. As Mrs. Middleton was at this time but little known at court, Grammont found some difficulty in obtaining an introduction to her as promptly as he desired; but feeling anxious to make her acquaintance, and being no laggard in love, he without hesitation applied to her porter for admittance, and took one of her lovers into his confidence. This latter gallant rejoiced in the name of Jones, and subsequently became Earl of Ranelagh. In the fulness of his heart towards one who experienced a fellow feeling, he resolved to aid Grammont in gaining the lady's favours. This generosity being prompted by the fact that the chevalier would rid him of a rival whom he feared, and at the same time relieve him of an expense he could ill afford, the lady having certain notions of magnificence which her husband's income was unable to sustain.

Mrs. Middleton received the chevalier with good grace; but he found her more ready to receive the presents he offered, than to grant the privileges he required. Miss Kirk, on the other hand, was not only flattered by his attentions, but was willing to use every means in her power to preserve a continuance of his friendship; Therefore out of gratitude for graces received from one of the ladies, and in expectation of favours desired from the other, Grammont made them the handsomest presents. Perfumed gloves, pocket looking-glasses, apricot paste, came every week from Paris for their benefit; whilst more substantial offerings in the shape of jewellery, diamonds, and guineas were procured for them in London, all of which they made no hesitation to accept.

It happened one night, whilst Grammont was yet in pursuit of Mrs. Middleton, that the queen gave a ball. In hope of winning her husband's affection, by studying his pleasures and suiting herself to his ways, her majesty had become a changed woman. She now professed a passion for dancing, wore decollete costumes, and strove to surpass those surrounding her in her desire for gaiety. Accordingly her balls were the most brilliant spectacles the court had yet witnessed; she taking care to assemble the fairest women of the day, and the most distinguished men. Now amongst the latter was the Chevalier de Grammont; and amidst the former, Mrs. Middleton and Miss Hamilton.

Of all the court beauties, "la belle Hamilton" was one of whom Grammont had seen least and heard most; but that which had been told him of her charms seemed, now that he beheld her, wholly inadequate to express her loveliness. Therefore, his eyes followed her alone, as her graceful figure glided in the dance adown the ballroom, lighted with a thousand tapers, and brilliant with every type of beauty. And when presently she rested, it was with an unusual flutter at his heart that this gallant, heretofore so daring in love, sought her company, addressed her, and listened with strange pleasure to the music of her voice. From that night he courted Mrs. Middleton no more, but devoted himself to "la belle Hamilton," who subsequently became his wife.

Meanwhile, the merry monarch behaved as if he had no higher purpose in life than that of following his pleasures. "The king is as decomposed [dissipated] as ever," the lord chancellor writes to the Duke of Ormond, in a letter preserved in the Bodleian library, "and looks as little after his business; which breaks my heart, and makes me and other of your friends weary of our lives. He seeks for his satisfaction and delight in other company, which do not love him so well as you and I do." His days were spent in pursuing love, feasting sumptuously, interchanging wit, and enjoying all that seemed good to the senses. Pepys, who never fails to make mention of the court when actual experience or friendly gossip enables him, throws many pleasant lights upon the ways of the monarch and his courtiers.

For instance, he tells us that one Lord's day--the same on which this excellent man had been to Whitehall chapel, and heard a sermon by the Dean of Ely on returning to the old ways, and, moreover, a most tuneful anthem sung by Captain Cooke, with symphonies between--whom should he meet but the great chirurgeon, Mr. Pierce, who carried him to Somerset House, and into the queen mother's presence-chamber. And there, on the left hand of Henrietta Maria, sat the young queen, whom Mr. Pepys had never seen before, and now thought that "though she be not very charming, yet she hath a good, modest, and innocent look, which is pleasing." Here, likewise, he saw the king's mistress, and the young Duke of Monmouth, "who, I perceive," Pepys continues, "do hang much upon my Lady Castlemaine, and is always with her; and I hear the queenes, both of them, are mighty kind to him. By-and-by in comes the king, and anon the duke and his duchesse; so that, they being all together, was such a sight as I never could almost have happened to see with so much ease and leisure. They staid till it was dark, and then went away; the king and his queene, and my Lady Castlemaine and young Crofts, in one coach, and the rest in other coaches. Here were great stores of great ladies. The king and queen were very merry; and he would have made the queene mother believe that the queene was with child, and said that she said so. And the young queene answered, 'You lye,' which was the first English word that I ever heard her say, which made the king good sport."

Others besides Mr. Pepys had begun to notice that the young Duke of Monmouth hung much upon the Countess of Castlemaine, and that her ladyship lavished caresses upon him. Whether this was to provoke the uneasiness of his majesty, who she hoped might find employment for the lad elsewhere, or to express her genuine affection for him, it is impossible to say. However, the duke being come to an age when the endearments of such a woman might have undesired effects upon him, the king resolved to remove him from her influence, and at the same time secure his fortune by marriage.

He therefore selected a bride for him, in the person of Lady Anne Scott, a young gentlewoman of virtue and excellence, who was only child of Francis, Earl of Buccleugh, and the greatest heiress in Great Britain. Their nuptials were celebrated on the 20th of April, 1663, the bridegroom at this time not having reached his fifteenth birthday, whilst the bride was younger by a year. The duke on his marriage assumed his wife's family name, Scott; and some years later--in 1673--both were created Duke and Duchess of Buccleugh. From this union the family now bearing that title has descended. A great supper was given at Whitehall on the marriage-night, and for many days there were stately festivities held to celebrate the event with becoming magnificence.

Now at one of the court balls held at this time, the woman of all others who attracted most attention and gained universal admiration was Frances Stuart, maid of honour to Queen Catherine. She was only daughter of a gallant gentleman, one Walter Stuart, and grand-daughter of Lord Blantyre. Her family had suffered sore loss in the cause of Charles I., by reason of which, like many others, it sought refuge in France. This young gentlewoman was therefore bred in that country, and was, moreover, attached to the court of the queen mother, in whose suite she travelled into England. Her beauty was sufficient to attract the attention of Louis XIV., who, loath to lose so fair an ornament from his court, requested her mother would permit her to remain, saying, he "loved her not as a mistress, but as one that would marry as well as any lady in France."

No doubt Mrs. Stuart understood the motives of his majesty's interested kindness, of which, however, she declined availing herself, and therefore departed with her daughter for England. At the time of her appearance at Whitehall, Frances Stuart was in her fifteenth year. Even in a court distinguished by the beauty of women, her loveliness was declared unsurpassed. Her features were regular and refined, her complexion fair as alabaster, her hair bright and luxuriant, her eyes of violet hue; moreover, her figure being tall, straight, and shapely, her movements possessed an air of exquisite grace. An exact idea of her lineaments may be gained unto this day, from the fact that Philip Rotier, the medallist, who loved her true, represented her likeness in the face of Britannia on the reverse of coins; and so faithful was the likeness, we are assured, that no one who had ever seen her could mistake who had sat as model of the figure.

Soon after her arrival in England, she was appointed one of the maids of honour to Queen Catherine, and as such was present at all festivities of the court. Now, at one of the great balls given in honour of the Duke of Monmouth's nuptials, the fair Frances Stuart appeared in the full lustre of her charms. Her beauty, her grace, and her youth completely eclipsed the more showy gifts of my Lady Castlemaine, who on this occasion looked pale and thin, she being in the commencement of another pregnancy, "which the king was pleased to place to his own account." The merry monarch had before this time been attracted by the fair maid of honour, but now it was evident his heart had found a new object of admiration in her surpassing beauty. Henceforth he boldly made love to her. The countess was not much disturbed by this, for she possessed great faith in her own charms and implicit belief in her power over the king. Besides, she had sufficient knowledge of mankind to comprehend that to offer opposition in pursuit of love is the most certain method to foster its growth. She therefore resolved to seek Miss Stuart's society, cultivate her friendship, and constantly bring her into contact with his majesty. This would not only prove to the satisfaction of the court she had no fear of losing her sovereignty over the monarch, but, by keeping him engaged with the maid of honour, would likewise divert his attention from an intrigue the countess was then carrying on with Henry Jermyn. Accordingly, she made overtures of friendship to Miss Stuart, invited her to private parties, and appeared continually with her in public.

Concerning these ladies and the merry monarch, Pepys narrates a strange story which Captain Ferrers told him as they "walked finely" in the park. This was, that at an entertainment given by my Lady Castlemaine, towards the end of which his majesty played at being married with fair Frances Stuart, "with ring and all other ceremonies of Church service, and ribbands, and a sack posset [A drink composed of milk, wine, and spices.] in bed, and flinging the stocking. My Lady Castlemaine looked on the while, evincing neither anger nor jealousy, but entering into the diversion with great spirit." Nor was this the only indiscretion of which she was culpable, for, in the full confidence of her charms, she frequently kept Miss Stuart to stay with her. "The king," says Hamilton, "who seldom neglected to visit the countess before she rose, seldom failed likewise to find Miss Stuart with her. The most indifferent objects have charms in a new attachment; however, the imprudent countess was not jealous of this rival's appearing with her, in such a situation, being confident that, whenever she thought fit, she could triumph over all the advantages which these opportunities could afford Miss Stuart."

No doubt Lady Castlemaine's imprudences arose from knowledge that Miss Stuart was devoid of tact, and incapable of turning opportunities to her own advantage in the king's regard. For though the maid of honour was richly endowed with beauty, she was wholly devoid of wit. She was not only a child in years, but likewise in behaviour. She laughed at every remark made her, delighted in playing blind man's buff, and was never more happy than when building castles of cards. At this latter amusement she continually employed herself whilst the deepest play was taking place in her apartments; being always attended by groups of courtiers, who were either attracted by the charm of her beauty, or were eager to make court through her favour. As she sat upon the floor, intent on her favourite occupation, they on their knees handed her cards, traced out designs for her, or built elaborate structures rivalling her own.

Amongst those who attended her in this manner was the gay, graceful, and profligate Duke of Buckingham, who became enamoured of her loveliness. Not only did he raise the most wonderful of card mansions for her delight, but having a good voice, and she possessing a passion for music, he invented songs and sung them to pleasure her. Moreover, he told her the wittiest stories, turned the courtiers into the greatest ridicule for her entertainment, and made her acquainted with the most diverting scandals. Finally, he professed his ardent love for her; but at this the fair Stuart either felt, or feigned, intense astonishment, and so repulsed him that he abandoned the pursuit of an amour over which he had wasted so much time, and thenceforth deprived himself of her company.

His attentions were, however, soon replaced by those of the Earl of Arlington, a lord of the bedchamber, and a man of grave address and great ambition. Owing to this latter trait his lordship was desirous of winning the good graces of Miss Stuart in the present, in hopes of governing his majesty in the future, when she became the king's mistress. But these sage and provident intentions of his were speedily overturned, for early in the course of their acquaintance, when he had commenced to tell her a story, his manner so forcibly reminded her of Buckingham's mimicry of him, that she burst out laughing in the earl's face. This being utterly uncalled for by the circumstances of his tale, and still less by the manner of its narration, Lord Arlington, who was serious, punctilious, and proud, became enraged, abruptly left her presence, and abandoned his schemes of governing the king through so frivolous a medium.

A man who had better chances of success in winning this beautiful girl was George Hamilton, whose name has been already mentioned. It was not, however, his graceful person, or elegant manner, but his performance of a trick which gained her attention. It happened one night that an Irish peer, old Lord Carlingford, was diverting her by showing how she might hold a burning candle in her mouth a considerable time without its being extinguished. This was a source of uncommon delight to her; seeing which, George Hamilton thought he would give her still further entertainment. For being furnished by nature with a wide mouth, he placed within it two lighted candles, and walked three times round the room without extinguishing them, whilst the fair Stuart clapped her pretty hands in delight, and shouted aloud with laughter.

A man who could accomplish such a feat was worthy of becoming a favourite. She at once admitted him to terms of familiarity; and he had a hundred chances of paying her the attentions he greatly desired, and which she freely accepted. Grammont, foreseeing that Hamilton would incur the royal displeasure if his love for Miss Stuart became known to the king, besought him to abandon his addresses; but this advice did not at first sound pleasant to the lover's ears. "Since the court has been in the country," said he, "I have had a hundred opportunities of seeing her, which I had not before. You know that the dishabille of the bath is a great convenience for those ladies, who, strictly adhering to all the rules of decorum, are yet desirous to display all their charms and attractions. Miss Stuart is so fully acquainted with the advantages she possesses over all other women, that it is hardly possible to praise any lady at court for a well-turned arm, and a fine leg but she is ever ready to dispute the point by demonstration; and I really believe that, with a little address, it would not be difficult to induce her to strip naked, without ever reflecting upon what she was doing. After all, a man must be very insensible to remain unconcerned and unmoved on such happy occasions."

Hamilton was therefore not willing to renounce Miss Stuart, but upon Grammont showing that attentions paid the lady would certainly provoke the king's anger, he resolved on sacrificing love to interest, and abandoning the company of the fair maid of honour for evermore. The truth was, his majesty loved her exceedingly, as was indeed evident, for he constantly sought her presence, talked to her at the drawing-rooms as if no one else were by, and kissed her "to the observation of all the world." But though she allowed Charles such liberties, she refused to become his mistress, notwithstanding the splendid settlements and high titles with which the monarch engaged to reward the sacrifice of her virtue. And so, though a king, it was not given him to be obeyed in all. And though generally loved for his easy ways and gracious manners, he was continually harassed by his mistresses, reproved by his chancellor, and ridiculed by his courtiers. Indeed, they now spoke of him in his absence as "Old Rowley;" the reason of which is given by Richardson. "There was an old goat," writes he, "in the privy garden, that they had given this name to; a rank lecherous devil, that everybody knew and used to stroke, because he was good-humoured and familiar; and so they applied this name to the king."

CHAPTER VIII.

The Duke of York's intrigues.--My Lady Chesterfield and his royal highness--The story of Lady Southesk's love.--Lord Arran plays the guitar.--Lord Chesterfield is jealous.--The countess is taken from court.--Mistress Margaret Brooke and the king.--Lady Denham and the duke.--Sir John goes mad.--My lady is poisoned.

The while his majesty devoted himself to pleasure and intrigue, neglectful of affairs of state, and heedless of public scandal, his brother of York, whose disposition was not less amorous, likewise followed the bent of his inclinations. Soon after her appearance at court he professed himself in love with the beautiful Elizabeth Hamilton, whom to behold was to admire. But the duke being a married man, and she a virtuous woman, he dared not address her on the subject of his affection, and was therefore obliged to confine the expression of his feelings to glances. These she refused to interpret; and he, becoming weary of a pursuit which promised no happy results, turned his attentions to the Countess of Chesterfield, who seemed in no way loath to receive them.

This charming woman had married my Lord Chesterfield in compliance with a family arrangement; and discovered too soon she had no place in the heart of him whose life she shared. His coldness to her was only equalled by his ardour for Lady Castlemaine, whose lover he continued to remain after his marriage. The affection his wife had offered and he had repulsed, in the dawn of their wedded life, changed by degrees to disdain and hatred.

Now as chamberlain to the queen my Lord Chesterfield had, apartments in the palace, by reason of which the countess became an habituee of the court. The moral atmosphere of Whitehall was not calculated to strengthen her conjugal virtue, but its perpetual gaiety was destined to dissipate her sense of neglect. It was not possible for a woman endowed with so much beauty, and possessed of such engaging manners, to be disregarded, in a court entirely devoted to love and gallantry; and accordingly she soon became an object of general admiration. This was by no means pleasing to my Lord Chesterfield, who, though he had wilfully repulsed her affections, was selfishly opposed to their bestowal upon others. Accordingly he became watchful of her conduct, and jealous of her admirers.

Prominent amongst these were James Hamilton and the Duke of York. The former was her cousin, and her husband's confidant, in consequence of which my lord failed to associate him with the suspicion he entertained towards all other men who approached her: the latter he regarded with the uttermost distrust. His royal highness had before now disturbed the happy confidence which husbands had placed in their wives, as my Lord Carnegy could testify.

The story which hangs thereby had, a little while before the duke fell in love with Lady Chesterfield, afforded vast amusement to the court, and was yet fresh in the recollection of many. It happened that his royal highness became enamoured of my Lady Carnegy, daughter of the gallant Duke of Hamilton, and friend of the gay Lady Castlemaine. Lady Carnegy loved pleasure mightily, painted her face "devilishly," and drove in the park flauntingly. She was endowed with considerable beauty of form and great tenderness of heart, as many gallants acknowledged with gratitude. Now when the Duke of York made advances to her, she received them with all the satisfaction he could desire; an intimacy therefore followed, which she was the better able to entertain on account of her husband's absence in Scotland. Whilst my Lord Carnegy was in that country, his father, the Earl of Southesk, died, and he succeeded to the title and estates. In due time the new earl returned to London and his wife, and was greeted by rumours of the friendship which in his absence had sprung up between my lady and the duke. These, as became a good husband, he refused to believe, until such time as he was enabled to prove their veracity. Now, though his royal highness did not cease to honour my lady with his visits on her husband's return, yet out of respect to decorum, and in order to silence scandalous tongues, he from that time invariably called on her accompanied by a friend.

It therefore came to pass that one day he requested an honest, foolish Irishman, Dick Talbot, afterwards Duke of Tyrconnel, to attend him in his visit to the lady. He could scarcely have selected a man more unfitted to the occasion, inasmuch as

Talbot was wholly devoid of tact, and possessed a mind apt to wander at large at critical moments. He had but recently returned from Portugal, and was not aware my Lord Carnegy had in the meantime become Earl of Southesk, nor had he ever met the lady who shared that title until introduced to her by the duke. When that ceremony had been duly performed and a few sentences interchanged between them, Talbot, acting on instructions previously received, retired into an ante-room and took his post at a window that he might divert himself by viewing the street, and observing those who approached the house.

Here he remained for some time, but the study of mankind which the view admitted did not afford sufficient interest to prevent him becoming absorbed in his own thoughts, and indifferent to all objects surrounding him. From this mental condition he was presently aroused by seeing a carriage draw up to the door, and its occupant descend and quickly enter the house. Talbot was so forgetful of his duty that he omitted apprising the duke of this fact or making any movement until the door of the ante-room opened, when he turned round to face the intruder. Then he started forward and cried out, "Welcome, Carnegy!" for it was no other than he. "Welcome my good fellow! Where the devil have you been, that I have never been able to set eyes on you since we were at Brussels! What business brought you here?" he continued in the same breath; and then added in a tone of banter, "Do you likewise wish to see Lady Southesk; if this is your intention, my poor friend, you may go away again; for I must inform you the Duke of York is in love with her, and I will tell you in confidence that at this very time he is in her chamber."

My Lord Southesk was overwhelmed with shame and confusion, and not knowing how to act, immediately returned to his coach, Talbot attending him to the door as his friend, and advising him to seek a mistress elsewhere. He then went back to his post, and with some impatience awaited the Duke's return, that he might tell him what had happened. And in due time, when he had narrated the story, he was much surprised that neither his royal highness nor the countess saw any humour in the fact of Lord Carnegy's discomfiture. It served, however, to make the duke break off his connection with the lady, and likewise to amuse the town.

Remembering this incident, my Lord Chesterfield kept a watchful eye upon the duke, who he observed made advances towards the countess, which she, in her generosity, had not the heart to repulse. But, as his royal highness could see her only in presence of the court, my lord derived some satisfaction from knowing he was witness to such civilities as had yet passed between them. The duke was, however, anxious to have a more particular occasion of conversing with my lady, and in accomplishing this desire her brother Lord Arran was willing to aid him.

It happened about this time an Italian, named Francisco Corbeta, who played with great perfection on the guitar, arrived at court. His performances excited the wonder and delight of all who heard him, and the instrument which produced such melody speedily became fashionable at court, to such an extent, that a universal strumming was heard by day and by night: throughout the palace of Whitehall. The Duke of York, being devoted to music, was amongst those who strove to rival Signor Francisco's performance; whilst my Lord Arran, by the delicacy of his execution, almost equalled the great musician. The while Francisco's popularity increased, his fame reaching its zenith when he composed a saraband, to learn which became the ambition of all delighting in the guitar.

Now one day the duke, not thinking himself perfect in this piece, requested Lord Arran to play it over for him. My lord being a courteous man, was anxious to oblige his royal highness, and in order that the saraband might be heard to greatest advantage, was desirous of performing it upon the best instrument at court, which it was unhesitatingly acknowledged belonged to my Lady Chesterfield. Accordingly, Lord Arran led the duke to his sister's apartments. Here they found not only the guitar and my lady, but likewise my lord, who was no less astonished than disturbed by their visit. Then my Lord Arran commenced the famous saraband, whilst the duke commenced to ogle my lady, and she to return his glances in kind, as if both were unconscious of her husband's presence. So delightful did they find the saraband, that Lord Arran was obliged to repeat it at least twenty times, to the great mortification of the earl, who could scarcely contain his violent rage and jealousy. His torture was presently increased to an immeasurable degree, by a summons he received from the queen to attend her in his capacity of lord chamberlain, during an audience she was about, to give the Muscovite ambassador.

He had from the first suspected the visit, with which he was honoured, to have been preconcerted by his wife and the duke; and he now began to think her majesty was likewise connected with a plot destined to rob him of his peace and blight his honour. However, he was obliged to obey the queen's summons and depart. Nor had he been many minutes absent when Lord Arran entered the presence-chamber where the audience was being held, unaccompanied by the duke, at which Lord Chesterfield's jealous fears were strengthened a thousandfold. Before night came he was satisfied he held sufficient proof of his wife's infidelity.

This conviction caused him intense anxiety and pain; he walked about his apartments abstracted and brooding on the wrongs from which he suffered; avoided all who came in his way; and maintained strict silence as to that which disturbed his peace, until next day, when he met James Hamilton. To him he confided an account of the troubles which beset him. After speaking of the visit paid by his royal highness, and the part enacted by my Lord Arran, whom he described as "one of the silliest creatures in England, with his guitar, and his other whims and follies," he went on to say that when Hamilton had heard him out, he would be enabled to judge whether the visit ended in perfect innocence or not. "Lady Chesterfield is amiable, it must be acknowledged," said he, "but she is far from being such a miracle of beauty as she supposes herself: you know she has ugly feet; but perhaps you are not acquainted that she has still worse legs. They are short and thick, and to remedy these defects as much as possible, she seldom wears any other than green stockings. I went yesterday to Miss Stuart's after the audience of those damned Muscovites: the king arrived there just before me; and as if the duke had sworn to pursue me wherever I went that day, he came in just after me. The conversation turned upon the extraordinary appearance of the ambassadors. I know not where that fool Crofts had heard that all these Muscovites had handsome wives; and that all their wives had handsome legs. Upon this the king maintained, that no woman ever had such handsome legs as Miss Stuart; and she to prove the truth of his majesty's assertion, with the greatest imaginable ease, immediately showed her leg above the knee. Some were ready to prostrate themselves in order to adore its beauty, for indeed none can be handsomer; but the duke alone began to criticize upon it. He contended that it was too slender, and that as for himself he would give nothing for a leg that was not thicker and shorter, and concluded by saying that no leg was worth anything without green stockings; now this in my opinion was a sufficient demonstration that he had just seen green stockings, and had them fresh in his remembrance."

At hearing this story, Hamilton, being deeply in love with Lady Chesterfield, was scarcely less agitated or less jealous than her lord; but he was obliged to conceal his feelings. Therefore, assuming the tone of an impartial hearer, he shrugged his shoulders, declared appearances were often deceitful, and maintained that even if she had given herself airs to encourage the duke, there were no grounds to show she had been culpable of improprieties. My lord expressed himself much obliged to his friend for the interest he had shown in his troubles, and after exchanging a few compliments they parted. Hamilton, full of wrath, returned home, and wrote a letter replete with violent expostulations and tender reproaches to the woman he loved. This he delivered to her secretly at the next opportunity. She received it from him with a smile, which scared all doubts of her frailty from his mind, and with a pressure of his hand which awoke the tenderest feelings in his heart.

He was now convinced her husband had allowed jealousy to blind him, and had magnified his unworthy suspicions to assurances of guilt. Is this view Hamilton was fully confirmed by a letter he received from her the following day in answer to his own. "Are you not," said she, "ashamed to give any credit to the visions of a jealous fellow, who brought nothing else with him from Italy? Is it possible that the story of the green stockings, upon which he has founded his suspicions, should have imposed upon you, accompanied as it is with such pitiful circumstances? Since he has made you his confidant, why did not he boast of breaking in pieces my poor harmless guitar? This exploit, perhaps, might have convinced you more than all the rest; recollect yourself, and if you are really in love with me, thank fortune for a groundless jealousy, which diverts to another quarter the attention he might pay to my attachment for the most amiable and the most dangerous man at court."

Anointed by this flattering unction, such wounds as Hamilton had experienced were quickly healed; alas, only to bleed afresh at the certain knowledge that this charming woman had been making him her dupe! For soon after, in a moment of indiscretion, and whilst the whole court, including her majesty, was assembled in the card-room, my lady there permitted the duke a liberty which confirmed her husband in his suspicions of their intimacy. Hamilton at hearing this was wild with fury, and advised Lord Chesterfield to carry her away from the allurements of the court, and seclude her in one of his country mansions. This was an advice to which the earl listened with complaisance, and carried out with despatch, to her intense mortification.

The whole court was amused by the story, but dismayed at the punishment my lord inflicted upon his lady. Anthony Hamilton declares that in England "they looked with astonishment upon a man who could be so uncivil as to be jealous of his wife; and in the city of London it was a prodigy, till that time unknown, to see a husband have recourse to violent means to prevent what jealousy fears, and what it always deserves." He adds, they endeavoured to excuse my lord by laying all the blame on his bad education, which made "all the mothers vow to God that none of their sons should ever set a foot in Italy, lest they should bring back with them that infamous custom of laying restraint upon their wives."

By the departure of Lady Chesterfield the court lost one of its most brilliant ornaments forever, for the unhappy countess never again returned to the gay scene of her adventures. For three long years she endured banishment at Bretby in Derbyshire, and then died, it was believed, from the effects of poison. For my lord, never having his suspicions of her intrigue cleared, insisted on her taking the sacrament by way of pledging her innocence; on which occasion he, in league with his chaplain, mixed poison in the sacred wine, as result of which she died. This shocking story gained credence not only with the public, but with members of his own family; inasmuch as his daughter-in-law, Lady Gertrude Stanhope, after she had quarrelled with him, would, when she sat at his table, drink only of such wine and water as a trusty servant of hers procured.

This intrigue of the duke had given much uneasiness to his duchess, who had complained to the king and to her father, and had, moreover, set a watch upon the movements of his royal highness. But such measures did not avail to make him a faithful husband, and no sooner was Lady Chesterfield removed from his sight, than Lady Denham took her place in his affections. This latter mentioned gentlewoman was daughter of a valiant baronet, Sir William Brooke, and niece to a worthless peer, the Earl of Bristol. The earl had, on the king's restoration, cherished ambitious schemes to obtain the merry monarch's favour; for which purpose he sought to commend himself by ministering to the royal pleasures.

Accordingly he entertained the king as became a loyal gentleman, giving him luxurious banquets and agreeable suppers, to which, by way of adding to his majesty's greater satisfaction, the noble host invited his nieces, Mistress Brooke and her sister. The wily earl had, indeed, conceived a plan the better to forward his interests with the king, and was desirous one of these gentlewomen should subdue his majesty's heart, and become his mistress. Margaret Brooke, the elder of the maidens, was at this time in her eighteenth year, and was in the full flower of such loveliness as was presented by a fair complexion, light brown hair, and dark grey eyes. The merry monarch's susceptible heart was soon won by her beauty; the charming lady's amorous disposition was speedily conquered by his gallantry, and nothing prevented her becoming his mistress save Lady Castlemaine's jealousy.

This, however, proved an insurmountable obstacle; for the countess, hearing rumours of the pleasures which were enjoyed at my Lord Bristol's table, insisted on attending the king thither, and soon gave his gracious majesty an intimation he dared not disregard--that she would not suffer Miss Brooke as a rival. Margaret Brooke was grievously disappointed; but the Duke of York beginning his attentions at the point where his majesty discontinued them, she was soon consoled for loss of the monarch's affection by the ardour of his brother's love. But a short time after, probably foreseeing the ambiguous position in which she stood, she forsook her lover, and accepted a husband in the person of Sir John Denham.

This worthy knight was a man of parts; inasmuch as he was a soldier, a poet, and a gamester. At the time of his marriage he had passed his fiftieth year; moreover, he limped painfully and carried a crutch. His appearance, indeed, was far from imposing. According to Aubrey, he was tall, had long legs, and was "incurvelting at his shoulders; his hair was but thin and flaxen, with a moist curl; his gait slow and rather astalking; his eye was a kind of light goose-grey, not big, but it had a strange piercingness, not as to shining and glory, but when he conversed he looked into your very thoughts." His personal defects, however, were to a great degree compensated for by his great wealth. Moreover he was surveyor-general of his majesty's works, had a town house in Scotland Yard, and a country residence at Waltham Cross in Essex. But there are some deficiencies for which wealth does not atone, as no doubt Lady Denham promptly discovered; for, before a year of her married life had passed, she renewed her intrigue with the Duke of York. His love for her seemed to have increased a thousandfold since fate had given her to the possession of another. At royal drawing-rooms he took her aside and talked to her "in the sight of all the world," and whenever she moved away from him he followed her like a dog.

Indeed, he made no effort to screen his passion, for not only did he make love to her in presence of the court, but he visited her at noonday, attended by his gentlemen, before all the town. Nor did Lady Denham desire to conceal the honour with which, she considered, this amour covered her, but openly declared she would "not be his mistress, as Mrs. Price, to go up and down the privy stairs, but will be owned publicly;" and in this respect she obtained her desire. Meanwhile Sir John was rendered miserable; and, indeed, his desperation soon overthrew his reason, and rendered him a lunatic. This affection first appeared during a journey he made to the famous free-stone quarries near Portland in Dorset. When he came within a mile of his destination, he suddenly turned back, and proceeded to Hounslow, where he demanded rents for lands he had disposed of years before; and then hastening to town sought out the king and informed him he was the Holy Ghost.

This madness lasted but a short time; and the first use he made of his recovered senses was to plot vengeance on his wife. Now there was one honour which she coveted above all others, that of being appointed a lady of the bedchamber to the Duchess of York. This her royal lover, following the example of his majesty, sought to obtain for her; but the duchess, who had already suffered many indignities by reason of her husband's improprieties, refused him this request, which would render her liable to continual insult in her own court. The duke, however, had a strong will, and the duchess was on the point of yielding to his demand, when rumour announced that Lady Denham had been taken suddenly ill, and scandal declared she had been poisoned. The wildest sensation followed. His royal highness, stricken with remorse and terror, hastened to Scotland Yard and sought his beloved mistress, who told him she believed herself poisoned, and felt she was now dying. The most eminent physicians were speedily summoned, but their skill proved of no avail, for she gradually became worse, and finally died, leaving instructions that her body should be opened after death, in order that search might be made for the fatal drug.

The surgeons followed these directions, as we learn from the Orrery state papers, but no trace of poison was discovered. For all that the public had no doubt her husband had destroyed her life, and Hamilton tells us the populace "had a design of tearing Sir John in pieces as soon as he should come abroad; but he shut himself up to bewail her death, until their fury was appeased by a magnificent funeral, at which he distributed four times more burnt wine than had ever been drunk at any burial in England."

As for the duke, he was sorely troubled for her loss, and declared he should never have a public mistress again.

CHAPTER IX.

Court life under the merry monarch.--Riding in Hyde Park.--Sailing on the Thames.--Ball at Whitehall.--Petit soupers.--What happened at Lady Gerrard's.--Lady Castlemaine quarrels with the king.--Flight to Richmond.--The queen falls ill.--The king's grief and remorse.--Her majesty speaks.--Her secret sorrow finds voice in delirium.--Frances Stuart has hopes.--The queen recovers.

Views of court life during the first years of the merry monarch's reign, obtainable from works of his contemporaries, present a series of brilliant, changeful, and interesting pictures. Scarce a day passed that their majesties, attended by a goodly throng of courtiers, went not abroad, to the vast delight of the town: and rarely a night sped by unmarked by some magnificent entertainment, to the great satisfaction of the court. At noon it was a custom of the king and queen, surrounded by maids of honour and gentlemen in waiting, the whole forming a gladsome and gallant crowd, to ride in coaches or on horseback in Hyde Park: which place has been described as "a field near the town, used by the king and nobility for the freshness of the air, and goodly prospect."

Here in a railed-off circle, known as the ring, and situated in the northern half of the park, the whole world of fashion and beauty diverted itself. Noble gallants wearing broad-brimmed hats and waving plumes, doublets of velvet, and ruffles of rich lace; and fair women with flowing locks and dainty patches, attired in satin gowns, and cloaks wrought with embroidery, drove round and round, exchanging salutations and smiles as they passed. Here it was good Mr. Pepys saw the Countess of Castlemaine, among many fine ladies, lying "impudently upon her back in her coach asleep, with her mouth wide open." And on another occasion the same ingenious gentleman observed the king and my lady pass and repass in their respective coaches, they greeting one another at every turn.

But Mr. Pepys gives us another picture, in which he shows us the king riding right gallantly beside his queen, and therefore presents him to better advantage. This excellent gossip, sauntering down Pall Mall one bright summer day, it being the middle of July, in the year 1663, met the queen mother walking there, led by her supposed husband, the Earl of St. Albans. And, hearing the king and queen rode abroad with the ladies of honour to the park, and seeing a great crowd of gallants awaiting their return, he also stayed, walking up and down the while. "By-and-by," says he, "the king and queene, who looked in this dress (a white laced waistcoate and a crimson short pettycoate, and her hair dressed A LA NEGLIGENCE) mighty pretty; and the king rode hand in hand with her. Here was also my Lady Castlemaine riding amongst the rest of the ladies; but the king took, methought, no notice of her; nor when they light did anybody press (as she seemed to expect, and staid for it) to take her down, but was taken down by her own gentlemen. She looked mighty out of humour, and had a yellow plume in her hat (which all took notice of), and yet is very handsome. I followed them up into Whitehall, and into the queene's presence, where all the ladies walked, talking and fiddling with their hats and feathers, and changing and trying one another's by one another's heads, and laughing. But it was the finest sight to me, considering their great beautys and dress, that ever I did see in my life. But, above all, Mrs. Stuart in this dresse with her hat cocked and a red plume, with her sweet eye, little Roman nose, and excellent taille, is now the greatest beauty I ever saw, I think, in my life; and, if ever woman can, do exceed my Lady Castlemaine, at least in this dresse: nor do I wonder if the king changes, which I verily believe is the reason of his coldness to my Lady Castlemaine."

Having returned from the park, dined at noon, walked in the palace gardens, or played cards till evening came, their majesties, surrounded by a brilliant and joyous court, would in summer time descend the broad steps leading from Whitehall to the Thames, and embark upon the water for greater diversion. Never was there so goodly a sight, seldom so merry a company. The barges in which they sailed were draped to the water's edge with bright fabrics, hung with curtains of rich silk, and further adorned with gay pennants. And, as the long procession of boats, filled with fair women and gallant men, followed their majesties adown the placid Thames towards pleasant Richmond, my Lord Arran would delight the ears of all by his performance on the guitar; the fair Stuart would sing French songs in her sweet childlike voice; or a concert of music would suddenly resound from the banks, being placed there to surprise by some ingenious courtier.

And presently landing on grassy meads, delightful to sight by freshness of their colour, and sweet to scent from odour of their herbs, the court would sup right heartily; laugh, drink, and make love most merrily, until early shadows stole across the summer sky, and night-dews fell upon the thirsty earth. Then king, queen, and courtiers once more embarking, would sail slowly back, whilst the moon rose betimes in the heavens, and the barges streaked the waters with silver lines.

At other times magnificent entertainments filled the nights with light and revelry. Pepys tells us of a great ball he witnessed in the last month of the year 1662 at the palace of Whitehall. He was carried thither by Mr. Povy, a member of the Tangier Commission, and taken at first to the Duke of York's chambers, where his royal highness and the duchess were at supper; and from thence "into a room where the ball was to be, crammed with fine ladies, the greatest of the court. By-and-by comes the king and queene, the duke and duchess, and all the great ones; and, after seating themselves, the king takes out the Duchess of York; and the duke the Duchess of Buckingham; the Duke of Monmouth my Lady Castlemaine; and so other lords other ladies; and they danced the bransle. After that, the king led a lady a single coranto; and then the rest of the lords, one after another, other ladies: very noble it was, and great pleasure to see. Then to country dances: the king leading the first. Of the ladies that danced, the Duke of Monmouth's lady, and my Lady Castlemaine, and a daughter of Sir Harry de Vicke's were the best. The manner was, when the king dances, all the ladies in the room, and his queene herself, stand up: and indeed he dances rarely, and much better than the Duke of York."

PETIT SOUPERS were another form of entertainments, greatly enjoyed by Charles, and accordingly much in vogue with his courtiers. The Chevalier de Grammont had principally helped to make them fashionable, his suppers being served With the greatest elegance, attended by the choicest wits, and occasionally favoured with the presence of majesty itself. Nor were Lady Gerrard's PETIT SOUPERS less brilliant, or her company less distinguished. Her ladyship boasted of French parentage and understood the art of pleasing to perfection; and accordingly at her board wine flowed, wit sparkled, and love obtained in the happiest manner. Now it happened one of her delightful entertainments was destined to gain a notoriety she by no means coveted, and concerning which the French ambassador, Count de Comminges, wrote pleasantly enough to the Marquis de Lionne.

It came to pass that Lady Gerrard, who loved the queen, requested the honour of their majesties to sup with her. She, moreover, invited some of the courtiers, amongst whom she did not include my Lady Castlemaine. On the appointed night the king and queen duly arrived; the other guests had already assembled; and the hour gave fair promise of entertainment. But presently, when supper was announced, his majesty was missing, and on inquiry it was discovered he had left the house for Lady Castlemaine's lodgings, where he spent the evening. Such an insult as this so openly dealt the queen, and such an indignity put upon the hostess, caused the greatest agitation to all present; and subsequently afforded subject for scandalous gossip to the town. It moreover showed that the monarch was yet an abject slave of his mistress, whose charms entangled him irresistibly. At least four times a week he supped with her, returning at early morning from her lodgings, in a stealthy way, through the privy gardens, a proceeding of which the sentries took much notice, joked unbecomingly, and gossiped freely.

Now in order to avoid further observation at such times, and silence rumours which consequently obtained, his majesty removed the countess from her lodgings in that part of the palace divided by the road leading to Westminster from the chief block, and furnished her with apartments next his own chamber. The poor queen, who had sought by every means in her power to win his affection, was sorely grieved at this action, and moreover depressed by the neglect to which she was continually subjected. Sometimes four months were allowed to pass without his deigning to sup with her, though the whole court was aware he constantly paid that honour to her infamous rival. But knowing how unavailing reproach would be, she held her peace; and feeling how obtrusive her sorrow would seem, she hid her tears. Now and again, however, a look would flash in her eyes, and an answer rise to her lips, which showed how deeply she felt her bitter wrongs. "I wonder your majesty has the patience to sit so long adressing," said my Lady Castlemaine to her one morning when she found her yet in the dresser's hands. "I have so much reason to use patience," answered the neglected wife, "that I can very well bear with it."

And so the countess continued to reign paramount in his majesty's favour until the middle of July, 1663, when a rumour spread through the town that she had quarrelled with the king, and had consequently fallen from her high estate. The cause of disagreement between the monarch and his mistress is narrated by the French ambassador in a letter to Louis XIV.

By this time the fair Stuart had so increased in his majesty's favour, that my Lady Castlemaine began to see the indiscretion of which she had been guilty in bringing her so constantly into his presence, and moreover to fear her influence over his fickle heart. Accordingly she refused to invite the maid of honour to her apartments, or entertain her at her assemblies. At this the king became exceedingly wrathful, and told my lady he would not enter her rooms again unless Miss Stuart was there. Thereon the charming countess flew into a violent passion, roundly abused his majesty, called her carriage, and protesting she would never again enter the palace of Whitehall, drove off in a rage to the residence of her uncle at Richmond. The monarch had not expected his words would cause such fury, nor did he desire her departure; and no sooner had she gone than he began to regret her absence and long for her return.

Therefore next morning he made pretence of hunting, and turning his horse's head in the direction of Richmond, called on his mistress, when he apologized to and made friends with her. She therefore returned and exercised her old ascendancy over him once more. It is probable his majesty was the more anxious to pacify her, from the fact that she was now far advanced in her third pregnancy; for two months later she gave birth to her second son, who was baptized Henry Fitzroy, and subsequently created Duke of Grafton.

And it happened about this time, that the queen, falling ill, drew near unto death. On Friday, the 14th October, 1663, a fever took possession of her, when the doctors were summoned, her head shaven, and pigeons put to her feet. Her illness, however, rapidly increased, and believing she was about to leave a world in which her young life had known so much sorrow, she made her will, put her affairs in order, and received extreme unction. Upon this the king, mindful of grievous injuries he had done her, was sorely troubled in his heart, and going to her chamber, flung himself at the foot of her bed and burst into tears; as the French ambassador narrates.

It is said women love best men who treat them worst. If this be so, God, alone who made them knows wherefore; for it is given no man to understand them in all. Now her majesty proved no exception to this rule regarding the unreasonableness of her sex in placing their affections most on those who regard them least; for she was devoted to the king. Therefore the evidence of his grief at prospect of her loss touched her deeper than all words can say, and with much sweetness she sought to soothe and console him.

She told him she had no desire to live, and no sorrow to die, save, indeed, that caused by parting from him. She hoped he would soon wed a consort more worthy of his love than she had been; one who would contribute more to his happiness and the satisfaction of the nation than she had. And now they were about to part, she had two requests to make: that he would never separate his interests from those of the king her brother, or cease to protect her distressed nation; and that her body might be sent back to Portugal and laid in the tomb of her ancestors. At this the king, yet on his knees beside her, interrupted her only by his sobs, hearing which she wept likewise; and so overcome was he by grief that he was obliged to be led from her room.

The court was saddened by her majesty's illness, for she had won the goodwill of all by the kindness of her disposition and gentleness of her manner; the city was likewise afflicted, for the people thought so good a queen could not fail in time to reclaim even so erratic a husband; and trade became suddenly depressed. Crowds gathered by night and by day outside the palace to learn the most recent change in her majesty's condition many thinking her death inevitable, because the doctors had pronounced her recovery impossible. And for days her soul hovered betwixt two worlds.

On the night of the 19th, a fierce storm raged over England; and Mr. Pepys, being waked by the roaring of mighty winds, turned to his wife and said: "I pray God I hear not of the death of any great person, this wind is so high." And fearing the queen might have departed, he rose betimes, and took coach to the palace that he might make inquiries concerning her, but found her majesty was still living. She was now, however, unconscious; and gave free voice to the secret sorrow which underlay her life, because she had not borne children to the king. Had she given him heirs, she felt assured he would certainly love her as well as he loved his mistresses; and would feel as proud of her offspring as of those borne him by other women. But though she had proved capable of becoming a mother on more than one occasion, it pleased heaven to leave her childless, to her great grief. Therefore in her delirium, desires shaped themselves to realities, and she believed she had given birth to three children, two boys and a girl. The latter she fancied much resembled the king, but she was troubled that one of the boys was plain featured. And seeing her grief at this, his majesty, who stood by, sought in pity to console her, saying the boy was indeed pretty; at which she brightened visibly, and answering him said: "Nay, if it be like you, it is a fine boy indeed, and I would be very well pleased with it." This delusion continued through her illness, and so strongly did it force itself upon her mind, that one morning when she was on her way to recovery, on waking suddenly and seeing the doctor bending over her, she exclaimed, "How do the children?"

Now all this time, whilst the shadow of death lay upon the palace, and laughter and music were no longer heard within its walls, there was one of its inmates who pondered much upon the great fortune which the future might have in keeping for her. This was fair Frances Stuart, who, not having yielded to the king's request by becoming his mistress, now entertained high hopes of being made his wife. In this dream she was, moreover, flattered by an unusual deference and high respect paid her by the court since the beginning of her majesty's illness. The king continued his attentions to her; for though he had proved himself "fondly disconsolate" and wept sorely for her majesty, he never during her sickness omitted an opportunity of conversing with Miss Stuart, or neglected supping with Lady Castlemaine. But the hopes entertained by the maid of honour were speedily overthrown, for contrary to all expectation the queen recovered, and was so well on the 10th November as to "bespeak herself a new gowne"

And so the court remained unchanged, and life went on as before; the queen growing gradually stronger, the king making love to Miss Stuart by day, and visiting Lady Castlemaine by night. And it happened one evening when he went to sup with the latter there was a chine of beef to roast, and no fire to cook it because the Thames had flooded the kitchen. Hearing which, the countess called out to the cook, "Zounds, you must set the house on fire but it shall be roasted!" And roasted it was.

CHAPTER X.

Notorious courtiers.--My Lord Rochester's satires.--Places a watch on certain ladies of quality.--His majesty becomes indignant.--Rochester retires to the country.--Dons a disguise and returns to town.--Practises astrology.--Two maids of honour seek adventure.--Mishaps which befell them.--Rochester forgiven.--The Duke of Buckingham.--Lady Shrewsbury and her victims.--Captain Howard's duel.--Lord Shrewsbury avenges his honour.--A strange story.--Colonel Blood attempts an abduction.--Endeavours to steal the regalia.--The king converses with him.

Prominent among the courtiers, and foremost amid the friends of his majesty, were two noblemen distinguished alike for their physical grace, exceeding wit, and notable eccentricity. These were the Earl of Rochester, and his Grace of Buckingham; gallants both, whose respective careers were so intimately connected with the court as to make further chronicle of them necessary in these pages.

My Lord Rochester, though younger in years than the duke, was superior to him in wit, comeliness, and attraction. Nor was there a more conspicuous figure observable in the palace of Whitehall than this same earl, who was ever foremost in pursuit of such pleasures as wine begets and love appeases. His mirth was the most buoyant, his conversation the most agreeable, his manner the most engaging in the world; whence he became "the delight and wonder of men, the love and dotage of women." A courtier possessed of so happy a disposition, and endowed with such brilliant talents, could not fail in pleasing the king; who vastly enjoyed his society, but was occasionally obliged to banish his person from court, when his eccentric conduct rendered him intolerable, or his bitter satire aimed at royalty. For it was given no other man in his age to blend merry wit and caustic ridicule so happily together; therefore those who read his lines were forced to laugh at his fancy, even whilst hurt by his irony.

Now in order to keep this talent in constant practice, he was wont to celebrate in inimitable verse such events, be they private or public, as happened at court, or befell the courtiers; and inasmuch as his subjects were frequently of a licentious nature, his lines were generally of a scandalous character. He therefore became the public censor of court folly; and so unerringly did his barbed shafts hit the weaknesses at which they aimed, that his productions were equally the terror of those he victimized, and the delight of those he spared.

This liberal use of satire he was wont to excuse on the plea there were some who could not be kept in order, or admonished, by other means. Therefore, having the virtue of his friends keenly at heart, an ingenious plan occurred to him by which he might secretly discover their vices, and publicly reprove them. In order that he might fulfil this purpose to his greater satisfaction, he promptly sought and found a footman, who, by virtue of his employment, was well acquainted with the courtiers. This man the "noble and beautiful earl" furnished with a red coat and a musket, that he might pass as a sentinel, and then placed him every night throughout one winter at the doors of certain ladies of quality whom he suspected of carrying on intrigues.

In this disguise the footman readily passed as a soldier stationed at his post by command of his officer, and was thus enabled to note what gentlemen called on the suspected ladies at unreasonable but not unfashionable hours. Accordingly, my lord made many surprising discoveries, and when he had gained sufficient information on such delicate points, he quietly retired into the country, that he might with greater ease devote himself to the composition of those lively verses which he subsequently circulated through the court, to the wonder and dismay of many, and the delight and profit of few.

To these lampoons no name was attached, and my lord took precautions that their authorship should not be satisfactorily proved, no matter how sagely suspected. Moreover, in his conversation he was judicious enough to keep the weapon of his satire in reserve; sheathing its fatal keenness in a bewitching softness of civility until occasion required its use; when forth it flashed all the brighter for its covering, all the sharper for its rest. And satire being absent from his speech, humour ever waited on his words; and never was he more extravagantly gay than when assisting at the pleasant suppers given by the merry monarch to his choicest friends.

Here, whilst drinking deep of ruddy wine from goblets of old gold, he narrated his strange experiences, and illustrated them with flashes of his wit. For it was the habit of this eccentric earl, when refinements of the court began to pall upon him, or his absence from Whitehall became a necessity, to seek fresh adventure and intrigue disguised as a porter, a beggar, or a ballad-monger. And so carefully did he hide his identity in the character he assumed, that his most intimate friends failed to recognise his personality.

No doubt the follies in which he indulged were in some measure due to the eccentricity ever attendant upon genius; but they were probably likewise occasioned by craving for excitement begotten of drink. For my lord loved wine exceedingly; and when he drew near unto death in the dawn of his manhood, confessed to Bishop Burnet that for five years he was continually drunk: "Not that he was all the while under the visible effects of it, but his blood was so inflamed, that he was not in all that time cool enough to be perfectly master of himself." Charles delighted in the society of this gay courtier, because of his erratic adventures, and his love of wine. Moreover, the licentious verses which it was the earl's good pleasure to compose, the names of some of which no decent lips would whisper in this age of happy innocence, afforded the monarch extravagant enjoyment. Withal his majesty's satisfaction in Lord Rochester's wit was not always to be counted upon, as it proved. For it came to pass one night at the close of a royal supper, during which the earl had drunk deep, that with great goodwill to afford the king diversion, he handed his majesty what he believed was a satire on a courtier, more remarkable for its humour than its decency. Whereon Charles, with anticipation of much delight, opened the folded page, when he was surprised to see, not a copy of verses, but an unflattering description of himself, which ran as follows:

> "Here lies our mutton-eating king,
>   Whose word no man relies on;
>   Who never said a foolish thing,
>   And never did a wise one."

Now the king, though the best tempered of men and most lenient of masters, was naturally wrathful at this verbal character: the more so because recognising its faithfulness at a glance. He therefore upbraided Rochester with ingratitude, and banished him from the court.

Nothing dismayed, my lord retired into the country; but in a short time, growing weary of pastoral solitude which gave him an appetite for adventure it could not wholly supply, he returned privately to town, and assuming a disguise, took up his residence in the city. Here exercising his characteristic tact, and great capacity for pleasing, he speedily made friends with wealthy merchants and worthy aldermen, who subsequently invited him to their hospitable tables, and introduced him to their gracious ladies.

And as his conversation had not failed to delight the husbands, neither were his charms unsuccessful in affording satisfaction to their wives. To the one he railed against the impotence of the king's ministers, to the other he declaimed upon the wickedness of his majesty's mistresses; and to both his denunciations were equally sincere and acceptable. But his bitterest words were reserved for such courtiers as Rochester, Buckingham, and Killigrew, whose dissipated lives were the scandal of all honest men, the terror of all virtuous women: insolent fellows, moreover, who had the impudence to boast that city ladies were not so faithful to their husbands as was generally supposed, and, moreover, the boldness to assert that they painted. Indeed, he marvelled much, that since such men were frequenters of Whitehall, sacred fire from heaven had not long since descended and consumed the royal palace to ashes. Such virtuous sentiments as these, expressed by so gallant a man, made him acceptable in many homes: and the result was he speedily became surfeited by banquets, suppers, and other hospitalities, to which the excellent but credulous citizens bade him heartily welcome.

He therefore disappeared from their midst one day as suddenly and unaccountably as he had come amongst them. He did not, however, take himself afar, but donning a new disguise, retreated to a more distant part of the city: for an idea had occurred to him which he determined speedily to put in practice. This was to assume the character and bearing of a sage astrologer and learned physician, at once capable of reading the past, and laying bare the future of all who consulted him; also of healing diseases of and preventing mishaps to such as visited him. Accordingly, having taken lodgings in Tower Street, at a goldsmith's house, situated next the Black Swan, he prepared himself for practice, adopted the title of doctor, the name of Alexander Bendo, and issued bills headed by the royal arms, containing the most remarkable and impudent manifesto perhaps ever set forth by any impostor.

Copies of this may yet be seen in early editions of his works. It was addressed to all gentlemen, ladies, and others, whether of the city, town, or country, to whom Alexander Bendo wished health and prosperity. He had come amongst them because the great metropolis of England had ever been infested by numerous quacks, whose arrogant confidence, backed by their ignorance, had enabled them to impose on the public; either by premeditated cheats in physic, chymical and galenic, in astrology, physiognomy, palmistry, mathematics, alchymy, and even government itself. Of which latter he did not propose to discourse, or meddle with, since it in no way belonged to his trade or vocation, which he thanked God he found much more safe, equally honest, and more profitable. But he, Alexander Bendo, had with unswerving faithfulness and untiring assiduity for years courted the arts and sciences, and had learned dark secrets and received signal favours from them. He was therefore prepared to take part against unlearned wretches, and arrant quacks, whose impudent addresses and saucy pretences had brought scandal upon sage and learned men.

However, in a wicked world like this, where virtue was so exactly counterfeited, and hypocrisy was generally successful, it would be hard for him, a stranger, to escape censure. But indeed he would submit to be considered a mountebank if he were discovered to be one. Having made which statement, he proceeded to draw an ingenious comparison between a mountebank and a politician, suitable to all ages and dimes, but especially to this century and country. Both, he intimated, are fain to supply the lack of higher abilities to which they pretend, with craft; and attract attention by undertaking strange things which can never be performed. By both the people are pleased and deluded; the expectation of good in the future drawing their eyes from the certainty of evil in the present.

The sage Alexander Bendo then discoursed of miraculous cures which he could effect, but he would set down no word in his bill which bore an unclean sound. It was enough that he made himself understood, but indeed he had seen physicians' bills containing things of which no man who walked warily before God could approve. Concerning astrological predictions, physiognomy, divination by dreams, and otherwise, he would say, if it did not look like ostentation, he had seldom failed, but had often been of service; and to those who came to him he would guarantee satisfaction. Nor would he be ashamed to avow his willingness to practise rare secrets, for the help, conservation, and augmentation of beauty and comeliness; an endowment granted for the better establishment of mutual love between man and woman, and as such highly valuable to both. The knowledge of secrets like this he had gathered during journeys through France and Italy, in which countries he had spent his life since he was fifteen years old. Those who had travelled in the latter country knew what a miracle art there performs in behalf of beauty; how women of forty bear the same countenance as those of fifteen, ages being in no way distinguished by appearances; whereas in England, by looking at a horse in the mouth and a woman in the face, it was possible to tell the number of their years. He could, therefore, give such remedies as would render those who came to him perfectly fair; clearing and preserving them from all spots, freckles, pimples, marks of small-pox, or traces of accidents. He would, moreover, cure the teeth, clear the breath, take away fatness, and add flesh.

A man who vouched to perform such wonders was not long without patients. At first these were drawn from his immediate neighbourhood, but soon his fame reached the heart of the city. Accordingly, many ladies of whose hospitality he had partaken, and of whose secrets he had become possessed, hurried to consult him; and the marvellous insight he betrayed regarding their past, and strange predictions he pronounced concerning their future, filled them with amazement, and occasionally with alarm. And they, proclaiming the marvels of his wisdom, widened the circle of his reputation, until his name was spoken within the precincts of Whitehall.

Curiosity concerning so remarkable a man at once beset the minds of certain ladies at court, who either feared or expected much from the future, and were anxious to peer into such secrets as it held concerning themselves. But dreading the notoriety their presence would naturally cause in the vicinity of Tower Street, a spot to them unknown, they, acting with a prudence not invariably characteristic of their conduct, sent their maids to ascertain from personal experience if the astrologer's wisdom was in truth as marvellous as reported. Now, when these appeared in fear and trembling before the great Alexander Bendo, the knowledge he revealed concerning themselves, and their mistresses likewise, was so wonderful that it exceeded all expectation. Accordingly, the maids returned to court with such testimonies concerning the lore of this star-reader, as fired afresh their mistresses' desires to see and converse with him in their proper persons.

It therefore came to pass that Miss Price and Miss Jennings, maids of honour both--the one to the queen, the other to the Duchess of York--boldly resolved to visit Doctor Bendo, and learn what the future held for them. Miss Price was a lady who delighted in adventure; Miss Jennings was a gentlewoman of spirit; both looked forward to their visit with excitement and interest. It happened one night, when the court had gone to the playhouse, these ladies, who had excused themselves from attending the queen and the duchess, dressed as orange girls, and taking baskets of fruit under their arms, quickly crossed the park, and entered a hackney-coach at Whitehall Gate. Bidding the driver convey them to Tower Street, they rattled merrily enough over the uneven streets until they came close to the theatre, when, being in high spirits and feeling anxious to test the value of their disguise, they resolved to alight from their conveyance, enter the playhouse, and offer their wares for sale in presence of the court.

Accordingly, paying the driver, they descended from the coach, and running between the lines of chairs gathered round the theatre, gained the door. Now, who should arrive at that moment but the beau Sidney, attired in the bravery of waving feathers, fluttering ribbons, and rich-hued velvets. And as he paused to adjust his curls to his greater satisfaction before entering the playhouse, Miss Price went boldly forward and asked him to buy her fine oranges; but so engaged was he in his occupation, that he did not deign to make reply, but passed into the theatre without turning his glance upon her. Miss Jennings, however, fared somewhat differently; and with less satisfaction to herself; for, perceiving another courtier, none other than Tom Killigrew, a rare wit and lover of pleasure, she went up to him and offered her fruit for sale. These he declined to buy; but chucking her under the chin, and glancing at her with an air of familiarity, invited her to bring her oranges to his lodgings next morning. On this Miss Jennings, who was as virtuous as lovely, pushed him away with violence, and forgetting the character she assumed, commenced rebuking his insolence, much to the amusement and surprise of the bystanders. Fearing detection of their identity, Miss Price pulled her forcibly away from the crowd.

Miss Jennings was after this incident anxious to forego her visit to the astrologer, and return to Whitehall, but her companion declaring this would be a shameful want of spirit, they once more entered a hackney-coach, and requested they might be driven to the lodgings of the learned Doctor Bendo. Their adventures for the evening were unfortunately not yet at an end; for just as they entered Tower Street they saw Henry Brinker, one of the gentlemen of the bedchamber to the Duke of York. Now it happened this courtier had been dining with a citizen of worth and wealth, whose house he was about to leave the moment the maids of honour drove by. They, knowing him to be a man remarkable for his gallantries, were anxious to avoid his observation, and therefore directed the driver to proceed a few doors beyond their destination; but he, having caught sight of two pretty orange wenches, followed the coach and promptly stepping up as they alighted, made some bold observations to them. On this both turned away their heads that they might avoid his gaze, a proceeding which caused him to observe them with closer scrutiny, when he immediately recognised them, without however intimating his knowledge. He therefore fell to teasing them, and finally left them with no very pleasant remarks ringing in their ears, concerning the virtue which obtained among maids of honour, for he did not doubt their disguise was assumed for purposes of intrigue.

Overwhelmed with confusion, they walked towards the goldsmith's shop, over which the oracle delivered wisdom; but being no longer in a humour to heed his words, they presently resolved on driving back to Whitehall with all possible speed. But alas! on turning round they beheld their driver waging war with a crowd which had gathered about his vehicle; for having left their oranges in the coach, some boys had essayed to help themselves, whereon the man fell foul of them. But he, being one against many, was like to fare badly at their hands; seeing which, the maids of honour persuaded him to let the crowd take the fruit and drive them back at once. This conduct had not the effect of appeasing those who profited by its generosity; for the gentlewomen were greeted with most foul abuse, and many unworthy charges were laid to their account in language more vigorous than polished. And having at last arrived in safety at Whitehall, they resolved never to sally forth in search of adventure again.

After various strange experiences in his character as doctor of medicine and teller of fortunes, of the weakness of human nature and strength of common credulity, the learned Alexander Bendo vanished from the city; and about the same time the gallant Earl of Rochester appeared at court, where he sought for and obtained the merry monarch's pardon. The wonderful stories he was enabled to relate, piquant in detail, and sparkling with wit, rendered it delightful to the king, in whose favour he soon regained his former supremacy. Nay, Charles even determined to enrich and reward him, not indeed from the resources of his privy purse, his majesty's income being all too little for his mistresses' rapacity, but by uniting him to a charming woman and an heiress.

The lady whom his majesty selected for this purpose was Elizabeth Mallett, daughter of Lord Hawley of Donamore. Now this gentlewoman had a fortune of two thousand five hundred a year, a considerable sum in those days, and one which gained her many suitors; amongst whom Lord Hinchingbrook was commended by her family, and Lord Rochester by the king. Now the latter nobleman, having but a poor estate, was anxious to obtain her wealth, and fearful of losing his suit: and being uncertain as to whether he could gain her consent to marry him by fair means, he resolved to obtain it by execution of a daring scheme.

This was to carry her off by force, an action which highly commended itself to his adventurous spirit. Accordingly he selected a night on which the heiress supped at Whitehall with her friend Miss Stuart, for conducting his enterprise. It therefore happened that as Elizabeth Mallett was returning home from the palace in company with her grandfather, their coach was suddenly stopped at Charing Cross. Apprehending some danger, Lord Hawley looked out, and by the red light of a score of torches flashing through darkness, saw he was surrounded by a band of armed men, both afoot and on horse. Their action was prompt and decisive, for before either my lord or his granddaughter was aware of their intention, the latter was seized, forcibly lifted from the coach, and transferred to another which awaited close at hand. This was driven by six horses, and occupied by two women, who received the heiress with all possible respect. No sooner had she been placed in the coach than the horses were set to a gallop, and away she sped, surrounded by a company of horsemen.

Lord Hawley was cast into the uttermost grief and passion by this outrage; but his condition did not prevent him speedily gathering a number of friends and retainers, in company with whom he gave chase to those who had abducted his granddaughter; and so fast did they ride that Mistress Mallett was overtaken at Uxbridge, and carried back in safety to town. For this outrageous attempt, my Lord Rochester was by the king's command committed to the Tower, there to await his majesty's good pleasure. It seemed now as if the earl's chance of gaining the heiress had passed away for ever; inasmuch as Charles regarded the attempted abduction with vast displeasure, and my Lord Hawley with terrible indignation.

But the ways of women being inexplicable, it happened in a brief while Mistress Mallett was inclined to regret my Lord Rochester's imprisonment, and therefore moved to have him released; and, moreover, she was subsequently pleased to regard his suit and accept him as her wedded lord. It speaks favourably for his character that with all his faults she loved him well: nor did Rochester, though occasionally unfaithful, ever treat her with unkindness. At times the old spirit of restlessness and passion for adventure would master him, when he would withdraw himself from her society for weeks and months. But she, though sadly afflicted by such conduct, did not resent it. "If I could have been troubled at anything, when I had the happiness of receiving a letter from you," she writes to him on one occasion when he had absented himself from her for long, "I should be so because you did not name a time when I might hope to see you, the uncertainty of which very much afflicts me." And again the poor patient wife tells him, "Lay your commands upon me, what I am to do, and though it be to forget my children, and the long hope I have lived in of seeing you, yet I will endeavour to obey you; or in memory only torment myself, without giving you the trouble of putting you in mind that there lives such a creature as your faithful humble servant." At length dissipation undermined his naturally strong constitution; and for months this once most gay and gallant man, this "noble and beautiful earl," lay dying of that cruel disease consumption. The while such thoughts as come to those who reason of life's vanities beset him; and as he descended into the valley of shadows, the folly of this world's ways was made clear to him. And repenting of his sins, he died in peace with God and man at the age of three-and-thirty.

George Villiers second Duke of Buckingham, was not less notable than my Lord Rochester. By turns he played such diverse parts in life's strange comedy as that of a spendthrift and a miser, a profligate and a philosopher, a statesman who sought the ruin of his country, and a courtier who pandered to the pleasures of his king. But inasmuch as this history is concerned with the social rather than the political life of those mentioned in its pages, place must be given to such adventures as were connected with the court and courtiers. Buckingham's were chiefly concerned with his intrigues, which, alas! were many and strange; for though his wife was loving and virtuous, she was likewise lean and brown, and wholly incapable of controlling his erring fancies. Perhaps it was knowledge of her lack of comeliness which helped her to bear the burden of his follies; for according to Madame Dunois, though the duchess knew he was continually engaged in amours, she, by virtue of a patience uncommon to her sex, forbore mentioning the subject to him, and "had complaisance enough to entertain his mistresses, and even lodge them in her house, all which she suffered because she loved him."

The most remarkable of his intrigues was that which connected his name with the Countess of Shrewsbury. Her ladyship, was daughter of the second Earl of Cardigan, and wife of the eleventh Earl of Shrewsbury. She was married a year previous to the restoration, and upon the establishment of the court at Whitehall had become one of its most distinguished beauties. Nor was she less famed for the loveliness of her person than for the generosity of her disposition; inasmuch as none who professed themselves desirous of her affection were ever allowed to languish in despair. She therefore had many admirers, some of whom were destined to suffer for the distinction her friendship conferred.

Now one of the first to gain her attachment was the young Earl of Arran, the grace of whose bearing and ardour of whose character were alike notable to the court. The verses he sung her to an accompaniment of his guitar, and the glances he gave her indicative of his passion, might have melted a heart less cold than hers. Accordingly they gained him a friendship which, by reason of her vast benevolence, many were subsequently destined to share. Now it chanced that the little Jermyn, who had already succeeded in winning the affections of such notable women as the poor Princess of Orange and my Lady Castlemaine, and had besides conducted a series of minor intrigues with various ladies connected with the court, was somewhat piqued that Lady Shrewsbury had accepted my Lord Arran's attentions without encouraging his. For Henry Jermyn, by virtue of the fascinations he exercised and the consequent reputation he enjoyed, expected to be wooed by such women as desired his love.

But when, later on, Lord Arran's devotion to the lady was succeeded by that of Thomas Howard, brother to the Earl of Carlisle, and captain of the guards, Jermyn was thoroughly incensed, and resolved to make an exception in favour of the countess by beginning those civilities which act as preludes to intrigue. My lady, who was not judicious enough to be off with the old love before she was on with the new, accepted Jermyn's advances with an eagerness that gave promise of further favours. This was highly displeasing to Howard, a brave and generous man, who under an exterior of passive calmness concealed a spirit of fearless courage. Though not desirous of picking a quarrel with his rival, he was unwilling to suffer his impertinent interference. Jermyn, on the other hand, not being aware of Howard's real character, sought an early opportunity of insulting him. Such being their dispositions, a quarrel speedily ensued, which happened in this manner.

One fair summer day Captain Howard gave an entertainment at Spring Gardens, in honour of the countess. These gardens were situated close by Charing Cross, and opened into the spacious walks of St. James's Park. Bounded on one side by a grove, and containing leafy arbours and numerous thickets, the gardens were "contrived to all the advantages of gallantry." The scene of many an intrigue, they were constantly frequented by denizens of the court and dwellers in the city, to whom they afforded recreation and pleasure. In the centre of these fair gardens stood a cabaret, or house of entertainment, where repasts were served at exceeding high prices, and much good wine was drunk. Here it was Captain Howard received my Lady Shrewsbury and a goodly company, spread a delicate banquet for them, and for their better diversion provided some excellent music played upon the bagpipes, by a soldier noted for his execution on that instrument.

Jermyn hearing of the great preparations Captain Howard made, resolved to be present on the occasion; and accordingly, before the hour appointed for dinner, betook himself to the garden, and as if he had arrived there by accident, strolled leisurely down the broad pleasant paths, bordered by pinks and fragrant roses clustering in the hedgerows. And presently drawing nigh the cabaret, he tarried there until the countess, rich in physical graces, with sunny smiles upon her lips, and amorous light in her eyes, stepped forth upon the balcony and greeted him. Whereon his heart took fire: and entering the house, he joined her where she stood, and held pleasant converse with her. Inflated by his success, he resolved on making himself disagreeable to the host, and therefore ventured to criticize the entertainment, and ridicule the music, which he voted barbarous to civilized ears. And to such an extent did he outrage Thomas Howard, that the gallant captain, being more of a soldier than a courtier, and therefore preferring passages at arms to those of wit, could scarce refrain from drawing his sword and demanding the satisfaction due to him.

However, he subdued his wrath till the day was spent, and early next morning sent a challenge to his rival. Accordingly they met with fierce intent, and the duel which followed ended almost fatally for Jermyn, who was carried from the scene of encounter bleeding from three wounds caused by his antagonist's sword.

The unfortunate issue of this fight deprived Lady Shrewsbury of two lovers; for Howard, having rendered Jermyn unable to perform the part of a gallant, was obliged to fly from the country and remain abroad some time.

In their stead the countess sought consolation in the companionship of Thomas Killigrew, a handsome man and a notable courtier. She therefore had no regrets for the past: and he was entirely happy in the present, so that he boasted of his felicities to all acquaintance, in general, and to his friend the Duke of Buckingham in particular. It was Killigrew's constant habit to sup with his grace, on which occasions his conversation invariably turned on her ladyship, when, his imagination being heated by wine, he freely endowed her with the perfections of a goddess. To such descriptions the duke could not listen unmoved; and therefore resolved to judge for himself if indeed the countess was such a model of loveliness as Killigrew represented. Accordingly, at the first opportunity which presented itself, the duke made love to her, and she, nothing averse to his attentions, encouraged his affections. Killigrew was much aggrieved at this unexpected turn of affairs, and bitterly reproached the countess; but she, being mistress of the situation, boldly denied all knowledge of him.

This was more than he expected or could endure, and he consequently abused her roundly in all companies, characterizing the charms of which he once boasted as faults he could not endure; ridiculing her airs, and denouncing her conduct. Reports of his comments and discourses speedily reached Lady Shrewsbury's ears; and he was privately warned that if he did not desist means would be taken to silence him effectually. Not being wise enough to accept this hint he continued to vilify her. The result was, one night when returning from the Duke of York's apartments he was suddenly waylaid in St. James's Park, and three passes of a sword made at him through his chair, one of which pierced his arm. Not doubting they had despatched him to a better world, His assailants made their escape; and my Lady Shrewsbury, who singularly enough happened to be passing at the time in her coach, and had stopped to witness the proceedings, drove off as speedily as six horses could carry her.

Knowing it would be impossible to trace the villainy which had prompted this deed to its source, Killigrew said not a word concerning the murderous attempt, and henceforth held his peace regarding his late mistress's imperfections. For some time she continued her intrigue with the Duke of Buckingham without interference. But in an evil hour it happened the Earl of Shrewsbury, who had long entertained a philosophical indifference towards her previous amours, now undertook to defend his honour, which it was clear his Grace of Buckingham had sadly injured.

Accordingly he challenged the duke to combat, and in due time they met face to face in a field by Barnes Elms. His grace had as seconds Sir Robert Holmes and Captain William Jenkins; the earl being supported by Sir John Talbot and Bernard Howard, son of my Lord Arundel. The fight was brief and bloody; Lord Shrewsbury, being run through the body, was carried from the field in an insensible condition. The duke received but a slight wound, but his friend Captain Jenkins was killed upon the spot. The while swords clashed, blood flowed, and lives hung in a balance, the woman who wrought this evil stood close by, disguised as a page, holding the bridle of her lover's horse, as Lord Orford mentions.

In consequence of this duel the Duke of Buckingham absented himself from the capital; but two months after its occurrence King Charles was pleased, "in contemplation of the services heretofore done to his majesty by most of the persons engaged in the late duel or rencontre, to graciously pardon the said offence." Three months after the day on which he fought, Lord Shrewsbury died from effects of his wounds, when the duke boldly carried the widow to his home. The poor duchess, who had patiently borne many wrongs, could not stand this grievous and public insult, and declared she would not live under the same roof with so shameless a woman. "So I thought, madam," rejoined her profligate lord, "and have therefore ordered your coach to convey you to your father."

The countess continued to live with her paramour; nor was the court scandalized. The queen, it is true, openly espoused the cause of the outraged duchess, and sought to enlist sympathy on her behalf; but so low was the tone of public morality that her words were unheeded, and no voice was raised in protest against this glaring infamy. Nay, the duke went further still in his efforts towards injuring the wife to whom he owed so much, and who loved him over-well; as he caused his chaplain, the Rev. Thomas Sprat, to marry him to my Lady Shrewsbury; and subsequently conferred on the son to which she gave birth, and for whom the king stood godfather, his second title of Earl of Coventry. His wife was henceforth styled by the courtiers Dowager Duchess of Buckingham. It is worthy of mention that the Rev. Thomas Sprat in good time became Bishop of Rochester, and, it is written, "an ornament to the church among those of the highest order."

One of the most extraordinary characters which figured in this reign was Thomas Blood, sometimes styled colonel. He was remarkable for his great strength, high courage, and love of adventure. The son of an Irish blacksmith, he had, on the outbreak of civil warfare in his native country, joined Cromwell's army; and for the bravery he evinced was raised to the rank of lieutenant, rewarded by a substantial grant of land, and finally made a justice of the peace. At the restoration he was deprived of this honour, as he was likewise of the property he called his, which was returned to its rightful owner, an honest royalist. Wholly dissatisfied with a government which dealt him such hardships, he organised a plot to raise an insurrection in Ireland, storm Dublin Castle, and seize the Duke of Ormond, then lord lieutenant. This dark scheme was discovered by his grace; the chief conspirators were accordingly seized, with the exception of Blood, who succeeded in making his escape to Holland. His fellow traitors were tried and duly executed.

From Holland, Blood journeyed into England, where, becoming acquainted with some republicans, he entered into projects with them calculated to disturb the nation's peace; which fact becoming known, he was obliged to seek refuge in Scotland. Here he found fresh employment for his restless energies, and in the year 1666 succeeded in stirring up some malcontents to rebellion. The revolt being quelled, he escaped to Ireland; and after a short stay in that country returned once more to England, where he sought security in disguise.

He lived here in peace until 1670, when he made an attempt no less remarkable for its ingenuity than notable for its villainy. Towards the end of that year the Prince of Orange, being in London, was invited by the lord mayor to a civic banquet. Thither the Duke of Ormond attended him, and subsequently accompanied him to St. James's, where the prince then stayed. A short distance from the palace gates stood Clarendon House, where the duke then resided, and towards which he immediately drove, on taking leave of his royal highness. Scarce had he proceeded a dozen yards up St. James's Street, when his coach was suddenly stopped by a band of armed and mounted men, who, hurriedly surrounding his grace, dragged him from the carriage and mounted him on a horse behind a stalwart rider. Word of command being then given, the gang started at a brisk pace down Piccadilly. Prompted by enemies of the duke, as well as urged by his own desires to avenge his loss of property and the death of his fellow-conspirators, Blood resolved to hang him upon the gallows at Tyburn. That he might accomplish this end with greater speed and security, he, leaving his victim securely buckled and tied to the fellow behind whom he had been mounted, galloped forward in advance to adjust the rope to the gallows, and make other necessary preparations.

No sooner did the echo of his horse's hoofs die away, than the duke, recovering the stupor this sudden attack had caused, became aware that now was his opportunity to effect escape, if, indeed, such were possible. He to whom his grace was secured was a burly man possessed of great strength; the which Lord Ormond, being now past his sixtieth year, had not. However, life was dear to him, and therefore he began struggling with the fellow; and finally getting his foot under the villain's, he unhorsed him, when both fell heavily to the ground. Meanwhile his grace's coach having driven to Clarendon House, the footmen had given an account of the daring manner in which his abduction had been effected. On this an alarm was immediately raised, and the porter, servants, and others hastened down Piccadilly in search of their master, fast as good horses could carry them.

They had proceeded as far as the village of Knightsbridge, when reports of muskets, cries for help, and sounds of a scuffle they could not see for darkness, fell upon their ears, and filled them with alarm. The whole neighbourhood seemed startled, lights flashed, dogs barked, and many persons rushed towards the scene of encounter. Aware of this, the miscreants who had carried off the duke discharged their pistols at him, and leaving him, as they supposed, for dead, fled to avoid capture, and were seen or heard of no more. His grace was carried in an insensible condition to a neighbouring house, but not having received serious hurt, recovered in a few days. The court and town were strangely alarmed by this outrage; nor as time passed was there any clue obtained to its perpetrators, though the king offered a thousand pounds reward for their discovery.

The duke and his family, however, had little doubt his grace of Buckingham was instigator of the deed; and Lord Ossory was resolved the latter should be made aware of their conviction. Therefore, entering the royal drawing-room one day, he saw the duke standing beside his majesty, and going forward addressed him. "My lord," said he in a bold tone, whilst he looked him full in the face, "I know well that you are at the bottom of this late attempt upon my father; and I give you fair warning, if my father comes to a violent end by sword or pistol, or if he dies by the hand of a ruffian, or by the more secret way of poison, I shall not be at a loss to know the first author of it: I shall consider you as the assassin; I shall treat you as such; and wherever I meet you I shall pistol you, though you stood behind the king's chair; and I tell you it in his majesty's presence, that you may be sure I shall keep my word." No further attempt was made upon the Duke of Ormond's life.

Scarce six months elapsed from date of the essayed abduction, before Blood endeavoured to steal the regalia and royal jewels preserved in the Tower. The courage which prompted the design is not more remarkable than the skill which sought to effect it; both were worthy a man of genius. In the month of April, 1671, Blood, attired in the cassock, cloak, and canonical girdle of a clergyman, together with a lady, whom he represented as his wife, visited the Tower on purpose to see the crown. With their desire Mr. Edwards, the keeper, an elderly man and a worthy, readily complied. It chanced they were no sooner in the room where the regalia was kept, than the lady found herself taken suddenly and unaccountably ill, and indeed feared she must die; before bidding adieu to life, she begged for a little whisky. This was promptly brought her, and Mrs. Edwards, who now appeared upon the scene, invited the poor gentlewoman to rest upon her bed. Whilst she complied with this kind request, the clergyman and Edwards had time to improve their acquaintance, which indeed bade fair towards speedily ripening into friendship.

And presently the lady recovering, she and her spouse took their leave with many expressions of gratitude and respect. Four days later, the good parson called on Mrs. Edwards, in order to present her with four pairs of fine new gloves, which she was pleased to receive. This gracious act paved the way to further friendship, which at last found its climax in a proposal of marriage made by the parson on behalf of his nephew, for the hand of young Mistress Edwards. "You have a pretty gentlewoman for your daughter," said the clergyman, "and I have a young nephew, who has two or three hundred pounds a year in land, and is at my disposal; if your daughter be free, and you approve of it, I will bring him hither to see her, and we will endeavour to make a match of it."

To this project Edwards readily consented, and invited the clergyman and the young man to spend a day with him when they could discourse on the subject with greater leisure and more satisfaction. This was cordially agreed to by the parson, who, with the bridegroom elect and two of his friends, presented themselves on the appointed date, as early as seven of the clock in the morning. Edwards was up betimes; but the good clergyman, apologizing for the untimely hour of their arrival, which he attributed to his nephew's eagerness for sight of his mistress, declared he would not enter the keeper's apartments until Mrs. Edwards was ready to receive them. However, in order to pass the time, he begged his host might show the jewels to their young friends.

With this petition Edwards complied readily enough. One of the men, protesting he did not care to see the treasures, waited at the door; the other three entered with the keeper, who was no sooner inside the room than a cloak was thrown over his head, a gag, constructed of wood with a hole in it by which he might breathe, clapped into his mouth, and the more effectually to prevent him making a noise, an iron ring was fastened to his nose. He was told if he attempted an alarm he would be instantly killed, but if he remained quiet his life should be spared. Blood and his two accomplices then seized upon the crown, orb, and sceptre, seeing which, Edwards made as much noise as he possibly could by stamping on the floor, whereon the robbers struck him with a mallet on the head, stabbed him with a short sword in the side, and left him, as they thought, for dead. Blood then secured the regalia under his cloak, one of his companions put the orb into his breeches pocket, whilst the other proceeded to file the sceptre that it might be more conveniently carried.

Now, at this moment it happened the keeper's son, who had been absent in Flanders, returned to his father's home. He who stood sentinel asked him with whom he would speak, whereon young Edwards said he belonged to the house, and so passed to the apartments where his family resided. The other giving notice of his arrival, the robbers hastened to depart, leaving the sceptre behind them. No sooner had they gone, than the old man struggled to his feet, dragged the gag from his mouth, and cried out in fright: "Treason--murder--murder--treason!" On this his daughter rushed down, and seeing the condition of her father, and noting the absence of the regalia, continued his cry, adding, "The crown is stolen--thieves--thieves!"

Young Edwards and another who heard her, Captain Beekman, now gave pursuit to the robbers, who had already got beyond the main guard. Word was instantly shouted to the warder of the drawbridge to stop the villains, but Blood was equal to this emergency; coolly advancing, he discharged his pistol at the man, who instantly fell. The thieves then crossed the bridge, passed through the outward gate, and made for the street close by, where their horses awaited them, crying the while, "Stop thief! stop thief!" Before they advanced far, Captain Beekman came up with Blood, who, turning quickly round, fired his second pistol at the head of his pursuer; but Beekman, suddenly stooping, escaped injury, and sprang at the throat of his intended assassin. A struggle then ensued. Blood was a man of powerful physique, but Beekman was lithe and vigorous, and succeeded in holding the rogue until help arrived. In the contest, the regalia fell to the ground, when a fair diamond and a priceless pearl were lost; they were, however, eventually recovered. The other thieves were likewise captured, and all of them secured in the Tower.

Certain death now faced Blood; but the wonderful luck which had befriended him during life did not desert him now. At this time the Duke of Buckingham was high in favour with the king, and desirous of saving one who had secretly served him; or fearing exposure if Blood made a full confession, his grace impressed Charles with a desire to see the man who had perpetrated so daring a deed, saying he must be one possessed of extraordinary spirit. Giving ready ear to his words, the monarch consented to have an interview with the robber, for which purpose he gave orders Blood should be brought to Whitehall.

Those who heard of the king's resolution felt satisfied Blood need not despair of life; "for surely," said Sir Robert Southwell, on becoming aware of his majesty's design, "no king should wish to see a malefactor but with intentions to pardon him."

Now Blood, being a man of genius, resolved to play his part during the audience in a manner which would favourably impress the king. Therefore when Charles asked him how he had dared attempt so bold a robbery, Blood made answer he had lost a fine property by the crown, and was resolved to recover it with the crown. Diverted by his audacity his majesty questioned him further, when Blood confessed to his attempted abduction of the Duke of Ormond, but refused to name his accomplices. Nay, he narrated various other adventures, showing them in a romantic light; and finally concluded by telling the king he had once entered into a design to take his sacred life by rushing upon him with a carbine from out of the reeds by the Thames side, above Battersea, when he went to swim there; but he was so awed by majesty his heart misgave him, and he not only relented, but persuaded the remainder of his associates from such an intention.

This strange interview resulted in Charles pardoning Blood his many crimes. The Duke of Ormond, at his majesty's request, likewise forgave him. Nor did the king's interest in the villain end here; for he gave him a pension of five hundred pounds a year, and admitted him to his private friendship. Blood was therefore constantly at court, and made one of that strange assembly of wits and profligates which surrounded the throne. "No man," says Carte the historian, "was more assiduous than he. If anyone had a business at court that stuck, he made his application to Blood as the most industrious and successful solicitor; and many gentlemen courted his acquaintance, as the Indians pray to the devil, that he may not hurt them. He was perpetually in the royal apartments, and affected particularly to be in the same room where the Duke of Ormond was, to the indignation of all others, though neglected and overlooked by his grace."

CHAPTER XI.

Terror falls upon the people.--Rumours of a plague.--A sign in the heavens.--Flight from the capital.--Preparations against the dreaded enemy.--Dr. Boghurst's testimony.--God's terrible voice in the city.--Rules made by the lord mayor.--Massacre of animals.--O, dire death!--Spread of the distemper.--Horrible sights.--State of the deserted capital.--"Bring out your dead."--ashes to ashes.--Fires are lighted.--Relief of the poor.--The mortality bills.

It came to pass during the fifth month of the year 1665, that a great terror fell upon the city of London; even as a sombre cloud darkens the midday sky. For it was whispered abroad a plague had come amongst the people, fears of which had been entertained, and signs of which had been obvious for some time. During the previous November a few persons had fallen victims to this dreaded pestilence, but the weather being cold and the atmosphere clear, it had made no progress till April. In that month two men had died of this most foul disease; and in the first week of May its victims numbered nine; and yet another fortnight and it had hurried seventeen citizens to the grave.

Now the memory of their wickedness rising before them, dread took up its abode in all men's hearts; for none knew but his day of reckoning was at hand. And their consternation was greater when it was remembered that in the third year of this century thirty-six thousand citizens of London had died of the plague, while twenty-five years later it had swept away thirty-five thousand; and eleven years after full ten thousand persons perished of this same pestilence. Moreover, but two years previous, a like scourge had been rife in Holland; and in Amsterdam alone twenty-four thousand citizens had died from its effects.

And the terror of the citizens of London was yet more forcibly increased by the appearance in April of a blazing star or comet, bearing a tail apparently six yards in length, which rose betimes in a lurid sky, and passed with ominous movement from west to east. [It is worthy of notice that Lilly in his "Astrological Predictions," published in 1648, declared the year 1656 would be "ominous to London, unto her merchants at sea, to her traffique at land, to her poor, to her rich, to all sorts of people inhabiting in her or her Liberties, by reason of sundry fires and a consuming plague."] The king with his queen and court, prompted by curiosity, stayed up one night to watch this blazing star pass above the silent city; the Royal Society in behalf of science embodied many learned comments regarding it in their "Philosophical Transactions;" but the great body of the people regarded it as a visible signal of God's certain wrath. They were more confirmed in this opinion, as some amongst them, whose judgments were distorted by fears, declared the comet had at times before their eyes assumed the appearance of a fiery sword threatening the sinful city. It was also noted in the spring of this year that birds and wild fowls had left their accustomed places, and few swallows were seen. But in the previous summer there had been "such a multitude of flies that they lined the insides of houses; and if any threads of strings did hang down in any place, they were presently thick-set with flies like ropes of onions; and swarms of ants covered the highways that you might have taken up a handful at a time, both winged and creeping ants; and such a multitude of croaking frogs in ditches that you might have heard them before you saw them," as is set down by one William Boghurst, apothecary at the White Hart in St. Giles-in-the-Fields, who wrote a learned "Treatis on the Plague" in 1666, he being the only man who up to that time had done so from experience and observation. [This quaint and curious production, which has never been printed, and which furnishes the following pages with some strange details, is preserved in the Sloane Collection of Manuscripts in the British Museum.] And from such signs, as likewise from knowledge that the pestilence daily increased, all felt a season of bitter tribulation was at hand.

 According to "Some Observations of the Plague," written by Dr. Hedges for use of a peer of the realm, the dread malady was communicated to London from the Netherlands "by way of contagion." It first made its appearance in the parishes of St. Giles and St. Martin's, Westminster, from which directions it gradually spread to Holborn, Fleet Street, the Strand, and the city, finally reaching to the east, bringing death invariably in its train.

The distemper was not only fatal in its termination, but loathsome in its progress; for the blood of those affected being poisoned by atmospheric contagion, bred venom in the body, which burst forth into nauseous sores and uncleanness; or otherwise preyed with more rapid fatality internally, in some cases causing death before its victims were assured of disease. Nor did it spare the young and robust any more than those weak of frame or ripe with years, but attacking stealthily, killed speedily. It was indeed the "pestilence that walketh in darkness, and the destruction that wasteth in the noonday." In the month of May, when it was yet uncertain if the city would be spared even in part, persons of position and wealth, and indeed those endowed with sufficient means to support themselves elsewhere, resolved to fly from the capital; whilst such as had neither home, friends, nor expectation of employment in other places, remained behind. Accordingly great preparations were made by those who determined on flight; and all day long vast crowds gathered round my lord mayor's house in St. Helen's, Bishopsgate, seeking certificates of health, so that for some weeks it was difficult to reach his door for the throng that gathered there, as is stated by John Noorthouck. Such official testimonies to the good health of those leaving London had now become necessary; for the inhabitants of provincial towns, catching the general alarm, refused to shelter in their houses, or even let pass through their streets, the residents of the plague-stricken city, unless officially assured they were free from the dreaded distemper. Nay, even with such certificates in their possession, many were refused admittance to inns, or houses of entertainment, and were therefore obliged to sleep in fields by night, and beg food by day, and not a few deaths were caused by want and exposure.

And now were the thoroughfares of the capital crowded all day long with coaches conveying those who sought safety in flight, and with waggons and carts containing their household goods and belongings, until it seemed as if the city mould be left without a soul. Many merchants and shipowners together with their families betook themselves to vessels, which they caused to be towed down the river towards Greenwich, and in which they resided for months; whilst others sought refuge in smacks and fishing-boats, using them as shelters by day, and lodging on the banks by night. Some few families remaining in the capital laid in stores of provisions, and shutting themselves up securely in their houses, permitted none to enter or leave, by which means some of them escaped contagion and death. The court tarried until the 29th of June, and then left for Hampton, none too soon, for the pestilence had reached almost to the palace gates. The queen mother likewise departed, retiring into France; from which country she never returned.

All through the latter part of May, and the whole of the following month, this flight from the dread enemy of mankind continued; presenting a melancholy spectacle to those who remained, until at last the capital seemed veritably a city of the dead. But for the credit of humanity be it stated, that not all possessed of health and wealth abandoned the town. Prominent amongst those who remained were the Duke of Albemarle, Lord Craven, the lord mayor, Sir John Laurence, some of his aldermen, and a goodly number of physicians, chirurgeons, and apothecaries, all of whom by their skill or exertions sought to check the hungry ravages of death. The offices which medical men voluntarily performed during this period of dire affliction were loathsome to a terrible degree. "I commonly dressed forty sores in a day," says Dr. Boghurst, whose simple words convey a forcible idea of his nobility; "held the pulse of patients sweating in their beds half a quarter of an hour together; let blood; administered clysters to the sick; held them up in their beds to keep them from strangling and choking, half an hour together commonly, and suffered their breathing in my face several times when they were dying; eat and drank with them, especially those that had sores; sat down by their bedsides and upon their beds, discoursing with them an hour together. If I had time I stayed by them to see them die. Then if people had nobody to help them (for help was scarce at such time and place) I helped to lay them forth out of the bed, and afterwards into the coffin; and last of all, accompanied them to the ground."

Of the physicians remaining in the city, nine fell a sacrifice to duty. Amongst those who survived was the learned Dr. Nathaniel Hodges, who was spared to meet a philanthropist's fate in penury and neglect. [Dr. Hodges subsequently wrote a work entitled "Loimologia; or, an Historical Account of the Plague of London," first published in 1672; of which, together with a collection of the bills of mortality for 1665, entitled "London's Dreadful Visitation," and a pamphlet by the Rev. Thomas Vincent, "God's Terrible Voice in the City," printed in 1667, De Foe largely availed himself in writing his vivid but unreliable "Journal of the Plague Year," which first saw the light in 1722.] The king had, on outbreak of the distemper, shown solicitude for his citizens by summoning a privy council, when a committee of peers was formed for "Prevention and Spreading of the Infection." Under their orders the College of Physicians drew up "Certain necessary Directions for the Prevention and Cure of the Plague, with Divers remedies for small Change," which were printed in pamphlet form, and widely distributed amongst the people. [We learn that at this time the College was stored with "men of learning, virtue, and probity, nothing acquainted with the little arts of getting a name by plotting against the honesty and credulity of the people." The prescriptions given by this worthy body were consequently received with a simple faith which later and more sceptical generations might deny them. Perhaps the most remarkable of these directions, given under the heading of "Medicines External," was the following: "Pull off the feathers from the tails of living cocks, hens, pigeons, or chickens, and holding their bills, hold them hard to the botch or swelling, and so keep them at that part until they die, and by that means draw out the poison. It is good to apply a cupping glass, or embers in a dish, with a handful of sorrel upon the embers."]

The lord mayor, having likewise the welfare of the people at heart, "conceived and published" rules to be observed, and orders to be obeyed, by them during this visitation. These directed the appointment of two examiners for every parish, who were bound to discover those who were sick, and inquire into the nature of their illness: and finding persons afflicted by plague, they, with the members of their family and domestics, were to be confined in their houses. These were to be securely locked outside, and guarded day and night by watchmen, whose duty it should be to prevent persons entering or leaving those habitations; as likewise to perform such offices as were required, such as conveying medicines and food. And all houses visited by the distemper were to be forthwith marked on the door by a red cross a foot long, with the words LORD HAVE MERCY UPON US set close over the same sacred sign. Female searchers, "such as are of honest reputation, and of the best sort as can be got of the kind," were selected that they might report of what disease people died; such women not being permitted during this visitation to use any public work or employment, or keep shop or stall, or wash linen for the people. Nurses to attend the afflicted deserted by their friends were also appointed. And inasmuch as multitudes of idle rogues and wandering beggars swarming the city were a great means of spreading disease, the constables had orders not to suffer their presence in the streets. And dogs and cats, being domestic animals, apt to run from house to house, and carry infection in their fur and hair, an order was made that they should be killed, and an officer nominated to see it carried into execution. It was computed that, in accordance with this edict, forty thousand dogs, and five times that number of cats, were massacred.

All plays bear-baitings, exhibitions, and games were forbidden; as were likewise "all public feasting, and particularly by the companies of the city, and dinners at taverns, alehouses, and other places of common entertainment; and the money thereby spared, be employed for the benefit and relief of the poor visited with the infection." Pest-houses were opened at Tothill Fields, Westminster, and at Bunhill Fields, near Old Street, for reception of the sick: and indeed every possible remedy calculated to check the disease was adopted. Some of these, though considered necessary to the well-being of the community, were by many citizens regarded as hardships, more especially the rule which related to closing of infected houses.

The misery endured by those in health suffering such confinement, was scarcely less than that realized by the afflicted. And fear making way for disease, it frequently occurred a whole family, when confined with one infected member, speedily became stricken by plague, and consequently overtaken by death. It therefore happened that many attempts were made by those in health to escape incarceration. In some cases they bribed, and in others ill-treated the watchmen: one of whom was actually blown up by gunpowder in Coleman Street, that those he guarded might flee unmolested. Again, it chanced that strong men, rendered desperate when brought face to face with loathsome death, lowered themselves from windows of their houses in sight of the watch, whom they threatened with instant death if they cried out or stirred.

The apprehension of the sick, who were in most cases deserted by their friends, was increased tenfold by the practices of public nurses: for being hardened to affliction by nature of their employment, and incapable of remorse for crime by reason of their vileness, they were guilty of many barbarous usages. "These wretches," says Dr. Hodges, "out of greediness to plunder the dead, would strangle their patients, and charge it to the distemper in their throats. Others would secretly convey the pestilential taint from sores of the infected to those who were well; and nothing indeed deterred these abandoned miscreants from prosecuting their avaricious purposes by all methods their wickedness could invent; who, although they were without witnesses to accuse them, yet it is not doubted but divine vengeance will overtake such wicked barbarities with due punishment. Nay, some were remarkably struck from heaven in the perpetration of their crimes; and one particularly amongst many, as she was leaving the house of a family, all dead, loaded with her robberies, fell down lifeless under her burden in the street. And the case of a worthy citizen was very remarkable, who, being suspected dying by his nurse, was beforehand stripped by her; but recovering again, he came a second time into the world naked."

But notwithstanding all precautions and care taken by the Duke of Albemarle and the worthy lord mayor, the dreadful pestilence spread with alarming rapidity; as may be judged from the fact that the number who died in the first week of June amounted to forty-three, whilst during the last week of that month two hundred and sixty-seven persons were carried to their graves. From the 4th of July to the 11th, seven hundred and fifty-five deaths were chronicled; the following eight days the death rate rose to one thousand and eighty-two; whilst the ensuing week this high figure was increased by over eight hundred. For the month of August, the mortality bill recorded seventeen thousand and thirty-six deaths; and during September, twenty-six thousand two hundred and thirty persons perished in the city.

The whole British nation was stricken with consternation at the fate of the capital. "In some houses," says Dr. Hodges, speaking from personal experience, "carcases lay waiting for burial, and in others were persons in their last agonies. In one room might be heard dying groans, in an other the ravings of delirium, and not far off relations and friends bewailing both their loss and the dismal prospect of their own sudden departure. Death was the sure midwife to all children, and infants passed immediately from the womb to the grave. Some of the infected run about staggering like drunken men, and fall and expire in the streets; whilst others lie half dead and comatose, but never to be waked but by the last trumpet." The plague had indeed encompassed the walls of the city, and poured in upon it without mercy. A heavy stifling atmosphere, vapours by day and blotting out all traces of stars and sky by night, hovered like a palpable shape of dire vengeance above the doomed city. During many weeks "there was a general calm and serenity, as if both wind and rain had been expelled the kingdom, so that there was not so much as to move a flame." The oppressive silence of brooding death, unbroken now even by the passing bell, weighed stupor-like upon the wretched survivors. The thoroughfares were deserted, grass sprang green upon side-paths and steps of dwellings; and the broad street in Whitechapel became like unto a field. Most houses bore upon their doors the dread sign of the red cross, with the supplication for mercy written above. Some of the streets were barricaded at both ends, the inhabitants either having fled into the country or been carried to their graves; and it was estimated in all that over seven thousand dwellings were deserted. All commerce, save that dealing with the necessaries of life, was abandoned; the parks forsaken and locked, the Inns of Court closed, and the public marts abandoned. A few of the church doors were opened, and some gathered within that they might humbly beseech pardon for the past, and ask mercy in the present. But as the violence of the distemper increased, even the houses of God were forsaken; and those who ventured abroad walked in the centre of the street, avoiding contact or conversation with friend or neighbour; each man dreading and avoiding his fellow, lest he should be to him the harbinger of death. And all carried rue and wormwood in their hands, and myrrh and zedoary in their mouths, as protection against infection. Now were the faces of all pale with apprehension, none knowing when the fatal malady might carry them hence; and moreover sad, as became those who stand in the presence of death.

And such sights were to be witnessed day after day as made the heart sick. "It would be endless," says the Rev. Thomas Vincent, "to speak what we have seen and heard; of some, in their frenzy, rising out of their beds and leaping about their rooms; others crying and roaring at their windows; some coming forth almost naked and running into the streets; strange things have others spoken and done when the disease was upon them: but it was very sad to hear of one, who being sick alone, and it is like frantic, burnt himself in his bed. And amongst other sad spectacles methought two were very affecting: one of a woman coming alone and weeping by the door where I lived, with a little coffin under her arm, carrying it to the new churchyard. I did judge that it was the mother of the child, and that all the family besides was dead, and she was forced to coffin up and bury with her own hands this her last dead child. Another was of a man at the corner of the Artillery Wall, that as I judge, through the dizziness of his head with the disease, which seized upon him there, had dashed his face against the wall; and when I came by he lay hanging with his bloody face over the rails, and bleeding upon the ground; within half an hour he died in that place."

And as the pestilence increased, it was found impossible to provide coffins or even separate graves for those who perished. And therefore, in order to bury the deceased, great carts passed through the streets after sunset, attended by linkmen and preceded by a bellman crying in weird and solemn tones, "Bring out your dead." At the intimation of the watchmen stationed before houses bearing red crosses upon their doors, the sad procession would tarry, When coffinless, and oftentimes shroudless, rigid, loathsome, and malodorous bodies were hustled into the carts with all possible speed. Then once more the melancholy cortege took its way adown the dark, deserted street, the yellow glare of links falling on the ghastly burden they accompanied, the dirge-like call of the bellman sounding on the ears of the living like a summons from the dead. And so, receiving additional freight upon its way, the cart proceeded to one of the great pits dug in the parish churchyards of Aldgate and Whitechapel, or in Finsbury Fields close by the Artillery Ground. These, measuring about forty feet in length, eighteen in breadth, and twenty in depth, were destined to receive scores of bodies irrespective of creed or class. The carts being brought to these dark and weirdsome gulphs, looking all the blacker from the flickering lights of candles and garish gleams of lanterns placed beside them, the bodies, without rite or ceremony, were shot into them, and speedily covered with clay. For the accomplishment of this sad work night was found too brief. And what lent additional horror to the circumstances of these burials was, that those engaged in this duty would occasionally drop lifeless during their labour. So that it sometimes happened the dead-carts were found without driver, linkman, or bell-man. And it was estimated that the parish of Stepney alone lost one hundred and sixteen gravediggers and sextons within that year.

During the month of September, the pestilence raged with increased fury; and it now seemed as if the merciless distemper would never cease whilst a single inhabitant remained in the city. The lord mayor, having found all remedies to stay its progress utterly fail, by advice of the medical faculty, ordered that great fires should be kindled in certain districts, by way of purifying the air, Accordingly, two hundred chaldrons of coal, at four pounds a chaldron, were devoted to this purpose. At first the fires were with great difficulty made to burn, through the scarcity, it was believed, of oxygen in the atmosphere; but once kindled, they continued blazing for three days and three nights, when a heavy downpour of rain falling they were extinguished. The following night death carried off four thousand souls, and the experiment of these cleansing fires was discontinued. All through this month fear and tribulation continued; the death rate, from the 5th of September to the 3rd of October, amounting to twenty-four thousand one hundred and seventy-one.

During October, the weather being cool and dry, the pestilence gave promise of rapid decrease. Hope came to the people, and was received with eager greeting. Once more windows were unshuttered, doors were opened, and the more venturous walked abroad. The great crisis had passed. In the middle of the month Mr. Pepys travelled on foot to the Tower, and records his impressions. "Lord," he says, "how empty the streets are and melancholy, so many poor sick people in the streets full of sores; and so many sad stories overheard as I walk, everybody talking of this dead, and that man sick, and so many in this place, and so many in that. And they tell me that in Westminster there is never a physician and but one apothecary left, all being dead; but that there are great hopes of a decrease this week. God send it."

The while, trade being discontinued, those who had lived by commerce or labour were supported by charity. To this good purpose the king contributed a thousand pounds per week, and Dr. Sheldon, Archbishop of Canterbury--who remained at Lambeth during the whole time--by letters to his bishops, caused great sums to be collected throughout the country and remitted to him for this laudable purpose. Nor did those of position or wealth fail in responding to calls made upon them at this time; their contributions being substantial enough to permit the lord mayor to distribute upwards of one hundred thousand pounds a week amongst the poor and afflicted for several months.

In October the death rate fell to nine thousand four hundred and forty-four; in November to three thousand four hundred and forty-nine; and in December to less than one thousand. Therefore, after a period of unprecedented suffering, the people took courage once more, for life is dear to all men. And those who had fled the plague-stricken city returned to find a scene of desolation, greater in its misery than words can describe. But the tide of human existence having once turned, the capital gradually resumed its former appearance. Shops which had been closed were opened afresh; houses whose inmates had been carried to the grave became again centres of activity; the sound of traffic was heard in streets long silent; church bells called the citizens to prayer; marts were crowded; and people wore an air of cheerfulness becoming the survivors of a calamity. And so all things went on as before.

The mortality bills computed the number of burials which took place in London during this year at ninety-seven thousand three hundred and six, of which sixty-eight thousand five hundred find ninety-six were attributed to the plague. This estimate has been considered by all historians as erroneous. For on the first appearance of the distemper, the number of deaths set down was far below that which truth warranted, in order that the citizens might not be affrighted; and when it was at its height no exact account of those shifted from the dead-carts into the pits was taken. Moreover, many were buried by their friends in fields and gardens. Lord Clarendon, an excellent authority, states that though the weekly bills reckoned the number of deaths at about one hundred thousand, yet "many who could compute very well, concluded that there were in truth double that number who died; and that in one week, when the bill mentioned only six thousand, there had in truth fourteen thousand died."

CHAPTER XII.

A cry of fire by night.--Fright and confusion.--The lord mayor is unmanned.--Spread of the flames.--Condition of the streets.--Distressful scenes.--Destruction of the Royal Exchange.--Efforts of the king and Duke of York.--Strange rumours and alarms.--St. Paul's is doomed.--The flames checked.--A ruined city as seen by day and night.--Wretched state of the people.--Investigation into the origin of the fire.--A new city arises.

Scarcely had the city of London recovered from the dire effects of the plague, ere a vast fire laid it waste. It happened on the 2nd of September, 1666, that at two o'clock in the morning, the day being Sunday, smoke and flames were seen issuing from the shop of a baker named Faryner, residing in Pudding Lane, close by Fish Street, in the lower part of the city. The house being built of wood, and coated with pitch, as were likewise those surrounding it, and moreover containing faggots, dried logs, and other combustible materials, the fire spread with great rapidity: so that in a short time not only the baker's premises, but the homesteads which stood next it on either side were in flames.

Accordingly, the watchman's lusty cry of "Fire, fire, fire!" which had roused the baker and his family in good time to save their lives, was now shouted down the streets with consternation, startling sleepers from their dreams, and awaking them to a sense of peril. Thereon they rose promptly from their beds, and hastily throwing on some clothes, rushed out to rescue their neighbours' property from destruction, and subdue the threatening conflagration.

And speedily was heard the tramp of many feet hurrying to the scene, and the shouting of anxious voices crying for help; and presently the bells of St. Margaret's church close by, ringing with wild uneven peals through the darkness, aroused all far and near to knowledge of the disaster. For already the flames, fanned by a high easterly wind, and fed by the dry timber of the picturesque old dwellings huddled close together, had spread in four directions.

One of these being Thames Street, the consequence was terrible, for the shops and warehouses of this thoroughfare containing inflammable materials, required for the shipping trade, such as oil, pitch, tar, and rosin, the houses at one side the street were immediately wrapped, from basement to garret, in sheets of angry flame. And now flaunting its yellow light skywards, as if exulting in its strength, and triumphing in its mastery over men's efforts, the fire rushed to the church of St. Magnus, a dark solid edifice standing at the foot of London Bridge. The frightened citizens concluded the conflagration must surely end here; or at least that whilst it endeavoured to consume a dense structure such as this, they might succeed in subduing its force; but their hopes were vain. At first the flames shot upwards to the tower of the building, but not gaining hold, retreated as if to obtain fresh strength for new efforts; and presently darting forward again, they seized the woodwork of the belfry windows. A few minutes later the church blazed at every point, and was in itself a colossal conflagration.

From this the fire darted to the bridge, burning the wooden houses built upon it, and the water machines underneath, and likewise creeping up Thames Street, on that side which was yet undemolished. By this time the bells of many churches rang out in sudden fright, as if appealing to heaven for mercy on behalf of the people; and the whole east end of the town rose up in alarm. The entire city seemed threatened with destruction, for the weather having long been dry and warm, prepared the homesteads for their fate; and it was noted some of them, when scorched by the approaching fire, ignited before the flames had time to reach them.

Sir Thomas Bludworth, the lord mayor, now arrived in great haste, but so amazed was he at the sight he beheld, and so bewildered by importunities of those who surrounded him, that he was powerless to act. Indeed, his incapacity to direct, and inability to command, as well as his lack of moral courage, have been heavily and frequently blamed. Bring a weak man, fearful of outstepping his authority, he at first forebore pulling down houses standing in the pathway of the flames, as suggested to him, a means that would assuredly have prevented their progress; but when urged to this measure would reply, he "durst not, without the consent of the owners." And when at last, after great destruction had taken place, word was brought him from the king to "spare no house, but pull them down everywhere before the fire," he cried out "like a fainting woman," as Pepys recounts, "Lord! what can I do? I am spent; people will not obey me."

Meanwhile, great bodies of the citizens of all classes had been at work; some upon the cumbrous engines, others carrying water, others levelling houses, but all their endeavours seemed powerless to quell the raging flames. And it was notable when first the pipes in the streets were opened, no water could be found, whereon a messenger was sent to the works at Islington, in order to turn on the cocks, so that much time was lost in this manner. All through Sunday morning the flames extended far and wide, and in a few hours three hundred houses were reduced to ashes. Not at midday, nor yet at night, did they give promise of abatement. The strong easterly wind continuing to blow, the conflagration worked its way to Cannon Street, from thence gradually encompassing the dwellings which lay between that thoroughfare and the Thames, till the whole seemed one vast plain of raging fire.

The streets now presented a scene of the uttermost confusion and distress. The affrighted citizens, whose dwellings were momentarily threatened with destruction, hurried to and fro, striving to save those of their families who by reason of infancy, age or illness were unable to help themselves. Women on the eve of childbirth were carried from their beds; mothers with infants clinging to their naked breasts fled from homes which would shelter them no more; the decrepit were borne away on the shoulders of the strong. The narrow thoroughfares were moreover obstructed by furniture dragged from houses, or lowered from windows with a reckless speed that oftentimes destroyed what it sought to preserve. Carts, drays, and horses laden with merchandise jostled each other in their hurried way towards the fields outside the city walls. Men young and vigorous crushed forward with beds or trunks upon their backs; children laboured under the weight of bundles, or rolled barrels of oil, wine, or spirits before them. And the air, rendered suffocating by smoke and flame, was moreover confused by the crackling of consuming timber, the thunder of falling walls, the crushing of glass, the shrieks of women, and the imprecations of men.

And those who lived near the waterside, or in houses on the bridges, hurried their goods and chattels into boats, barges, and lighters, in which they likewise took refuge. For the destruction of wharfs and warehouses, containing stores of most inflammable nature, was brief and desperate. The Thames, now blood-red from reflection of the fierce sky, was covered with craft of all imaginable shape and size. Showers of sparks blown by the high wind fell into the water with hissing sounds, or on the clothes and faces of the people with disastrous and painful effects; and the smoke and heat were hard to bear. And it was remarked that flocks of pigeons, which for generations had found shelter in the eaves and roofs of wooden houses by the riverside, were loath to leave their habitations; and probably fearing to venture afar by reason of the unwonted aspect of the angry sky, lingered on the balconies and abutments of deserted houses, until in some cases, the flames enwrapping them, they fell dead into the waters below.

On Sunday evening Gracechurch Street was on fire; and the flames spread onwards till they reached, and in their fury consumed, the Three Cranes in the Vintry. Night came, but darkness had fled from the city; and for forty miles round all was luminous. And there were many who in the crimson hue of the heavens, beheld an evidence of God's wrath at the sins of the nation, which it was now acknowledged were many and great.

Throughout Sunday night the fire grew apace, and those who, in the morning had carried their belongings to parts of the city which they believed would by distance ensure safety, were now obliged to move them afresh, the devastation extending for miles. Therefore many were compelled to renew their labours, thereby suffering further fatigue; and they now trusted to no protection for their property save that which the open fields afforded. Monday morning came and found the flames yet raging. Not only Gracechurch Street, but Lombard Street, and part of Fenchurch street, were on fire. Stately mansions, comfortable homes, warehouses of great name, banks of vast wealth, were reduced to charred and blackened walls or heaps of smoking ruins. Buildings had been pulled down, but now too late to render service; for the insatiable fire, yet fed by a high wind, had everywhere marched over the dried woodwork and mortar as it lay upon the ground, and communicated itself to the next block of buildings; so that its circumvention was regarded as almost an impossibility.

During Monday the flames attacked Cornhill, and then commenced to demolish the Royal Exchange. Having once made an entrance in this stately building it revelled in triumph; climbing up the walls, roaring along the courts and galleries, and sending through the broken windows volleys of smoke and showers of sparks, which threatened to suffocate and consume those who approached. Then the roof fell with a mighty crash, which seemed for a time to subdue the powerful conflagration; the walls cracked, parted, and fell; statues of kings and queens were flung from their niches; and in a couple of hours this building, which had been the pride and glory of British Merchants, was a blackened ruin.

The citizens were now in a state of despair. Upwards of ten thousand houses were in a blaze, the fire extending, according to Evelyn, two miles in length and one in breadth, and the smoke reaching near fifty miles in length. Mansions, churches, hospitals, halls, and schools crumbled into dust as if at blighting touch of some most potent and diabolical magician. Quite hopeless now of quenching the flames, bewildered by loss, and overcome by terror, the citizens, abandoning themselves to despair, made no further effort to conquer this inappeasable fire; but crying aloud in their distraction, behaved as those who had lost their wits. The king and the Duke of York, who on Sunday had viewed the conflagration from the Thames, now alarmed at prospect of the whole capital being laid waste, rode into the city, and by their presence, coolness and example roused the people to fresh exertions. Accordingly, citizens and soldiers worked with renewed energy and courage; whilst his majesty and his brother, the courtiers and the lord mayor, mixed freely with the crowd, commanding and directing them in their labours.

But now a new terror rose up amongst the citizens, for news spread that the Dutch and French--with whom England was then at war--and moreover the papists, whom the people then abhorred, had conspired to destroy the capital. And the suddenness with which the flames had appeared in various places, and the rapidity with which they spread, leading the distracted inhabitants to favour this report, a strong desire for immediate revenge took possession of their hearts.

Accordingly all foreigners were laid hold of, kicked, beaten, and abused by infuriated mobs, from which they were rescued only to be flung into prison. And this conduct was speedily extended to the catholics, even when such were known to be faithful and well-approved good citizens. For though at first it spread as a rumour, it was now received as a certainty that they, in obedience to the wily and most wicked Jesuits, had determined to lay waste an heretical city. Nor were there wanting many ready to bear witness they had seen these dreaded papists fling fire-balls into houses of honest citizens, and depart triumphing in their fiendish deeds. So that when they ventured abroad they were beset by great multitudes, and their lives were imperilled. And news of this distraction, which so forcibly swayed the people, reaching the king, he speedily despatched the members of his privy council to several quarters of the city, that in person they might guard such of his subjects as stood in danger.

Lord Hollis and Lord Ashley were assigned Newgate Market and the streets that lie around, as parts where they were to station themselves. And it happened that riding near the former place they saw a vast number of people gathered together, shouting with great violence, and badly using one who stood in their midst. Whereon they hastened towards the spot and found the ill-treated man to be of foreign aspect. Neither had he hat, cloak, nor sword; his face was covered with blood, his jerkin was torn in pieces, and his person was bedaubed by mud. And on examination it was found he was unable to speak the English tongue; but Lord Hollis, entering into conversation with him in the French language, ascertained that he was a servant of the Portuguese ambassador, and knew not of what he was accused, or why he had been maltreated.

Hereon a citizen of good standing pressed forward and alleged he had truly seen this man put his hand in his pocket and throw a fire-ball into a shop, upon which the house immediately took flame; whereon, being on the other side of the street, he called aloud that the people might stop this abominable villain. Then the citizens had seized upon him, taking away his sword, and used him according to their will. My Lord Hollis explaining this to the foreigner, he was overcome by amazement at the charge; and when asked what he had thrown into the house, made answer he had not flung anything. But he remembered well, whilst walking in the street, he saw a piece of bread upon the ground, which he, as was the custom in his country took up. Afterwards he laid it upon a shelf in a neighbouring house, which being close by, my Lords Hollis and Ashley, followed by a dense crowd, conducted him thither, and found the bread laid upon a board as he had stated. It was noted the next house but one was on fire, and on inquiry it was ascertained that the worthy citizen, seeing a foreigner place something inside a shop without tarrying, and immediately after perceiving a dwelling in flames, which in his haste he took to be the same, he had charged the man with commission of this foul deed. But even though many were convinced of his innocence, my Lord Hollis concluded the stranger's life would be in safer keeping if he were committed to prison, which was accordingly done.

Meanwhile the fire continued; and on Monday night and Tuesday raged with increasing violence. The very heart of the city was now eaten into by this insatiable monster: Soper Lane, Bread Street, Friday Street, Old Change, and Cheapside being in one blaze. It was indeed a spectacle to fill all beholding it with consternation; but that which followed was yet more terrible, for already St. Paul's Cathedral was doomed to destruction.

Threatened on one side by the flames devastating Cheapside, and on the other from those creeping steadily up from Blackfriars to this great centre, it was now impossible to save the venerable church, which Evelyn terms "one of the most ancient pieces of early Christian piety in the world." Seen by this fierce light, and overhung by a crimson sky, every curve of its dark outline, every stone of its pillars and abutments, every column of its incomparable portico, stood clearly defined, so that never had it looked so stately and magnificent, so vast and majestic, as now when beheld for the last time.

Too speedily the fire advanced, watched by sorrowful eyes; but even before it had reached the scaffolding now surrounding the building, the vaulted roof, ignited by showers of sparks, burst into flames. Then followed a scene unspeakably grand, yet melancholy beyond all telling. In a few moments a pale yellow light had crept along the parapets, sending faint clouds of smoke upwards, as if more forcibly marking the course of destruction. Then came the crackling, hissing sounds of timber yielding to the fire, and soon a great sheet of lead which covered the roof, and was said to measure six acres, melting by degrees, down came on every side a terrible rain of liquid fire that seamed and burned the ground, and carried destruction with it in its swift course towards the Thames.

And now, by reason of the fearful heat, great projections of Portland stone, cornices, and capitals of columns, flew off before the fire had time to reach them. Windows melted in their frames, pillars fell to the ground, ironwork bent as wax; nay, the very pavements around glowed so that neither man nor horse dared tread upon them. And the flames, gradually gaining ground, danced fantastically up and down the scaffolding, and covered the edifice as with one blaze; whilst inside transom beams were snapped asunder, rafters fell with destruction, and the fire roaring through chapels and aisles as in a great furnace, could be heard afar. And that which had been a Christian shrine was now, a smoking ruin.

Raging onward in their fierce career, the flames darted towards such buildings in the neighbourhood as had been previously untouched, so that Paternoster Row, Newgate Street, the Old Bailey and Ludgate Hill were soon in course of destruction. And from the latter spot the conflagration, urged by the wind, rapidly rushed onwards towards Fleet Street. On the other hand, it extended from Cheapside to Ironmongers' Lane, Old Jewry, Lawrence Lane, Milk Street, Wood Street, Gutter Lane, and Foster Lane; and again spreading from Newgate Street, it surrounded and destroyed Christ Church, burned through St. Martin's-le-Grand towards Aldgate, and threatened to continue its triumphant march to the suburbs.

For several miles nothing but raging fire and smoking ruins was visible, for desolation had descended on the city. It was now feared the flames would reach the Palace of Whitehall, and extend towards Westminster Abbey, a consideration which caused much alarm to his majesty, who prized the sacred fane exceedingly. And now the king was determined the orders he had already issued should be obeyed, and that houses standing in direct path of the fire should be demolished by gunpowder; so that, a greater gap being effected than any previously made by pulling them down, the conflagration might have no further material wherewith to strengthen and feed its further progress.

This plan, Evelyn states, had been proposed by some stout seamen early enough to have saved nearly the whole city; "but this some tenacious and avaricious men, aldermen, etc., would not permit, because their houses would have been the first." Now, however, this remedy was tried, and with greater despatch, because the fire threatened the Tower and the powder magazine it contained. And if the flames once reached this, London Bridge would assuredly be destroyed, the vessels in the river torn and sunk, and incalculable damage to life and property effected.

Accordingly Tower Street, which had already become ignited, was, under supervision of the king, blown up in part, and the fire happily brought to an end by this means in that part of the town. Moreover, on Wednesday morning the east wind, which had continued high from Sunday night, now subsided, so that the flames lost much of their vehemence, and by means of explosions were more easily mastered at Leadenhall and in Holborn, and likewise at the Temple, to which places they had spread during Wednesday and Thursday.

During these latter days, the king and the Duke of York betrayed great vigilance, and laboured with vast activity; the latter especially, riding from post to post, by his example inciting those whose courage had deserted them, and by his determination overcoming destruction. On Thursday the dread conflagration, after raging for five consecutive days and nights, was at length conquered.

On Friday morning the sun rose like a ball of crimson fire above a scene of blackness, ruin, and desolation. Whole streets were levelled to the ground, piles of charred stones marked where stately churches had stood, smoke rose in clouds from smouldering embers. With sorrowful hearts many citizens traversed the scene of desolation that day; amongst others Pepys and Evelyn. The latter recounts that "the ground and air, smoke and fiery vapour, continu'd so intense, that my haire was almost sing'd, and my feete unsuffurably surbated. The people who now walk'd about ye ruines appear'd like men in some dismal desert, or rather in some greate citty laid waste by a cruel enemy; to which was added that stench that came from some poore creatures' bodies, beds, and other combustible goods."

It would have been impossible to trace the original course of the streets, but that some gable, pinnacle, or portion of walls, of churches, halls, or mansions, indicated where they had stood. The narrower thoroughfares were completely blocked by rubbish; massive iron chains, then used to prevent traffic at night in the streets, were melted, as were likewise iron gates of prisons, and the hinges of strong doors. Goods stored away in cellars and subterranean passages of warehouses yet smouldered, emitting foul odours; wells were completely choked, fountains were dried at their sources. The statues of monarchs which had adorned the Exchange, were smashed; that of its founder, Sir Thomas Gresham, alone remaining entire. The ruins of St. Paul's, with its walls standing black and cheerless, presented in itself a most melancholy spectacle. Its pillars were embedded in ashes, its cornices irretrievably destroyed, its great bell reduced to a shapeless mass of metal; whilst its general air of desolation was heightened by the fact that a few monuments, which had escaped destruction, rose abruptly from amidst the charred DEBRIS.

But if the ruins of the capital looked sad by day, their appearance was more appalling when seen by light of the moon, which rose nightly during the week following this great calamity. From the city gates, standing gaunt, black, and now unguarded, to the Temple, the level waste seemed sombre as a funeral pall; whilst the Thames, stripped of wharves and warehouses, quaintly gabled homes, and comfortable inns--wont to cast pleasant lights and shadows on its surface--now swept past the blackened ruins a melancholy river of white waters.

In St. George's Fields, Moorfields, and far as Highgate for several miles, citizens of all degrees, to the number of two hundred thousand, had gathered: sleeping in the open fields, or under canvas tents, or in wooden sheds which they hurriedly erected. Some there were amongst them who had been used to comfort and luxury, but who were now without bed or board, or aught to cover them save the clothes in which they had hastily dressed when fleeing from the fire. And to many it seemed as if they had only been saved from one calamity to die by another: for they had nought wherewith to satisfy their hunger, yet had too much pride to seek relief.

And whilst yet wildly distracted by their miserable situation, weary from exhaustion, and nervous from lack of repose, a panic arose in their midst which added much to their distress. For suddenly news was spread that the French, Dutch and English papists were marching on them, prepared to cut their throats. At which, broken-spirited as they were, they rose up, and leaving such goods that they had saved, rushed towards Westminster to seek protection from their imaginary foes. On this, the king sought to prove the falsity of their alarm, and with infinite difficulty persuaded them to return to the fields: whence he despatched troops of soldiers, whose presence helped to calm their fears.

And the king having, moreover, tender compassion for their wants, speedily sought to supply them. He therefore summoned a council that it might devise means of relief; and as a result, it published a proclamation ordering that bread and all other provisions, such as could be furnished, should be daily and constantly brought, not only to the markets formerly in use, but also to Clerkenwell, Islington, Finsbury Fields, Mile End Green, and Ratcliffe, for greater convenience of the citizens. For those who were unable to buy provisions, the king commanded the victualler of his navy to send bread into Moorfields, and distribute it amongst them. And as divers distressed people had saved some of their goods, of which they knew not where to dispose, he ordered that churches, chapels, schools, and such like places in and around Westminster, should be free and open to receive and protect them. He likewise directed that all cities and towns should, without contradiction or opposition, receive the citizens and permit them free exercise of their manual labours: he promising, when the present exigency had passed away, to take care the said persons should be no burden to such towns as received them.

The people were therefore speedily relieved. Many of them found refuge with their friends and relatives in the country, and others sought homes in the districts of Westminster and Southwark: so that in four days from the termination of the fire, there was scarce a person remaining in the fields, where such numbers had taken refuge.

The first hardships consequent to the calamity having passed away, people were anxious to trace the cause of their sufferings, which they were unwilling to consider accidental. A rumour therefore sprang up, that the great fire resulted from a wicked plot, hatched by Jesuits, for the destruction of an heretical city. At this the king was sorely troubled; for though there was no evidence which led him to place faith in the report, yet a great body of the citizens and many members of his council held it true. Therefore, in order to appease such doubts as arose in his mind, and likewise to satisfy the people, he appointed his privy council to sit morning and evening to inquire into the matter, and examine evidences set forth against those who had been charged with the outrage and cast into prison during the conflagration.

And in order that the investigation might be conducted with greater rigour he sent into the country for the lord chief justice, who was dreaded by all for his unflinching severity. The lord chancellor, in his account of these transactions, assures us many of the witnesses who gave evidence against those indicted with firing the capital "were produced as if their testimony would remove all doubts, but made such senseless relations of what they had been told, without knowing the condition of the persons who told them, or where to find them, that it was a hard matter to forbear smiling at their declarations." Amongst those examined was one Roger Hubert, who accused himself of having deliberately set the city on fire. This man, then in his twenty-fifth year, was son of a watchmaker residing in Rouen. Hubert had practised the same trade both in that town and in London, and was believed by his fellow workmen to be demented. When brought before the chief justice and privy council, Hubert with great coolness stated he had set the first house on fire: for which act he had been paid a year previously in Paris. When asked who had hired him to accomplish this evil deed, he replied he did not know, for he had never seen the man before: and when further questioned regarding the sum he had received, he declared it was but one pistole, but he had been promised five pistoles more when he should have done his work. These ridiculous answers, together with some contradictory statements he made, inclined many persons, amongst whom was the chief justice, to doubt his confession. Later on in his examinations, he was asked if he knew where the house had stood which he set on fire, to which he replied in the affirmative, and on being taken into the city, pointed out the spot correctly.

In the eyes of many this was regarded as proof of his guilt; though others stated that, having lived in the city, he must necessarily become acquainted with the position of the baker's shop. Opinion was therefore somewhat divided regarding him. The chief justice told the king "that all his discourse was so disjointed that he did not believe him guilty." Yet having voluntarily accused himself of a monstrous deed, and being determined as it seemed to rid himself of life, he was condemned to death and speedily executed.

Lord Clarendon says: "Neither the judges nor any present at the trial did believe him guilty; but that he was a poor distracted wretch, weary of his life, and chose to part with it in this way. Certain it is that upon the strictest examination that could be afterwards made by the king's command, and then by the diligence of the House, that upon the jealousy and rumour made a committee, that was very diligent and solicitous to make that discovery, there was never any probable evidence (that poor creature's only excepted) that there was any other cause of that woful fire than the displeasure of God Almighty: the first accident of the beginning in a baker's house, where there was so great a stock of faggots, and the neighbourhood of such combustible matter, of pitch and rosin, and the like, led it in an instant from house to house, through Thames Street, with the agitation of so terrible a wind to scatter and disperse it."

But belief that the dreaded papists had set fire to the city, lingered in the minds of many citizens. When the city was rebuilt, this opinion found expression in an inscription cut over the doorway of a house opposite the spot where the fire began, which ran as follows:

"Here, by the permission of heaven, hell broke loose on this protestant city from the malicious hearts of barbarous papists, by the hand of their agent Hubert, who confessed, and on the ruins of this place declared the fact, for which he was hanged. Erected in the mayoralty of Sir Patience Ward, Knight."

The loss caused by this dreadful conflagration was estimated at ten million sterling. According to a certificate of Jonas Moore and Ralph Gatrix, surveyors appointed to examine the ruins, the fire overrun 373 acres within the walls, burning 13,200 houses, 89 parish churches, numerous chapels, the Royal Exchange, Custom House, Guildhall, Blackwell Hall, St. Paul's Cathedral, Bridewell, fifty-two halls of the city companies, and three city gates.

As speedily as might be, the king and his parliament then sitting at Oxford, sought to restore the city on a scale vastly superior to its former condition. And the better to effect this object, an act of parliament was passed that public buildings should be rebuilt with public money, raised by a tax on coals; that the churches and the cathedral of St. Paul's should be reconstructed from their foundations; that bridges, gates and prisons should be built anew; the streets made straight and regular, such as were steep made level, such as were narrow made wide; and, moreover, that every house should be built with party walls, such being of stone or brick, and all houses raised to equal height in front.

And these rules being observed, a stately and magnificent city rose phoenix-like from ruins of the old; so that there was naught to remind the inhabitants of their great calamity save the Monument. This, designed by Sir Christopher Wren, and built at a cost of fourteen thousand five hundred pounds, was erected near where the fire broke out, the better to perpetuate a memory of this catastrophe in the minds of future generations, which purpose it fulfils unto this day.

CHAPTER XIII.

The court repairs to Oxford.--Lady Castlemaine's son.--Their majesties return to Whitehall.--The king quarrels with his mistress.--Miss Stuart contemplates marriage.--Lady Castlemaine attempts revenge.--Charles makes an unpleasant discovery.--The maid of honour elopes.--His majesty rows down the Thames.--Lady Castlemaine's intrigues.--Fresh quarrels at court.--The king on his knees.

The while such calamities befell the citizens, the king continued to divert himself in his usual fashion. On the 29th of June, 1665, whilst death strode apace through the capital, reaping full harvests as he went, their majesties left Whitehall for Hampton Court, From here they repaired to Salisbury, and subsequently to Oxford, where Charles took up his residence in Christchurch, and the queen at Merton College.

Removed from harrowing scenes of ghastliness and distress, the court made merry. Joined by fair women and gallant men, their majesties played at bowls and tennis in the grassy meads of the college grounds; rode abroad in great hawking parties; sailed through summer days upon the smooth waters of the river Isis; and by night held revelry in the massive-beamed oak-panelled halls, from which scarce five-score candles served to chase all gloom.

It happened whilst life thus happily passed, at pleasant full-tide flow, my Lady Castlemaine, who resided in the same college with her majesty, gave birth on the 28th of December to another son, duly baptized George Fitzroy, and subsequently created Duke of Northumberland. By this time, the plague having subsided in the capital, and all danger of infection passed away, his majesty was anxious to reach London, yet loth to leave his mistress, whom he visited every morning, and to whom he exhibited the uttermost tenderness. And his tardiness to return becoming displeasing to the citizens, and they being aware of its cause, it was whispered in taverns and cried in the streets, "The king cannot go away till my Lady Castlemaine be ready to come along with him," which truth was found offensive on reaching the royal ears.

Towards the end of January, 1666, he returned to Whitehall, and a month later the queen, who had been detained by illness, joined him. Once more the thread of life was taken up by the court at the point where it had been broken, and woven into the motley web of its strange history. Unwearied by time, unsatiated by familiarity, the king continued his intrigue with the imperious Castlemaine, and with great longing likewise made love to the beautiful Stuart. But yet his pursuit of pleasure was not always attended by happiness; inasmuch as he found himself continually involved in quarrels with the countess, which in turn covered him with ridicule in the eyes of his courtiers, and earned him contempt in the opinions of his subjects.

One of these disturbances, which occurred soon after his return from Oxford, began at a royal drawing-room, in presence of the poor slighted queen and ladies of the court. It happened in the course of conversation her majesty remarked to the countess she feared the king had taken cold by staying so late at her lodgings; to which speech my Lady Castlemaine with some show of temper answered aloud, "he did not stay so late abroad with her, for he went betimes thence, though he do not before one, two, or three in the morning, but must stay somewhere else." The king, who had entered the apartment whilst she was speaking, came up to her, and displeased with the insinuations she expressed, declared she was a bold, impertinent woman, and bade her begone from the court, and not return until he sent for her. Accordingly she whisked from the drawing-room, and drove at once to Pall Mall, where she hired apartments.

Her indignation at being addressed by Charles in such a manner before the court, was sufficiently great to beget strong desires for revenge; when she swore she would be even with him and print his letters to her for public sport. In cooler moments, however, she abandoned this idea; and in course of two or three days, not hearing from his majesty, she despatched a message to him, not entreating pardon, but asking permission to send for her furniture and belongings. To this the monarch, who had begun to miss her presence and long for her return, replied she must first come and view them; and then impatient for reconciliation, he sought her, and they became friends once more. And by way of sealing the bond of pacification, the king soon after agreed to pay her debts, amounting to the sum of thirty thousand pounds, which had been largely incurred by presents bestowed by her upon her lovers.

His majesty was not only rendered miserable by the constant caprices and violent temper of the countess, but likewise by the virtue and coldness Miss Stuart betrayed since her return from Oxford. The monarch was sorely troubled to account for her bearing, and attributing it to jealousy, sought to soothe her supposed uneasiness by increasing his chivalrous attentions. Her change of behaviour, however, proceeded from another cause. The fair Stuart, though childlike in manner, was shrewd at heart; and was moreover guided invariably by her mother, a lady who reaped wisdom from familiarity with courts. Therefore the maid of honour, seeing she had given the world occasion to think she had lost her virtue, declared she was ready to "marry any gentleman of fifteen hundred a year that would have her in honour."

This determination she was obliged to keep-secret from the king, lest his anger should fall upon such as sought her, and so interfere with her matrimonial prospects. Now with such intentions in her mind she pondered well on an event which had happened to her, such as no woman who has had like experience ever forgets; namely, that amongst the many who professed to love her, one had proposed to marry her. This was Charles Stuart, fourth Duke of Richmond, a man possessed of neither physical gifts nor mental abilities; who was, moreover, a widower, and a sot.

However, the position which her union with him would ensure was all she could desire, and he renewing his suit at this time, she consequently consented to marry him. Now though it was probable she could keep her design from knowledge of her royal lover, it was scarcely possible she could hide it from observation of his mistress. And the latter, knowing the extent to which fair Frances Stuart shared his majesty's heart, and being likewise aware of the coldness with which his protestations were by her received, scorned the king and detested the maid. Lady Castlemaine therefore resolved to use her knowledge of Miss Stuart's contemplated marriage, for purpose of enraging the jealousy of the one, and destroying the influence of the other. In order to accomplish such desirable ends she quietly awaited her opportunity. This came in due time.

It happened one evening when his majesty had been visiting Frances Stuart in her apartments, and had returned to his own in a condition of ill-humour and disappointment, the countess, who had been some days out of favour, suddenly presented herself before him, and in a bantering tone, accompanied by ironical smiles, addressed him.

"I hope," said she, "I may be allowed to pay you my homage, although the angelic Stuart has forbidden you to see me at my own house. I will not make use of reproaches and expostulations which would disgrace myself; still less will I endeavour to excuse frailties which nothing can justify, since your constancy for me deprives me of all defence, considering I am the only person you have honoured with your tenderness, who has made herself unworthy of it by ill-conduct. I come now, therefore, with no other intent than to comfort and condole with you upon the affliction and grief into which the coldness or new-fashioned chastity of the inhuman Stuart has reduced your majesty."

Having delivered herself of this speech she laughed loud and heartily, as if vastly amused at the tenour of her words; and then before the impatient monarch had time to reply, continued in the same tone, with quickening breath and flashing eyes, "Be not offended that I take the liberty of laughing at the gross manner in which you are imposed upon; I cannot bear to see that such particular affection should make you the jest of your own court, and that you should be ridiculed with such impunity. I know that the affected Stuart has sent you away under pretence of some indisposition, or perhaps some scruple of conscience; and I come to acquaint you that the Duke of Richmond will soon be with her, if he is not there already. I do not desire you to believe what I say, since it might be suggested either through resentment or envy. Only follow me to her apartment, either that, no longer trusting calumny and malice you may honour her with a just preference, if I accuse her falsely; or, if my information be true, you may no longer be the dupe of a pretended prude, who makes you act so unbecoming and ridiculous a part."

The king, overwhelmed with astonishment, was irresolute in action; but Lady Castlemaine, determined on not being deprived of her anticipated triumph, took him by the hand and forcibly pulled him towards Miss Stuart's apartments. The maid of honour's servants, surprised at his majesty's return, were unable to warn their mistress without his knowledge; whilst one of them, in pay of the countess, found means of secretly intimating to her that the Duke of Richmond was already in Miss Stuart's chamber. Lady Castlemaine, having with an air of exultation led the king down the gallery from his apartments to the threshold of Miss Stuart's door, made him a low courtesy savouring more of irony than homage, bade him goodnight, and with a subtle smile promptly retired.

The scene which followed is best painted by Hamilton's pen. "It was near midnight; the king on his way met the chambermaids, who respectfully opposed his entrance, and, in a very low voice, whispered his majesty that Miss Stuart had been very ill since he left her; but that being gone to bed, she was, God be thanked, in a very fine sleep. 'That I must see,' said the king, pushing her back, who had posted herself in his way. He found Miss Stuart in bed, indeed, but far from being asleep; the Duke of Richmond was seated at her pillow, and in all probability was less inclined to sleep than herself. The perplexity of the one party, and the rage of the other, were such as may easily be imagined upon such a surprise. The king, who of all men was one of the most mild and gentle, testified his resentment to the Duke of Richmond in such terms as he had never before used. The duke was speechless and almost petrified; he saw his master and his king justly irritated. The first transports which rage inspires on such occasions are dangerous. Miss Stuart's window was very convenient for a sudden revenge, the Thames flowing close beneath it; he cast his eyes upon it, and seeing those of the king more incensed than fired with indignation than he thought his nature capable of, he made a profound bow, and retired without replying a single word to the vast torrent of threats and menaces that were poured upon him.

"Miss Stuart having a little recovered from her first surprise, instead of justifying herself, began to talk in the most extravagant manner, and said everything that was most capable to inflame the king's passion and resentment: that if she were not allowed to receive visits from a man of the Duke of Richmond's rank, who came with honourable intentions, she was a slave in a free country; that she knew of no engagement that could prevent her from disposing of her hand as she thought proper; but, however, if this were not permitted her in his dominions, she did not believe that there was any power on earth that could hinder her from going over to

France, and throwing herself into a Convent, to enjoy there that tranquillity which was denied her in his court. The king, sometimes furious with anger, sometimes relenting at her tears, and sometimes terrified at her menaces, was so greatly agitated that he knew not how to answer either the nicety of a creature who wanted to act the part of Lucretia under his own eye, or the assurance with which she had the effrontery to reproach him. In this suspense love had almost entirely vanquished all his resentments, and had nearly induced him to throw himself upon his knees, and entreat pardon for the injury he had done her, when she desired him to retire, and leave her in repose, at least for the remainder of that night, without offending those who had either accompanied him, or conducted him to her apartments, by a longer visit. This impertinent request provoked and irritated him to the highest degree: he went out abruptly, vowing never to see her more, and passed the most restless and uneasy night he had ever experienced since his restoration."

Next morning, his majesty sent orders to the Duke of Richmond to quit the court, and never appear again in his presence. His grace, however, stayed not to receive this message, having betaken himself with all possible speed into the country. Miss Stuart, who likewise feared the king's resentment, hastened to the queen, and throwing herself at her majesty's feet, entreated forgiveness for the pain and uneasiness she had caused her in the past, and besought her care and protection in the future.

She then laid bare her intentions of marrying the Duke of Richmond, who had loved her long, and was anxious to wed her soon; but since the discovery of his addresses had caused his banishment, and created disturbances prejudicial to her good name, she begged the queen would obtain his majesty's consent to her retiring from the vexations of a court to the tranquillity of a convent. The queen raised her up, mingled her tears with those of the troubled maid, and promised to use her endeavours towards averting the king's displeasure.

On consideration, however, the fair Stuart did not wait to hear his majesty's reproaches, or receive his entreaties; for the duke, being impatient to gain his promised bride, quietly returned to town, and secretly communicated with her. It was therefore agreed between them she should steal away from the palace, meet him at the "Bear at the Bridge Foot," situated on the Southwark side of the river, where he would have a coach awaiting her, in order they might ride away to his residence at Cobham Hall, near Gravesend, and then be legally and happily united in the holy bonds of matrimony. And all fell out as had been arranged: the time being the month of March, 1667.

Now when the king discovered her flight, his anger knew no bounds, though it sought relief in uttering many violent threats against the duke, and in sending word to the duchess he would see her no more. In answer to this message, she, with some show of spirit, returned him the jewels he had given her, principal amongst which were a necklace of pearls, valued at over a thousand pounds, and a pair of diamond pendants of rare lustre.

Neither she nor her husband paid much heed to the royal menaces, for before a year elapsed they both returned to town, and took up their residence at Somerset House. Here, as Pepys records, she kept a great court, "she being visited for her beauty's sake by people, as the queen is at nights: and they say also she is likely to go to court again and there put my Lady Castlemaine's nose out of joint. God knows that would make a great turn." But to such proposals as were made regarding her return to Whitehall, her husband would not pay heed, and she therefore remained a stranger to its drawing-rooms for some time longer. And when two years later she appeared there, her beauty had lost much of its famed lustre, for meantime she was overtaken by smallpox, a scourge ever prevalent in the capital. During her illness the king paid her several visits, and was sorely grieved that the loveliness he so much prized should be marred by foul disease. But on her recovery, the disfigurement she suffered scarce lessened his admiration, and by no means abated his love; which seemed to have gained fresh force from the fact of its being interrupted awhile.

This soon became perceptible to all, and rumour whispered that the young duchess would shortly return to Whitehall in a position which she had declined before marriage. And amongst other stories concerning the king's love for her, it was common talk that one fair evening in May, when he had ordered his coach to be ready that he might take an airing in the park, he, on a sudden impulse, ran down the broad steps leading from his palace gardens to the riverside. Here, entering a boat alone, he rowed himself adown the placid river now crossed by early shadows, until he came to Somerset House, where his lady-love dwelt; and finding the garden-door locked, he, in his impatience to be with her, clambered over the wall and sought her. Two months after the occurrence of this incident, the young duchess was appointed a lady of the bedchamber to the queen, and therefore had apartments at Whitehall. There was little doubt now entertained she any longer rejected his majesty's love; and in order to remove all uncertainties on the point which might arise in her husband's mind, the king one night, when he had taken over much wine, boasted to the duke of her complaisancy. Lord Dartmouth, who tells this story, says this happened "at Lord Townshend's, in Norfolk, as my uncle told me, who was present." Soon after his grace accepted an honourable exile as ambassador to Denmark, in which country he died.

During the absence of the Duchess of Richmond, my Lady Castlemaine, then in the uninterrupted possession of power, led his majesty a sorry life. Her influence, indeed, seemed to increase with time, until her victim became a laughing-stock to the heartless, and an object of pity to the wise. Mr. Povy, whose office as a member of the Tangier Commission brought him into continual contact with the court, and whose love of gossip made him observant of all that passed around him, in telling of "the horrid effeminacy of the king," said that "upon any falling out between my Lady Castlemaine's nurse and her woman, my lady hath often said she would make the king make them friends, and they would be friends and be quiet--which the king had been fain to do." Nor did such condescension on his majesty's part incline his mistress to treat him with more respect; for in the quarrels which now became frequent betwixt them she was wont to term him a fool, in reply to the kingly assertion that she was a jade.

The disturbances which troubled the court were principally caused by her infidelities to him, and his subsequent jealousies of her. Chief among those who shared her intrigues at this time was Harry Jermyn, with whom she renewed her intimacy from time to time, without the knowledge of his majesty. The risks she frequently encountered in pursuit of her amours abounded in comedy. Speaking of Harry Jermyn, Pepys tells us the king "had like to have taken him abed with her, but that he was fain to creep under the bed into the closet." It being now rumoured that Jermyn was about to wed my Lady Falmouth, the countess's love for one whom she might for ever lose received a fresh impulse, which made her reckless of concealment. The knowledge of her passion, therefore, coming to Charles's ears, a bitter feud sprang up between them, during which violent threats and abusive language were freely exchanged.

At this time my lady was far gone with child, a fact that soon came bubbling up to the angry surface of their discourse; for the king avowed he would not own it as his offspring. On hearing this, her passion became violent beyond all decent bounds. "God damn me, but you shall own it!" said she, her cheeks all crimson and her eyes afire; and moreover she added, "she should have it christened in the Chapel Royal, and owned as his, or otherwise she would bring it to the gallery in Whitehall, and dash its brains out before his face."

After she had hectored him almost out of his wits, she fled in a state of wild excitement from the palace, and took up her abode at the residence of Sir Daniel Harvey, the ranger of Richmond Park. News of this scene spread rapidly through the court, and was subsequently discussed in the coffee-houses and taverns all over the town, where great freedom was made with the lady's name, and great sport of the king's passion. And now it was said the monarch had parted with his mistress for ever, concerning which there was much rejoicement and some doubt. For notwithstanding the king had passed his word to this effect, yet it was known though his spirit was willing his flesh was weak. Indeed, three days had scarcely passed when, mindful of her temper, he began to think his words had been harsh, and, conscious of her power, he concluded his vows had been rash. He therefore sought her once more, but found she was not inclined to relent, until, as Pepys was assured, this monarch of most feeble spirit, this lover of most ardent temper, "sought her forgiveness upon his knees, and promised to offend her no more."

CHAPTER XIV.

The kingdom in peril.--The chancellor falls under his majesty's displeasure.--The Duke of Buckingham's mimicry.--Lady Castlemaine's malice.--Lord Clarendon's fall.--The Duke of Ormond offends the royal favourite.--She covers him with abuse.--Plots against the Duke of York.--Schemes for a royal divorce.--Moll Davis and Nell Gwynn.--The king and the comedian.--Lady Castlemaine abandons herself to great disorders.--Young Jack Spencer.--The countess intrigues with an acrobat.--Talk of the town.--The mistress created a duchess.

At this time the kingdom stood in uttermost danger, being brought to that condition by his majesty's negligence towards its concerns. The peril was, moreover, heightened from the fact of the king being impatient to rid himself of those who had the nation's credit at heart, and sought to uphold its interests. To this end he was led in part by his own inclinations, and furthermore by his friends' solicitations. Foremost amongst those with whose services he was anxious to dispense, were the chancellor, my Lord Clarendon, and the lord lieutenant of Ireland, his grace the Duke of Ormond.

The king's displeasure against these men, who had served his father loyally, himself faithfully, and their country honestly, was instigated through hatred borne them by my Lady Castlemaine. From the first both had bewailed the monarch's connection with her, and the evil influence she exercised over him. Accordingly, after the pattern of honest men, they had set their faces against her.

Not only, as has already been stated, would the chancellor refuse to let any document bearing her name pass the great seal, but he had often prevailed with the king to alter resolutions she had persuaded him to form. And moreover had his lordship sinned in her eyes by forbidding his wife to visit or hold intercourse with her. These were sufficient reasons to arouse the hatred and procure the revenge of this malicious woman, who was now virtually at the head of the kingdom. For awhile, however, Charles, mindful of the services the chancellor had rendered him, was unwilling to thrust him from his high place. But as time sped, and the machinations of a clique of courtiers in league with the countess were added to her influence, the chancellor's power wavered. And finally, when he was suspected of stepping between his majesty and his unlawful pleasures--concerning which more shall be said anon--he fell.

At the head and front of the body which plotted against Lord Clarendon, pandered to Lady Castlemaine, and, for its own purposes--politically and socially--sought to control the king, was his grace the Duke of Buckingham. This witty courtier and his friends, when assembled round the pleasant supper table spread in the countess's apartments, and honoured almost nightly by the presence of the king, delighted to vent the force of their humour upon the chancellor, and criticize his influence over the monarch until Charles smarted from their words. In the height of their mirth, if his majesty declared he would go a journey, walk in a certain direction, or perform some trivial action next day, those around him would lay a wager he would not fulfil his intentions; and when asked why they had arrived at such conclusions, they would reply, because the chancellor would not permit him. On this another would remark with mock gravity, he thought there were no grounds for such an imputation, though, indeed, he could not deny it was universally believed abroad his majesty was implicitly governed by Lord Clarendon. The king, being keenly sensitive to remarks doubting his authority, and most desirous of appearing his own master, would exclaim on such occasions that the chancellor "had served him long, and understood his business, in which he trusted him; but in any other matter than his business, he had no more credit with him than any other man." And presently the Duke of Buckingham--who possessed talents of mimicry to a surpassing degree--would arise, and, screwing his face into ridiculous contortions, and shaking his wig in a manner that burlesqued wisdom to perfection, deliver some ludicrous speech brimming with mirth and indecencies, assuming the grave air and stately manner of the chancellor the while. And finally, to make the caricature perfect, Tom Killigrew, hanging a pair of bellows before him by way of purse, and preceded by a friend carrying a fireshovel to represent a mace, would walk round the room with the slow determined tread peculiar to Lord Clarendon. At these performances the king, his mistress, and his courtiers would laugh loud and long in chorus, with which was mingled sounds of chinking glasses and flowing wine. ["Came my lord chancellor (the Earl of Clarendon) and his lady, his purse and mace borne before him, to visit me"--Evelyn's "Diary."]

In this manner was the old man's power undermined; but a circumstance which hastened his fall occurred in the early part of 1667. In that year Lady Castlemaine had, for a valuable consideration, disposed of a place at court, which ensured the purchaser a goodly salary. However, before the bargain could finally be ratified, it was necessary the appointment should pass the great seal. This the chancellor would not permit, and accompanied his refusal by remarking, "he thought this woman would sell every thing shortly." His speech being repeated to her, she, in great rage, sent him word she "had disposed of this place, and had no doubt in a little time to dispose of his." And so great was the malice she bore him, that she railed against him openly and in all places; nor did she scruple to declare in the queen's chamber, in the presence of much company, "that she hoped to see his head upon a stake, to keep company with those of the regicides on Westminster Hall."

And some political movements now arising, the history of which lies not within the province of this work, the king seized upon them as an excuse for parting with his chancellor. The monarch complained that my Lord Clarendon "was so imperious that he would endure no contradiction; that he had a faction in the House of Commons that opposed everything that concerned his majesty's service, if it were not recommended to them by him; and that he had given him very ill advice concerning the parliament, which offended him most."

Therefore there were rumours in the air that the chancellor's fall was imminent; nor were the efforts of his son-in-law, the Duke of York, able to protect him, for the friends of my Lady Castlemaine openly told his majesty "it would not consist with his majesty's honour to be hectored out of his determination to dismiss the chancellor by his brother, who was wrought upon by his wife's crying." It therefore happened on the 26th of August, 1667, as early as ten o'clock in the morning, Lord Clarendon waited at Whitehall on the king, who presently, accompanied by his brother, received him with characteristic graciousness. Whereon the old man, acknowledging the monarch's courtesy, said he "had no suit to make to him, nor the least thought to dispute with him, or to divert him from the resolution he had taken; but only to receive his determination from himself, and most humbly to beseech him to let him know what fault he had committed, that had drawn this severity upon him from his majesty."

In answer to this Charles said he must always acknowledge "he had served him honestly and faithfully, and that he did believe never king had a better servant; that he had taken this resolution for his good and preservation, as well as for his own convenience and security; that he was sorry the business had taken so much air, and was so publicly spoken of, that he knew not how to change his purpose." To these words of fair seeming the troubled chancellor replied by doubting if the sudden dismissal of an old servant who had served the crown full thirty years, without any suggestion of crime, but rather with a declaration of innocence, would not call his majesty's justice and good nature into question. He added that men would not know how to serve him, when they should see it was in the power of three or four persons who had never done him any notable service to dispose him to ungracious acts. And finally, he made bold to cast some reflections upon my Lady Castlemaine, and give his majesty certain warnings regarding her influence.

At this the king, not being well pleased, rose up, and the interview, which had lasted two hours, terminated. Lord Clarendon tells us so much concerning his memorable visit, to which Pepys adds a vivid vignette picture of his departure. When my lord passed from his majesty's presence into the privy garden, my Lady Castlemaine, who up to that time had been in bed, "ran out in her smock into her aviary looking into Whitehall--and thither her woman brought her nightgown--and stood joying herself at the old man's going away; and several of the gallants of Whitehall, of which there were many staying to see the chancellor return, did talk to her in her birdcage--among others Blaneford, telling her she was the bird of paradise."

A few days after this occurrence the king sent Secretary Morrice to the chancellor's house, with a warrant under a sign manual to require and receive the great seal. This Lord Clarendon at once delivered him with many expressions of duty which he bade the messenger likewise convey his majesty. And no sooner had Morrice handed the seals to the king, than Baptist May, keeper of the privy purse, and friend of my Lady Castlemaine, sought the monarch, and falling upon his knees, kissed his hand and congratulated him on his riddance of the chancellor. "For now."

said he, availing himself of the liberty Charles permitted his friends, "you will be king--what you have never been before." Finally, the chancellor was, through influence of his enemies, impeached in the House of Commons; and to such length did they pursue him, that he was banished the kingdom by act of parliament.

His grace the Duke of Ormond was the next minister whom my Lady Castlemaine, in the strength of her evil influence, sought to undermine. By reason of an integrity rendering him too loyal to the king to pander to his majesty's mistress, he incurred her displeasure in many ways; but especially by refusing to gratify her cupidity. It happened she had obtained from his majesty a warrant granting her the Phoenix Park, Dublin, and the mansion situated therein, which had always been placed at service of the lords lieutenants, and was the only summer residence at their disposal. The duke, therefore, boldly refusing to pass the warrant, stopped the grant. [According to O'Connor's "Bibliotheca Stowensis," Lady Castlemaine soon after received a grant of a thousand pounds per annum in compensation for her loss of Phoenix Park.] This so enraged the countess, that soon after, when his grace returned to England, she, on meeting him in one of the apartments in Whitehall, greeted him with a torrent of abusive language and bitter reproaches, such as the rancour of her heart could suggest, or the license of her tongue utter, and concluded by hoping she might live to see him hanged. The duke heard her with the uttermost calmness, and when she had exhausted her abusive vocabulary quietly replied, "Madam, I am not in so much haste to put an end to your days; for all I wish with regard to you is, that I may live to see you grow old." And, bowing low, the fine old soldier left her presence. It may be added, though the duke was deprived of the lord lieutenancy, the countess's pious wish regarding him was never fulfilled.

It now occurred to those who had relentlessly persecuted the chancellor, that though they were safe as long as Charles reigned, his death would certainly place them in peril. For they sufficiently knew the Duke of York's character to be aware when he ascended the throne he would certainly avenge the wrongs suffered by his father-in-law. Accordingly these men, prominent amongst whom were the Duke of Buckingham, Sir Thomas Clifford, Lords Arlington, Lauderdale, and Ashley, and Baptist May, resolved to devise means which would prevent the Duke of York ever attaining the power of sovereignty. Therefore scarce a year had gone by since Lord Clarendon's downfall, ere rumours were spread abroad that his majesty was about to put away the queen, This was to be effected, it was said, by the king's acknowledgment of a previous marriage with Lucy Walters, mother of the Duke of Monmouth, or by obtaining a divorce on ground of her majesty's barrenness.

The Duke of Buckingham, who was prime mover in this plot, aware of the king's pride in, and fondness for the Duke of Monmouth, favoured the scheme of his majesty's admission of a marriage previous to that which united him with Catherine of Braganza. And according to Burnet, Buckingham undertook to procure witnesses who would swear they had been present at the ceremony which united him with the abandoned Lucy Walters. Moreover, the Earl of Carlisle, who likewise favoured the contrivance, offered to bring this subject before the House of Lords. However, the king would not consent to trifle with the succession in this vile manner, and the idea was promptly abandoned. But though the project was unsuccessful, it was subsequently the cause of many evils; for the chances of sovereignty, flashing before the eyes of the Duke of Monmouth, dazzled him with hopes, in striving to realize which, he, during the succeeding reign, steeped the country in civil warfare, and lost his head.

The king's friends, ever active for evil, now sought other methods by which he might rid himself of the woman who loved him well, and therefore be enabled to marry again, when, it was trusted, he would have heirs to the crown. It was suggested his union might, through lack of some formality, be proved illegal; but as this could not be effected without open violation of truth and justice, it was likewise forsaken. The Duke of Buckingham now besought his majesty that he would order a bill to divorce himself from the queen to be brought into the House of Commons. The king gave his consent to the suggestion, and the affair proceeded so far that a date was fixed upon for the motion. However, three days previous, Charles called Baptist May aside, and told him the matter must be discontinued.

But even yet my Lord Buckingham did not despair of gaining his wishes. And, being qualified by his character for the commission of abominable deeds, and fitted by his experience for undertaking adventurous schemes, he proposed to his majesty, as Burnet states, that he would give him leave to abduct the queen, and send her out of the kingdom to a plantation, where she should be well and carefully looked to, but never heard of more. Then it could be given out she had deserted him, upon which grounds he might readily obtain a divorce. But the king, though he permitted such a proposal to be made him, contemplated it with horror, declaring "it was a wicked thing to make a poor lady miserable only because she was his wife and had no children by him, which was no fault of hers."

Ultimately these various schemes resolved themselves into a proposition which Charles sanctioned. This was that the queen's confessor should persuade her to leave the world, and embrace a religious life. Whether this suggestion was ever made to her majesty is unknown, for the Countess of Castlemaine, hearing of these schemes, and foreseeing she would be the first sacrificed to a new queen's jealousy, opposed them with such vigour that they fell to the ground and were heard of no more. The fact was, the king took no active part in these designs, not being anxious, now the Duchess of Richmond had accepted his love, to unite himself with another wife. Whilst her grace had been unmarried, the idea had indeed occurred to him of seeking a divorce that he might be free to lay his crown at the feet of the maid of honour. And with such a view in mind he had consulted Dr. Sheldon, Archbishop of Canterbury, as to whether the Church of England "would allow of a divorce, when both parties were consenting, and one of them lay under a natural incapacity of having children." Before answering a question on which so much depended, the archbishop requested time for consideration, which, with many injunctions to secrecy, was allowed him. "But," says Lord Dartmouth, who vouches for truth of this statement, "the Duke of Richmond's clandestine marriage, before he had given an answer, made the king suspect he had revealed the secret to Clarendon, whose creature Sheldon was known to be; and this was the true secret of Clarendon's disgrace." For the king, believing the chancellor had aided the duke in his secret marriage, in order to prevent his majesty's union with Miss Stuart, and the presumable exclusion of the Duke and Duchess of York and their children from the throne, never forgave him.

Though the subject of the royal divorce was no longer mentioned, the disturbances springing from it were far from ended; for the Duke of Buckingham, incensed at Lady Castlemaine's interference, openly quarrelled with her, abused her roundly, and swore he would remove the king from her power. To this end he therefore employed his talents, and with such tact and assiduity that he ultimately fulfilled his menaces. The first step he took towards accomplishing his desires, was to introduce two players to his majesty, named respectively Moll Davis and Nell

Gwynn.

The former, a member of the Duke of York's troupe of performers, could boast of goodly lineage, though not of legitimate birth, her father being Thomas Howard, first Earl of Berkshire. She had, early in the year 1667, made her first appearance at the playhouse, and had by her comely face and shapely figure challenged the admiration of the town. Her winsome ways, pleasant voice, and graceful dancing soon made her a favourite with the courtiers, who voted her an excellent wench; though some of her own sex, judging harshly of her, as is their wont towards each other, declared her "the most impertinent slut in the world."

Now the Duke of Buckingham knowing her well, it seemed to him no woman was more suited to fulfil his purpose of thwarting the countess; for if he succeeded in awaking the king's passion for the comedian, such a proceeding would not only arouse my lady's jealousy, but likewise humble her pride. Therefore, when this court Mephistopheles accompanied his majesty to the playhouse, he was careful to dwell on Moll Davis's various charms, the excellency of her figure, the beauty of her face, the piquancy of her manner. So impressed was the monarch by Buckingham's descriptions, that he soon became susceptible to her fascinations. The amour once begun was speedily pursued; and she was soon enabled to boast, in presence of the players, that the king--whose generosity was great to fallen women--had given her a ring valued at seven hundred pounds, and was about to take, and furnish most richly, a house in Suffolk Street for her benefit and abode. Pepys heard this news in the first month of the year 1668; and soon afterwards a further rumour reached him that she was veritably the king's mistress, "even to the scorn of the world."

This intrigue affected Lady Castlemaine in a manner which the Duke of Buckingham had not expected. Whilst sitting beside Charles in the playhouse, she noticed his attention was riveted upon her rival, when she became melancholy and out of humour, in which condition she remained some days. But presently rallying her spirits, she soon found means to divert her mind and avenge her wrongs, of which more shall be recorded hereafter. Meanwhile, the poor queen, whose feelings neither the king nor his courtiers took into consideration, bore this fresh insult with such patience as she could summon to her aid, on one occasion only protesting against her husband's connection with the player. This happened when the Duke of York's troupe performed in Whitehall the tragedy of "Horace," "written by the virtuous Mrs. Phillips." The courtiers assembled on this occasion presented a brilliant and goodly sight. Evelyn tells us "the excessive gallantry of the ladies was infinite, those jewels especially on Lady Castlemaine esteemed at forty thousand pounds and more, far outshining ye queene." Between each act of the tradgedy a masque and antique dance was performed. When Moll Davis appeared, her majesty, turning pale from sickness of heart, and trembling from indignation at the glaring insult thrust upon her, arose and left the apartment boisterous with revelry, where she had sat a solitary sad figure in its midst. As a result of her intimacy with the king, Moll Davis bore him a daughter, who subsequently became Lady Derwentwater. But the Duke of Buckingham's revenge upon my Lady Castlemaine was yet but half complete; and therefore whilst the monarch carried on his intrigue with Moll Davis, his grace, enlarging upon the wit and excellency of Nell Gwynn, besought his majesty to send for her. This request the king complied with readily enough, and she was accordingly soon added to the list of his mistresses. Nell Gwynn, who was at this period in her eighteenth year, had joined the company of players at the king's house, about the same time as Moll Davis had united her fortunes with the Duke of York's comedians. Her time upon the stage was, however, but of brief duration; for my Lord Buckhurst, afterwards Earl of Dorset, a witty and licentious man, falling in love with her, induced her to become his mistress, quit the theatre, and forsake the society of her lover, Charles Hart, a famous actor and great-nephew of William Shakespeare. And she complying with his desires in these matters, he made her an allowance of one hundred pounds a year, on which she returned her parts to the manager, and declared she would act no more.

Accordingly in the month of July, 1667, she was living at Epsom with my Lord Buckhurst and his witty friend Sir Charles Sedley, and a right merry house they kept for a time. But alas, ere the summer had died there came a day when charming Nell and his fickle lordship were friends no more, and parting from him, she was obliged to revert to the playhouse again.

Now Nell Gwynn being not only a pretty woman, but moreover an excellent actress, her return was welcomed by the town. Her achievements in light comedy were especially excellent, and declared entertaining to a rare degree. Pepys, who witnessed her acting "a comical part," in the "Maiden Queen," a play by Dryden, says he could "never hope to see the like done again by man or woman. So great performance of a comical part," he continues, "was never, I believe, in the world before as Nell do this, both as a mad girle, then most and best of all when she comes in like a young gallant; and hath the motions and carriage of a spark the most that ever I saw any man have. It makes me, I confess, admire her." In the part of Valeria, in "Tyrannic Love," she was also pronounced inimitable; especially in her delivery of the epilogue. The vein of comedy with which she delivered the opening lines, addressed to those about to bear her dead body from the stage, was merry beyond belief. "Hold!" she cried out to one of them, as she suddenly started to life--

"Hold! are you mad? you damned confounded dog! I am to rise and speak the epilogue."

Before the year 1667 ended, she had several times visited his majesty at Whitehall. The king was now no less assured of her charms as a woman, than he had previously been convinced of her excellence as an actress. In due time, her intimacy with the monarch resulted in the birth of two sons; the elder of which was created Duke of St. Albans, from whom is descended the family now bearing that title: the second died young and unmarried.

Through influence of these women, my Lady Castlemaine's power over the king rapidly diminished, and at last ceased to exist; seeing which, as Burnet says, "She abandoned herself to great disorders; one of which by the artifice of the Duke of Buckingham was discovered by the king in person, the party concerned leaping out of the window." The gallant to whom the worthy bishop refers was John Churchill, afterwards the great Duke of Marlborough, at this time a handsome stripling of eighteen summers. In his office as page to the Duke of York, he frequently came under notice of her ladyship, who, pleased with the charms of his boyish face and graceful figure, intimated his love would not prove unacceptable to her. Accordingly he promptly made love to the countess, who, in the first fervour of her affection, presented him with five thousand pounds. With this sum he purchased a life annuity of five hundred pounds, which, as Lord Chesterfield writes, "became the foundation of his subsequent fortune." Nor did her generosity end here: at a cost of six thousand crowns she obtained for him the post of groom of the bedchamber to the Duke of York, and was instrumental in subsequently forwarding his advancements in the army.

My Lady Castlemaine was by no means inclined to spend her days in misery because the royal favour was no longer vouchsafed her; and therefore, by way of satisfying her desires for revenge, conducted intrigues not only with John Churchill and Harry Jermyn, but likewise with one Jacob Hall, a noted acrobat. This man was not only gifted with strength and agility, but likewise with grace and beauty: so that, as Granger tells us, "The ladies regarded him as a due composition of Hercules and Adonis." His dancing on the tight rope at Bartholomew Fair was "a thing worth seeing and mightily followed;" whilst his deeds of daring at Southwark Fair were no less subjects of admiration and wonder. The countess was so charmed by the performance of this athlete in public, that she became desirous of conversation with him in private; and he was accordingly introduced to her by Beck Marshall, the player. The countess found his society so entertaining that she frequently visited him, a compliment he courteously returned. Moreover, she allowed him a yearly salary, and openly showed her admiration for him by having their portraits painted in one picture: in which she is represented playing a fiddle, whilst he leans over her, touching the strings of a guitar.

Her amours in general, and her intimacy with the rope-dancer in particular, becoming common talk of the town, his majesty became incensed; and it grieved him the more that one who dwelt in his palace, and was yet under his protection, should divide her favours between a king and a mountebank. Accordingly bitter feuds arose between her and the monarch, when words of hatred, scorn, and defiance were freely exchanged. His majesty upbraiding her with a love for the rope-dancer, she replied with much spirit, "it very ill became him to throw out such reproaches against her: that he had never ceased quarrelling unjustly with her, ever since he had betrayed his own mean low inclinations: that to gratify such a depraved taste as his, he wanted the pitiful strolling actresses whom he had lately introduced into their society." Then came fresh threats from the lips of the fury, followed by passionate storms of tears.

The king, who loved ease greatly, and valued peace exceedingly, became desirous of avoiding such harrowing scenes. Accordingly, he resolved to enter into a treaty with his late mistress, by which he would consent to grant her such concessions as she desired, providing she promised to discontinue her intrigues with objectionable persons, and leave him to pursue his ways without reproach. By mutual consent, his majesty and the countess selected the Chevalier de Grammont to conduct this delicate business; he being one in whose tact and judgment they had implicit confidence. After various consultations and due consideration, it was agreed the countess should abandon her amours with Henry Jermyn and Jacob Hall, rail no more against Moll Davis or Nell Gwynn, or any other of his majesty's favourites, in consideration for which Charles would create her a duchess, and give her an additional pension in order to support her fresh honours with becoming dignity.

And as the king found her residence in Whitehall no longer necessary to his happiness, Berkshire House was purchased for her as a suitable dwelling This great mansion, situated at the south-west corner of St. James's Street, facing St. James's Palace, was surrounded by pleasant gardens devised in the Dutch style, and was in every way a habitation suited for a prince. This handsome gift was followed by a grant of the revenues of the Post Office, amounting to four thousand seven hundred pounds a year, which was at first paid her in weekly instalments. On the 3rd of August, 1670, Barbara, Countess of Castlemaine, was created Baroness Nonsuch, of Nonsuch Park, Surrey; Countess of Southampton; and Duchess of Cleveland in the peerage of England. The reasons for crowding these honours thick upon her were, as the patent stated, "in consideration of her noble descent, her father's death in the service of the crown, and by reason of her personal virtues."

Nor did his majesty's extravagant favours to her end here. She was now, as Mr. Povy told his friend Pepys, "in a higher command over the king than ever--not as a mistress, for she scorns him, but as a tyrant, to command him." In consequence of this power, she was, two months after her creation as duchess, presented by the monarch with the favourite hunting seat of Henry VIII., the magnificent palace and great park of Nonsuch, in the parishes of Cheam and Malden, in the county of Surrey. And yet a year later, she received fresh proofs of his royal munificence by the gift of "the manor, hundred, and advowson of Woking, county Surrey; the manor and advowson of Chobham, the hundred of Blackheath and Wootton, the manor of Bagshot (except the park, site of the manor and manor-house, and the Bailiwick, and the office of the Bailiwick, called Surrey Bailiwick, otherwise Bagshot Bailiwick), and the advowson of Bisley, all in the same county."

Her wealth, the more notable at a time when the king was in debt, and the nation impoverished from expenditure necessary to warfare, was enormous. Andrew Marvell, writing in August, 1671, states: "Lord St. John, Sir R. Howard, Sir

John Bennet, and Sir W. Bicknell, the brewer, have farmed the customs. They have signed and sealed ten thousand pounds a year more to the Duchess of Cleveland; who has likewise near ten thousand pounds a year out of the new farm of the country excise of Beer and Ale; five thousand pounds a year out of the Post Office; and they say, the reversion of all the King's Leases, the reversion of places all in the Custom House, the green wax, and indeed what not? All promotions spiritual and temporal pass under her cognizance."

CHAPTER XV.

Louise de Querouaille.--The Triple Alliance.--Louise is created Duchess of Portsmouth.--Her grace and the impudent comedian.--Madam Ellen moves in society.--The young Duke of St. Albans.--Strange story of the Duchess of Mazarine.--Entertaining the wits at Chelsea.--Luxurious suppers.--Profligacy and wit.

The Duchess of Cleveland having shared the fate common to court favourites, her place in the royal affections was speedily filled by a mistress whose influence was even more baneful to the king, and more pernicious to the nation. This woman was Louise de Querouaille, the descendant of a noble family in Lower Brittany. At an early age she had been appointed maid of honour to Henrietta, youngest sister of Charles II., soon after the marriage of that princess, in 1661, with the Duke of Orleans, brother to Louis XIV. Fate decreed that Mademoiselle de Querouaille should be brought into England by means of a political movement; love ordained she should reign mistress of the king's affections.

It happened in January, 1668, that a Triple Alliance had been signed at the Hague, which engaged England, Sweden, and the United Provinces to join in defending Spain against the power of France. A secret treaty in this agreement furthermore bound the allies to check the ambition of Louis XIV., and, if possible, reduce his encroaching sway. That Charles II. should enter into such an alliance was galling to the French monarch, who resolved to detach his kinsman from the compact, and bind him to the interests of France. To effect this desired purpose, which he knew would prove objectionable to the British nation, Louis employed Henrietta, Duchess of Orleans, to visit England on pretext of pleasure and affection, and secretly persuade and bribe her brother to the measures required.

The young duchess, though an English princess, had at heart the interests of the country in which she had been reared, and which on her marriage she had adopted as her own. She therefore gladly undertook this mission, confident of her success from the fact that of all his family she had ever been the most tenderly beloved by Charles. Therefore she set out from France, and in the month of May, 1670, arrived at Dover, to which port the king, Queen, and court hastened, that they might greet and entertain her. For full ten days in this merry month, high revelry was held at Dover, during which time Henrietta skilfully and secretly effected the object of her visit. And her delight was now the greater, inasmuch as one item which this agreement entrusted her to make, engaged that Charles would, as soon as he could with safety, follow the example of his brother the Duke of York, and become a Catholic. In carrying out this purpose Louis promised him substantial aid and sure protection. Likewise, it may be mentioned, did the French king engrage to grant him a subsidy equal to a million a year, if Charles joined him in an attack on Holland.

The prospect of his sister's return filled the king with sorrow, which increased as the term of her visit drew to an end. "He wept when he parted with her," wrote Monsieur Colbert, the French ambassador, who significantly adds, "whatever favour she asked of him was granted."

Now Louis knowing the weakness of the English monarch's character, and aware of his susceptibility to female loveliness, had despatched Mademoiselle de Querouaille in the train of Henrietta. Satisfied that Charles could not resist her charms, the French monarch had instructed this accomplished woman, who was trusted in his councils, to accept the royal love, which it was surmised would be proffered her; so that by the influence which she would consequently obtain, she might hold him to the promises he might make the Duchess of Orleans.

As had been anticipated, the king became enamoured of this charming woman, who, before departing with the princess, faithfully promised to return and become his mistress. In his desire to possess her the merry monarch was upheld by his grace of Buckingham, who, continuing in enmity with the Duchess of Cleveland, resolved to prevent her regaining influence over the king by adding the beautiful Frenchwoman to the number of his mistresses. He therefore told Charles, in the sarcastic manner it was occasionally his wont to use, "it was a decent piece of tenderness for his sister to take care of some of her servants;" whilst on being sent into France, he assured Louis "he could never reckon himself sure of the king, but by giving him a mistress that should be true to his interests." But neither king required urging to a resolution on which both had separately determined; and soon Mademoiselle Querouaille was ready for her journey to England. A yacht was therefore sent to Dieppe to convey her, and presently she was received at Whitehall by the lord treasurer, and her arrival celebrated in verse by Dryden. Moreover, that she might have apartments in the palace, the king at once appointed her a maid of honour to her majesty, this being the first of a series of favours she was subsequently to receive. Evelyn, writing in the following October, says it was universally reported a ceremonious espousal, devoid of the religious rite, had taken place between his majesty and Mademoiselle Querouaille at Lord Arlington's house at Euston. "I acknowledge," says this trustworthy chronicler "she was for the most part in her undresse all day, and that there was fondnesse and toying with that young wanton; nay, 'twas said I was at the former ceremony, but 'tis utterly false; I neither saw nor heard of any such thing whilst I was there, tho' I had ben in her chamber, and all over that apartment late enough, and was myself observing all passages with much curiosity."

She now became a central figure in the brilliant court of the merry monarch, being loved by the king, flattered by the wits, and tolerated by the queen, to whom--unlike the Duchess of Cleveland--she generally paid the greatest respect. Her card tables were thronged by courtiers eager to squander large sums for the honour of playing with the reigning sultana; her suppers were attended by wits and gallants as merry and amorous as those who had once crowded round my Lady Castlemaine in the zenith of her power. No expense was too great for his majesty to lavish upon her; no honour too high with which to reward her affection. The authority just mentioned says her apartments at Whitehall were luxuriously furnished "with ten times the richnesse and glory beyond the Queene's; such massy pieces of plate, whole tables and stands of incredible value." After a residence of little more than three years at court she was raised by King Charles to the peerage as Baroness of Petersfield, Countess of Farnham, and Duchess of Portsmouth; whilst the French king, as a mark of appreciation for the services she rendered France, conferred upon her the Duchy of Aubigny, in the province of Berri in France, to which he added the title and dignity of Duchess and Peeress of France, with the revenues of the territory of Aubigny. And two years later King Charles, prodigal of the honours he conferred upon her, ennobled the son she had borne him in 1672. The titles of the Duke of

Richmond and Lennox having lately reverted to the crown by the death of Frances Stuart's husband, who was last of his line, the bastard son of the French mistress was created Duke of Richmond and Earl of March in England, and Duke of Lennox and Earl of Darnley in Scotland. To these proud titles the present head of the noble house of Richmond and Lennox--by virtue of the grant made by Louis XIV. to his ancestress likewise adds that of Duc d'Aubigny in the peerage of France.

But though honoured by the king, and flattered by the court, the Duchess of Portsmouth was far from enjoying uninterrupted happiness; inasmuch as her peace was frequently disturbed by jealousy. The principal cause of her uneasiness during the first five years of her reign was the king's continued infatuation for Nell Gwynn; now, by reason of the elevated position she enjoyed, styled Madam Ellen. This "impudent comedian," as Evelyn calls her, was treated by his majesty with, extreme indulgence and royal liberality. In proof of the latter statement, it may be mentioned that in less than four years from the date of her first becoming his mistress, he had wantonly lavished sixty thousand pounds upon her, as Burnet affirms. Moreover, he had purchased as a town mansion for her "the first good house on the left-hand side of St. James's Square, entering Pall Mall," now the site of the Army and Navy Club; had given her likewise a residence situated close by the Castle at Windsor; and a summer villa located in what was then the charming village of Chelsea. To such substantial gifts as these he added the honour of an appointment at court: when the merry player was made one of the ladies of the privy chamber to the queen. Samuel Pegg states this fact, not generally known, and assures us he discovered it "from the book in the lord chamberlain's office."

From her position as the king's mistress, Madam Ellen moved on terms of perfect equality with the Duchess of Portsmouth's friends--supping with my Lady Orrery, visiting my Lord Cavendish, and establishing a friendship with the gay Duchess of Norfolk. This was a source of deep vexation to the haughty Frenchwoman; but Nell Gwynn's familiarity with the king was a cause of even greater mortification. Sir George Etherege records in verse when the monarch was "dumpish" Nell would "chuck the royal chin;" and it is stated that, mindful of her former conquests over Charles Hart and Charles Lord Buckley, it was her habit to playfully style his majesty "Charles the Third." Her wilfulness, wit, and beauty enabled her to maintain such a strong hold upon the king's heart, that he shared his time equally between her and the Duchess of Portsmouth. Indignant that a woman from the playhouse should receive such evidences of the royal affection, her grace lost no opportunity of insulting Nell, who responded by mimicry and grimaces, which threw those who witnessed the comedy into fits of laughter, and covered the wrathful duchess with confusion.

But though the light-hearted actress frequently treated disdain with ridicule, she could occasionally analyze the respective positions held by herself and the duchess with seriousness, Madame de Sevigne tells us, Nell would reason in this manner: "This duchess pretends to be a person of quality: she affirms she is related to the best families in France, and when any person of distinction dies she puts herself in mourning. If she be a lady of such quality, why does she demean herself to be a courtesan? She ought to die with shame. As for me, it is my profession. I do not pretend to anything better. The king entertains me, and I am constant to him at present. He has a son by me; I contend that he ought to acknowledge him--and I am well assured that he will, for he loves me as well as the duchess."

To have her son ennobled, and by this means raise him to an equality with the offspring of her grace, became the desire of Nell Gwynn's life. To her request that this favour might be granted, the king had promised compliance from time to time, but had as frequently postponed the fulfilment of his word. At last, weary of beseeching him, she devised a speech which she trusted might have the desired effect. Accordingly, when the monarch came to see her one day, he found her in a pensive mood, playing with her pretty boy; and the lad, being presently set upon his feet, he promptly tottered down the room, whereon she cried out to him, "Come here, you little bastard!" Hearing this word of evil import applied to his son, the monarch begged she would not use the expression, "I am sorry," said she regretfully, "but, alas, I have no other name to give him!" His majesty took the hint, and soon after bestowed on him that of Charles Beauclerk, and created him Baron of Heddington, in Oxon, and Earl of Burford in the same county; and finally, when he had reached the age of ten years, raised him to the dignity of Duke of St. Albans.

After a reign of five years in the court of the merry monarch, her Grace of Portsmouth was destined to encounter a far more formidable rival than Nell Gwynn, in the person of the Duchess of Mazarine. This lady, on her arrival in England in 1675, possessed most of the charms which had rendered her notable in youth.

To the attraction they lent was added an interest arising from her personal history, in which King Charles had once figured, and to which fate had subsequently added many pages of romance.

Hortensia Mancini, afterwards Duchess of Mazarine, was descendant of a noble Roman family, and niece of the great Julius Mazarine, cardinal of the church, and prime minister of France. Her parents dying whilst she, her sister and brother were young, they had been reared under the care of his eminence. According to the memoirs of the duchess, the cardinal's peace must have frequently been put to flight by his charges, whose conduct, he declared, exhibited neither piety nor honour. Mindful of this, he placed his nieces under the immediate supervision of Madame de Venelle, who was directed to have the closest guard over them. A story related by the duchess shows in what manner this lady's duty was carried out, and what unexpected results attended it on one occasion.

When the court visited Lyons, in the year 1658, the cardinal's nieces and their governess lodged in a commodious mansion in one of the public squares. "Our chamber windows, which opened towards the market-place," writes Hortensia, "were low enough for one to get in with ease. Madame de Venelle was so used to her trade of watching us, that she rose even in her sleep to see what we were doing. One night, as my sister lay asleep with her mouth open, Madame de Venelle, after her accustomed manner, coming, asleep as she was, to grope in the dark, happened to thrust her finger into her mouth so far that my sister, starting out of her sleep, made her teeth almost meet in her finger. Judge you the amazement they both were in to find themselves in this posture when they were thoroughly awake. My sister was in a grievous fret. The story was told the king the next day, and the court had the divertisement of laughing at it."

Whilst the great minister's nieces were yet extremely young, Louis XIV. fell passionately in love with the elder, Maria, and his marriage with her was frustrated only by the united endeavours of the queen mother and the cardinal. A proposal to raise Hortensia to the nominal dignity of queen was soon after made on behalf of Charles II., who sought her as his bride. But he being at the time an exile, banished from his kingdom, and with little hope of regaining his throne, the offer was rejected by Cardinal Mazarine as unworthy of his favourite niece.

His eminence was, however, anxious to see her married, and accordingly sought amongst the nobility of France a husband suitable to her merits and equal to her condition, she being not only a beautiful woman but, through his bounty, the richest heiress in Christendom. It happened the cardinal's choice settled upon one who had fallen in love with Hortensia, and who had declared, with amorous enthusiasm, that if he had but the happiness of being married to her, it would not grieve him to die three months afterwards.

The young noble was Armand Charles de la Porte, Duke de Meilleraye, who had the sole recommendation of being one of the richest peers of France. On condition that he and his heirs should assume the name of Mazarine and arms of that house, the cardinal consented to his becoming the husband of his niece. And the great minister's days rapidly approaching their end, the ceremony was performed which made Hortensia, then at the age of thirteen, Duchess of Mazarine. A few months later the great cardinal expired, leaving her the sum of one million six hundred and twenty-five thousand pounds sterling. Alas that she should have died in poverty, and that her body should have been seized for debt!

Scarce had the first weeks of her married life passed away, when the young wife found herself mated to one wholly unsuited to her character. She was beautiful, witty, and frivolous; he jealous, dull, and morose. The incompatibility of their dispositions became as discernible to him, as they had become intolerable to her; and, as if to avenge the fate which had united them, he lost no opportunity of thwarting her desires, by such means striving to bend her lissom quality to the gnarled shape of his unhappy nature.

With such a purpose in view no opportunity was neglected to curb her pleasures or oppose her inclinations. He continually forced her to leave Paris, and even when her condition required rest and care, compelled her to accompany him on long and weary journeys, undertaken by him in consequence of his diplomatic missions. If she received two successive visits from one man, he was instantly forbidden the house. If she called her carriage, the coachman received orders not to obey. If she betrayed a preference for one maid more than another, the favourite was instantly dismissed, moreover, the duchess was surrounded by spies, her movements being rigorously watched, and invariably reported. Nor would the duke vouchsafe an explanation to his young wife regarding the cause of this severe treatment, but continued the even course of such conduct without intermission or abatement.

After displaying these eccentricities for some years, they suddenly associated themselves with religion, when he became a fanatic. Her condition was now less endurable than before; his whims more ludicrous and exasperating. With solemnity he declared no one could in conscience visit the theatre; that it was a sin to play blind man's buff, and a heinous crime to retire to bed late. And presently, his fanaticism increasing, he prohibited the woman who nursed his infant to suckle it on Fridays or Saturdays; that instead of imbibing milk, it might, in its earliest life, become accustomed to fasting and mortification of the flesh.

The young duchess grew hopeless of peace. All day her ears were beset by harangues setting forth her wickedness, by exortations calling her to repentance, and by descriptions of visions vouchsafed him. By night her condition was rendered scarcely less miserable. "No sooner," says St. Evremond, "were her eyes closed, than Monsieur Mazarine (who had the devil always present in his black imagination) wakes his best beloved, to make her partaker--you will never be able to guess of what--to make her partaker of his nocturnal visions. Flambeaux are lighted, and search is made everywhere; but no spectre does Madame Mazarine find, except that which lay by her in the bed."

The distresses to which she was subjected were increased by the knowledge that her husband was squandering her vast fortune. In what manner the money was spent she does not state. "If" she writes, "Monsieur Mazarine had only taken delight in overwhelming me with sadness and grief, and in exposing my health and my life to his most unreasonable caprice, and in making me pass the best of my days in an unparalleled slavery, since heaven had been pleased to make him my master, I should have endeavoured to allay and qualify my misfortunes by my sighs and tears. But when I saw that by his incredible dilapidations and profuseness, my son, who might have been the richest gentleman in France, was in danger of being the poorest, there was no resisting the force of nature; and motherly love carried it over all other considerations of duty, or the moderation I proposed to myself. I saw every day vast sums go away: moveables of inestimable prices, offices, and all the rich remains of my uncle's fortune, the fruits of his labours, and the rewards of his services. I saw as much sold as came to three millions, before I took any public notice of it; and I had hardly anything left me of value but my jewels, when Monsieur Mazarine took occasion to seize upon them."

She therefore sought the king's interference, but as the duke had interest at court, she received but little satisfaction. Then commenced disputes, which, after months of wrangling, ended by the duchess escaping in male attire out of France, in company with a gay young cavalier, Monsieur de Rohan. After various wanderings through Italy and many adventures in Savoy, she determined on journeying to England. That her visit was not without a political motive, we gather from St. Evremond; who, referring to the ascendancy which the Duchess of Portsmouth had gained over his majesty, and the uses she made of her power for the interests of France, tells us, "The advocates for liberty, being excluded from posts and the management of affairs, contrived several ways to free their country from that infamous commerce; but finding them ineffectual, they at last concluded that there was no other course to take than to work the Duchess of Portsmouth out of the king's favour, by setting up against her a rival who should be in their interest. The Duchess of Mazarine was thought very fit for their purpose, for she outshined the other, both in wit and beauty."

Charles de St. Denis, Seigneur de St. Evremond, was a soldier, philosopher, and courtier, who had distinguished himself by his bravery, learning, and politeness. Having fallen under the displeasure of the French court, he had, in the year 1662, sought refuge in England, where he had been welcomed with the courtesy due to his rank, and the esteem which befitted his merits. Settling in the capital, he mixed freely in the companionship of wits, gallants, and courtiers who constituted its society; and delighted with London as a residence, he determined on making England his country by adoption. An old friend and fervent admirer of the Duchess of Mazarine, he had received the news of her visit with joy, and celebrated her arrival in verse.

The reputation of her loveliness and the history of her life having preceded her, the court became anxious to behold her; the king, mindful of the relationship he had once sought; with the duchess, grew impatient to welcome her. After a few days' rest, necessary to remedy the fatigue of her journey, she appeared at Whitehall. By reason of her beauty, now ripened rather than impaired by time, and those graces which attracted the more from the fascination they had formerly exercised, she at once gained the susceptible heart of the monarch. St. Evremond tells us her person "contained nothing that was not too lovely." In the "Character of the Duchess of Mazarine," which he drew soon after her arrival in London, he has presented a portrait of her worth examining not only for sake of the object it paints, but for the quaint workmanship it contains. "An ill-natured curiosity," he writes, "makes me scrutinize every feature in her face, with a design either to meet there some shocking irregularity, or some disgusting disagreeableness. But how unluckily do I succeed in my design. Every feature about her has a particular beauty, that does not in the least yield to that of her eyes, which, by the consent of all the world, are the finest in the universe. One thing there is that entirely confounds me: her teeth, her lips, her mouth, and all the graces that attend it, are lost amongst the great variety of beauties in her face and what is but indifferent in her, will not suffer us to consider what is most remarkable in others. The malice of my curiosity does not stop here. I proceed to spy out some defect in her shape; and I find I know not what graces of nature so happily and so liberally scattered in her person, that the genteelness of others only seems to be constraint and affectation."

The king--to whom the presence of a beautiful woman was as sunshine to the earth--at once offered her his affections, the gallants tendered their homage, the ladies of the court volunteered the flattery embodied in imitation. And by way of practically proving his admiration, his majesty graciously allotted her a pension of four thousand pounds a year, with apartments in St. James's Palace.

The sovereignty which the Duchess of Portsmouth had held for five years over the monarch's heart was now in danger of downfall; and probably would have ended, but for Madame Mazarine's indiscretions. It happened a few months after her arrival in London, the Prince of Monaco visited the capital. Young in years, handsome in person, and extravagant in expenditure, he dazzled the fairest women at court; none of whom had so much power to please him in all as the Duchess of Mazarine. Notwithstanding the king's generosity, she accepted the prince's admiration; and resolved to risk the influence she had gained, that she might freely love where she pleased. Her entertainment of a passion, as sudden in development as fervid in intensity, enraged the king; but his fury served only to increase her infatuation, seeing which, his majesty suspended payment of her pension.

The gay Prince of Monaco in due time ending his visit to London, and leaving the Duchess of Mazarine behind him, she, through the interposition of her friends, obtained his majesty's pardon, was received into favour, and again allowed her pension.

She now ruled, not only mistress of the king's heart, but queen of a brilliant circle of wits and men of parts, whose delight it became to heed the epigrams and eccentricities which fell from her lips. Her rooms at St. James's, and her house in Chelsea, became the rendezvous of the most polite and brilliant society in England. In the afternoons, seated amongst her monkeys, dogs, parrots, and pets, she discoursed on philosophy, love, religion, politics, and plays; whilst at night her saloons were thrown open to such as delighted in gambling. Then the duchess, seated at the head of the table, her dark eyes flashing with excitement, her red lips parted in expectation, followed the fortunes of the night with anxiety: all compliments being suspended and all fine speeches withheld the while, nought being heard but the rustle of cards and the chink of gold.

Dainty and luxurious suppers followed, when rare wines flowed, and wit long suppressed found joyous vent. Here sat Charles beside his beautiful mistress, happy in the enjoyment of the present, careless of the needs of his people; and close beside him my Lord of Buckingham, watchful of his majesty's face, hatching dark plots whilst he turned deft compliments. There likewise were my Lord Dorset, the easiest and wittiest man living; Sir Charles Sedley, one learned in intrigue; Baptist May, the monarch's favourite; Tom Killigrew who jested on life's follies whilst he enjoyed them; the Countess of Shrewsbury, beautiful and amorous; and Madam Ellen, who was ready to mimic or sing, dance or act, for his majesty's diversion.

And so, whilst a new day stole upon the world without, tapers burned low within the duchess's apartments; and the king, his mistress, and a brave and gallant company ate, drank, and made merry.

CHAPTER XVI.

A storm threatens the kingdom.--The Duke of York is touched in his conscience.--His interview with Father Simons.--The king declares his mind.--The Duchess of York becomes a catholic.--The circumstances of her death.--The Test Act introduced.--Agitation of the nation.--The Duke of York marries again.--Lord Shaftesbury's schemes.--The Duke of Monmouth.--William of Orange and the Princess Mary.--Their marriage and departure from England.

Whilst the surface life of the merry monarch sped onward in its careless course, watchful eyes took heed of potent signs boding storms and strife. The storm which shook the kingdom to its centre came anon; the strife which dethroned a monarch was reserved for the succeeding reign. These were not effected by the king's profligacy, indolence, or extravagance, but because of a change in the religious belief of the heir-apparent to the crown.

The cloud, no bigger than a man's hand, which presently spread and overcast the political horizon, was first observed towards the beginning of the year 1669. The Rev. J. S. Clarke, historiographer to George III., chaplain to the royal household, and librarian to the Prince Regent, in his "Life of James II., collected out of Memoirs writ of his own hand," tells us that about this time the Duke of York "was sensibly touched in his conscience, and began to think seriously of his salvation." Accordingly, the historian states, "he sent for one Father Simons, a Jesuit, who had the reputation of a very learned man, to discourse with him upon that subject; and when he came, he told him the good intentions he had of being a catholic, and treated with him concerning his being reconciled to the church. After much discourse about the matter, the Jesuit very sincerely told him, that unless he would quit the communion of the Church of England, he could not be received into the Catholic Church. The duke then said he thought it might be done by a dispensation from the pope, alleging the singularity of his case, and the advantage it might bring to the catholic religion in general, and in particular to those of it in England, if he might have such dispensation for outwardly appearing a protestant, at least till he could own himself publicly to be a catholic, with more security to his own person and advantage to them. But the father insisted that even the pope himself had not the power to grant it, for it was an unalterable doctrine of the Catholic Church, not to do ill that good might follow. What this Jesuit thus said was afterwards confirmed to the duke by the pope himself, to whom he wrote upon the same subject. Till this time his royal highness believed (as it is commonly believed, or at least said by the Church of England doctors) that dispensations in any such cases are by the pope easily granted; but Father Simons's words, and the letter of his holiness, made the duke think it high time to use all the endeavours he could, to be at liberty to declare himself, and not to live in so unsafe and so uneasy a condition."

Inasmuch as what immediately followed touches a point of great delicacy and vast importance, the words of the historian, mainly taken from the "Stuart Papers," are best given here, "His royal highness well-knowing that the king was of the same mind, and that his majesty had opened himself upon it to Lord Arundel of Wardour, Lord Arlington, and Sir Thomas Clifford, took an occasion to discourse with him upon that subject about the same time, and found him resolved as to his being a catholic, and that he intended to have a private meeting with those persons above named at the duke's closet, to advise with them about the ways and methods fit to be taken for advancing the catholic religion in his dominions, being resolved not to live any longer in the constraint he was under. The meeting was on the 25th of January. When they were met according to the king's appointment, he declared his mind to them on the matter of religion, and said how uneasy it was to him not to profess the faith he believed; and that he had called them together to have their advice about the ways and methods fittest to be taken for the settling of the catholic religion in his kingdoms, and to consider of the time most proper to declare himself, telling them withal that no time ought to be lost; that he was to expect to meet with many and great difficulties in bringing it about, and that he chose rather to undertake it now, when he and his brother were in their full strength and able to undergo any fatigue, than to delay it till they were grown older and less fit to go through with so great a design. This he spoke with great earnestness, and even with tears in his eyes; and added, that they were to go about it as wise men and good catholics ought to do. The consultation lasted long, and the result was, that there was no better way for doing this work than to do it in conjunction with France, and with the assistance of his Most Christian majesty." Accordingly the secret treaty with France was entered into, as already mentioned.

No further movement towards professing the catholic religion was made by the king or his brother for some time. The tendencies of the latter becoming suspected, his actions were observed with vigilance, when it was noted, that although he attended service as usual with the king, he no longer received the sacrament. It was also remarked the Duchess of York, whose custom it had been to communicate once a month, soon followed his example. Her neglect of this duty was considered the more conspicuous as she had been bred a staunch protestant, and ever appeared zealous in her support of that religion. Moreover, it was noted that, from the beginning of the year 1670, she was wont to defend the catholic faith from such errors as it had been charged withal.

These matters becoming subjects of conversation at court soon reached the ears of Bishop Morley, who had acted as her confessor since her twelfth year, confession being then much practised in the English Church. Thereon he hastened to her, and spoke at length of the inferences which were drawn from her neglect of receiving the sacrament, in answer to which she pleaded business and ill-health as sufficient excuses. But he, suspecting other causes, gave her advice, and requested she would send for him in case doubts arose in her mind concerning the faith she professed. Being now free from all uncertainties, she readily promised compliance with his desire, and added, "No priest had ever taken the confidence to speak to her on those matters."

The fact that she no longer communicated becoming more noticed as time passed, the king spoke to his brother concerning the omission, when the duke told him she had become a catholic. Hearing this, Charles requested him to keep her change of faith a secret, which was accordingly done, none being aware of the act but Father Hunt, a Franciscan friar, Lady Cranmer, one of her women of the bedchamber, and Mr. Dupuy, servant to the duke. In a paper she drew up relative to her adoption of the catholic religion, preserved in the fifth volume of the "Harleian Miscellany," she professes being one of the greatest enemies that faith ever had. She likewise declares no man or woman had said anything, or used the least persuasion to make her change her religion. That had been effected, she adds, by a perusal of Dr. Heylin's "History of the Reformation;" after which she spoke severally to Dr. Sheldon, Archbishop of Canterbury and Dr. Blandford, Bishop of Worcester, who told her "there were many things in the Roman Church which it was very much to be wished they had kept--as confession, which was no doubt commanded by God; and praying for the dead, which was one of the ancient things in Christianity--that for their parts they did it daily, though they would not own to it."

The duchess pondered over what she had read and heard, and being a woman accustomed to judge for herself, and act upon her decisions, she, in the month of August, 1670 became a member of the Catholic Church, in which communion she died seven months later. For fifteen months previous to her demise she had been suffering from a complication of diseases, with which the medical skill of that day was unable to cope, and these accumulating, in March, 1671, ended her days. The "Stuart Papers" furnish an interesting account of her death. Seeing the hour was at hand which would sever her from all earthly ties, she besought her husband not to leave her whilst life remained. She likewise requested that in case Dr. Blandford or any other of the bishops should come to visit her, he would tell them she had become a member of the Catholic Church; but if they insisted on seeing her she was satisfied to admit them, providing they would not distress her by arguments or controversy.

Soon after she had expressed these desires, Bishop Blandford arrived, and begged permission to see her, hearing which the duke went into the drawing-room, where his lordship waited, and delivered the message with which the duchess had charged him. Thereon the bishop said, "he made no doubt but that she would do well since she was fully convinced, and had not changed out of any worldly end." He then went into the room, and having made "a short Christian exhortation suitable to the condition she was in," took his departure. Presently the queen came and sat by the dying woman, with whom she had borne many wrongs in common; and later on, the Franciscan friar being admitted, the duchess "received all the last sacraments of the Catholick Church, and dyed with great devotion and resignation."

Though no mystery was now made concerning the faith in which she died, the duke, from motives of prudence, continued to preserve the secret of his having embraced the same religion. He still publicly attended service on Sundays with the king, but continued to absent himself from communion. At last, the Christmastide of the year 1672 being at hand, his majesty besought Lord Arundel and Sir Thomas (now Lord) Clifford to persuade the duke to take the sacrament with him, "and make him sensible of the prejudice it would do to both of them should he forbear so to do, by giving the world so much reason to believe he was a catholick." To this request these honest gentlemen replied it would be difficult to move the duke to his majesty's desires; but even if they succeeded, it would fail to convince the world his royal highness was not a catholic. With these answers Charles seemed satisfied; but again on Christmas Eve he urged Lord Clifford to advise the duke to publicly communicate on the morrow. His royal highness, not being so unscrupulous as the king, refused compliance with his wishes.

The following Easter he likewise refrained from communicating. Evelyn tells us that "a most crowded auditorie" had assembled in the Chapel Royal on this Sunday; possibly it had been drawn there to hear the eloquence of Dr. Sparrow, Bishop of Exeter--probably to observe the movements of the king's brother. "I staied to see," writes Evelyn, "whether, according to costome, the Duke of York received the communion with the king; but he did not, to the amazement of everybody. This being the second year he had forborn and put it off, and within a day of the parliament sitting, who had lately made so severe an act against ye increase of poperie, gave exceeding griefe and scandal to the whole nation, that the heyre of it, and ye sonn of a martyr for ye Protestant religion, should apostatize. What the consequence of this will be God only knows, and wise men dread."

That the nation might no longer remain in uncertainty concerning the change the duke was suspected to have made, a bill, commonly called the "Test Act," was, at the instigation of Lord Shaftesbury, introduced into the House of Commons, on its reassembling. In substance this set forth, that all persons holding office, or place of trust, or profit, should take the oaths of supremacy and allegiance in a public court; receive the sacrament according to the Church of England in some parish church on the Lord's Day; and deliver a certificate of having so received communion, signed by the respective ministers and church-wardens, and proved by two credible witnesses on oath. After prolonged debates upon this singular bill, it was passed through both houses of parliament, and received a reluctant consent from the king. [This act continued in force until the reign of George IV.]

A great commotion followed the passing of this Act. Immediately the Duke of York resigned his post of lord high admiral of England. Suspicion now became certainty; he was truly a papist. His enemies were elated with triumph, his friends dejected by regret. Before public feeling had time to subside, it was thoroughly startled by the news that Lord Clifford, who was supposed to be a staunch protestant, had delivered up his staff of office as lord treasurer; and Lord Bellasis and Sir Thomas Strickland, papists both, "though otherwise men of quality and ability," had relinquished their places at court. The king was perplexed, the parliament divided into factions, the nation disturbed. No man knew who might next proclaim himself a papist. As days passed, excitement increased; for hundreds who held positions in the army, or under the crown--many of whom had fought for the king and his father--by tendering their resignations, now proved themselves slaves of what a vigorous writer calls the "Romish yoke: such a thing," he adds, "as cannot, but for want of a name to express it, be called a religion."

Public agitation steadily rose. Evelyn tells us, "he dare not write all the strange talk of the town." Distrust of the king, fear of his brother, hatred of popery and papists, filled men's minds and blinded their reason with prejudice. That the city had seven years ago been destroyed by fire, in accordance with a scheme of the wicked Jesuits, was a belief which once more revived: the story of the gunpowder plot was again detailed. Fearful suspicions sprang up and held possession of the vulgar mind, that the prosecutions suffered by protestants under Queen Mary might be repeated in the reign of the present monarch, or of his brother. That heaven might defend the country from being overrun by popery, the House of Commons besought his majesty to order a day of fasting and humiliation. And by way of adding fury to the gathering tempest, the bishops, Burnet states, "charged the clergy to preach against popery, which alarmed the court as well as the city, and the whole nation."

The king therefore complained to Dr. Sheldon, Archbishop of Canterbury, that the discourse heard in every pulpit throughout the capital and the kingdom was "calculated to inflame the people, and alienate them from him and his government." Upon which Dr. Sheldon called the bishops together, that he might consult with them as to what answer he had best make. Whereon these wise men declared "since the king himself professed the protestant religion, it would be a thing without a precedent that he should forbid his clergy to preach in defence of a religion, while he himself said he was of it." The next action which served to inflame public prejudice against catholicism, was the marriage of the Duke of York to a princess professing that faith.

Soon after the death of his wife, it was considered wise and well his royal highness should marry again. Of the four sons and four daughters the duchess had borne him, three sons and one daughter had died before their mother, and the surviving son and another daughter quickly followed her to the tomb; therefore, out of eight children but two survived, Mary and Anne, at this time respectively aged nine and seven. It being desirable there should be a male heir-presumptive to the crown, the king was anxious his brother should take unto himself a second wife. And that a lady might be found worthy of the exalted station to which such a union would raise her, the Earl of Peterborough was sent incognito to report on the manners and appearance of the princesses of the courts of Neuburg and of Modena. Not being impressed by the merits of those belonging to the former, he betook himself to the latter, where, seeing the young Princess d'Este, then in her fifteenth year, he came to the conclusion no better choice could be made on behalf of the duke than this fair lady. On communicating this opinion to his royal highness and to his majesty, the king commissioned him to demand the hand of the princess in marriage for his brother.

Difficulties regarding this desired union now arose. The young lady, having been bred in great simplicity and ignorance, had never heard of such a country as England, or such a person as the Duke of York; and therefore had no mind to adventure herself in a distant land, or wed a man of whom she knew nought. Moreover, she had betrayed an inclination to spend her days in the seclusion of a convent, and had no thought of marriage. Her mother, the Duchess of Modena, then regent, by reason of her husband's death and her son's minority, was anxious for so advantageous an alliance. And being unable to gain her daughter's consent, she sought the interference of the pope, who wrote to the young princess, that compliance with her mother's request would "most conduce to the service of God and the public good." On this, Mary Beatrice Eleonora, Princess d'Este, daughter of the fourth Duke of Modena, consented to become Duchess of York. Whereon the Earl of Peterborough made a public entry into Modena, as ambassador extraordinary of Charles II.; and having agreed to all the articles of marriage, wedded her by proxy for the royal duke.

Meanwhile, news that the heir to the crown was about to wed a papist spread with rapidity throughout the kingdom, carrying alarm in its course. If sons were born of the union, they would, it was believed, undoubtedly be reared in the religion of their parents, and England in time became subject to a catholic king. The possibility of such a fate was to the public mind fraught with horror; and the House of Commons, after some angry debates on the subject, presented an address to the king, requesting he would abandon this proposed marriage. To this he was not inclined to listen, his honour being so far involved in the business; but notwithstanding his unwillingness, his councillors urged him to this step, and prayed he would stop the princess, then journeying through France on her way to England. This so incensed him that he immediately prorogued parliament, and freed himself from further interference on the subject.

On the 21st of November, 1673, the future duchess landed at Dover, where the duke awaited her, attended by a scant retinue. For the recent protestations, made in the House of Commons against the marriage, having the effect of scaring the courtiers, few of the nobility, and but one of the bishops, Dr. Crew of Oxford, ventured to accompany him, or greet his bride. On the day of her arrival the marriage was celebrated, "according to the usual form in cases of the like nature." The "Stuart Papers" give a brief account of the ceremony. "The Duke and Duchess of York, with the Duchess of Modena her mother, being together in a room where all the company was present, as also my Lord Peterborough, the bishop asked the Duchess of Modena and the Earl of Peterborough whether the said earl had married the Duchess of York as proxy of the duke? which they both affirming, the bishop then declared it was a lawful marriage."

This unpopular union served to strengthen the gathering storm; Protests against popery were universally heard; an article in the marriage settlement, which guaranteed the duchess a public chapel, was broken; and the duke was advised by Lord Berkshire to retire into the country, "where he might hunt and pray without offence to any or disquiet to himself." This counsel he refused to heed. Until his majesty should command him to the contrary, he said, he would always attend upon him, and do such service as he thought his duty and the king's security required of him. His enemies became more wrathful at this reply, more suspicious of popery, and more fearful of his influence with the king, They therefore sought to have him removed from his majesty's councils and presence by act of parliament.

Consequently, when both Houses assembled on the 7th of January, 1674, the lords presented an address to the monarch, praying he would graciously issue a proclamation, requiring all papists, or reputed papists, within five miles of London, Westminster, or Southwark, to depart ten miles from these respective cities, and not return during this session of Parliament. A few days afterwards an act was introduced into the House of Commons proposing a second test, impossible for catholics to accept, the refusal of which would not only render them incapable of holding any office, civil or military, or of sitting in either House of Parliament, but "of coming within five miles of the court." This unjust bill, to which, if it passed both houses, Charles dared not refuse assent, threw the court and country into a state of renewed excitement. Knowing it was a blow levelled at the duke, his friends gathered round him, determined to oppose it by might and main; and after great exertions caused a clause to be inserted excepting his royal highness from the test. This was ultimately carried by a majority of two votes, which, says Clarke, "put the little Earl of Shaftesbury so out of humour, that he said he did not care what became of the bill, having that proviso in it."

This noble earl, who was chief among the royal duke's enemies, was a prominent figure in the political history of the time. Mr. Burnet tells us his lordship's strength lay in the knowledge of England, and of all considerable men. "He understood," says the bishop, "the size of their understandings and their tempers; and he knew how to apply himself to them so dexterously, that though by his changing sides so often it was very visible how little he was to be depended on, yet he was to the last much trusted by all the discontented party. He had no regard to truth or justice." As rich in resources as he was poor in honour, he renewed a plan for depriving the Duke of York from succession to the crown; which, though it had failed when formerly attempted, he trusted might now succeed. This was to declare the Duke of Monmouth the king's legitimate son and heir to the throne of England, a scheme which the ambitious son of Lucy Walters was eager to forward.

His majesty's affection for him had strengthened with time, and his favours had been multiplied by years. On the death of the Duke of Albemarle, Captain General of the Forces, Monmouth had been appointed to that high office; and some time later had been made General of the Kingdom of Scotland, posts of greatest importance. Relying on the monarch's love and the people's admiration for this illegitimate scion of royalty, Lord Shaftesbury hoped to place him on the throne. As the first step necessary in this direction was to gain his majesty's avowal of a union with Lucy Walters, he ventured on broaching the subject to the king; at which Charles was so enraged that he declared, "much as he loved the Duke of Monmouth, he had rather see him hanged at Tyburn than own him as his legitimate son." There was, however, another man engaged in a like design to the noble earl, who, if not less scrupulous, was more daring.

This was one Ross, a Scotsman, who had been made governor of the young duke on his first coming into England, and who had since acted as his friend and confidant. Now Ross, who had not failed to whisper ambitious thoughts into his pupil's head, at this time sought Dr. Cosin, Bishop of Durham, and according to the "Stuart Papers," told him "he might do a great piece of service to the Church of England in keeping out popery, if he would but sign a certificate of the king's marriage to the Duke of Monmouth's mother, with whom that bishop was acquainted in Paris. Ross also told the bishop, to make the thing more easy to him, that during his life the certificate should not be produced or made use of." The same papers state that, as a bishop's certificate is a legal proof of marriage, Dr. Cosin's compliance would have been invaluable to the duke and his friends. His lordship, however, rejected the proposition, and laid the matter before the king, who expelled Ross from court.

Horror of popery and fear of a papist sovereign increased with time, care having been taken by my Lord Shaftesbury and his party that the public mind, once inflamed, should be kept ignited. For this purpose he spread reports abroad that the Irish were about to rise in rebellion, backed by the French; and that the papists in London had entered into a vile conspiracy to put their fellow citizens to the sword on the first favourable opportunity. To give this latter statement a flavour of reality he, assuming an air of fright, betook himself one night to the city, and sought refuge in the house of a fanatic, in order, he said, that he might escape the catholics, who had planned to cut his throat.

A tempest, dark and dangerous, was gathering fast, which the court felt powerless to subdue. The king's assurance to parliament that "he would endeavour to satisfy the world of his steadfastness for the security of the protestant religion," had little avail in soothing the people. Many of them suspected him to be a catholic at heart; others knew he had accepted the bounty of a country feared and detested by the nation. Deeds, not words, could alone dispel the clouds of prejudice which came between him and his subjects; and accordingly he set about the performance of such acts as might bring reconciliation in their train.

The first of these was the confirmation, according to the Protestant Church, of the Lady Mary, eldest daughter of the Duke of York, and after him heir presumptive to the crown; the second and more important was the marriage of that princess to William of Orange. This prince was son of the king's eldest sister, and therefore grandson of Charles I. As a hero who, by virtue of his statesmanship and indomitable courage, had rescued Holland from the hateful power of France, he was regarded not only as the saviour of his country, but as the protector of protestantism. Already a large section of the English nation turned their eyes towards him as one whom they might elect some day to weald the sceptre of Great Britain. Subtle, ambitious, and determined, a silent student of humanity, a grave observer of politics, a sagacious leader in warfare, he had likewise begun to look forward towards the chances of succeeding his uncle in the government of England--in hopes of which he had been strengthened by the private overtures made him by Shaftesbury, and sustained by the public prejudices exhibited against the Duke of York.

The proposed union between him and the heiress presumptive to the crown was regarded by the nation with satisfaction, and by the prince as an act strongly favouring the realization of his desires for sovereignty. Cold and grave in temperament, sickly and repulsive in appearance, blunt and graceless in manner, he was by no means an ideal bridegroom for a fair princess; but neither she nor her father had any choice given them in a concern so important to the pacification of the nation. She, it was whispered at court, had previously given her heart to a brave young Scottish laird; and her father, it was known, had already taken an instinctive dislike to the man destined to usurp his throne. In October, 1677, the Prince of Orange came to England, ostensibly to consult with King Charles regarding the establishment of peace between France and the Confederates; but the chief motive of his visit was to promote his marriage, which had some time before been proposed, and owing to political causes had been coolly received by him. Now, however, his anxiety for the union was made plain to the king, who quickly agreed to his desires. "Nephew," said he to the sturdy Dutchman, "it is not good for man to be alone, and I will give you a help meet for you; and so," continues Burnet, "he told him he would bestow his niece on him."

The same afternoon the monarch informed his council that "the Prince of Orange, desiring a more strict alliance with England by marriage with the Lady Mary, he had consented to it, as a thing he looked on as very proper to unite the family, and which he believed would be agreeable to his people, and show them the care he had of religion, for which reason he thought it the best alliance he could make." When his majesty had concluded this speech, the Duke of York stepped forward, and declared his consent to the marriage. He hoped "he had now given a sufficient testimony of his right intentions for the public good, and that people would no more say he designed altering the government in church or state; for whatever his opinion on religion might be, all that he desired was, that men might not be molested merely for conscience' sake."

The duke then dined at Whitehall with, the king, the Prince of Orange, and a noble company; after which he returned to St. James's, where he then resided. Dr. Edward Luke, at this time tutor to the Lady Mary, and subsequently Archdeacon of Exeter, in his interesting manuscript diary, informs us that on reaching the palace, the duke, with great tenderness and fatherly affection, took his daughter aside, "and told her of the marriage designed between her and the Prince of Orange; whereupon her highness wept all that afternoon and the following day." Her tears had not ceased to flow when, two days after the announcement of her marriage, Lord Chancellor Finch, on behalf of the council, came to congratulate her; and Lord Chief Justice Rainsford, on the part of the judges, complimented her in extravagant terms.

This union, which the bride regarded with so much repugnance, was appointed to take place on the 4th of November, that date being the bridegroom's birthday, as likewise the anniversary of his mother's nativity. Dr. Luke gives a quaint account of the ceremony. "At nine o'clock at night," he writes, "the marriage was solemnized in her highness's bedchamber. The king; who gave her away, was very pleasant all the while; for he desired that the Bishop of London would make haste lest his sister [the Duchess of York] should be delivered of a son, and so the marriage be disappointed. And when the prince endowed her with all his worldly goods [laying gold and silver on the book], he willed to put all up in her pockett, for 'twas clear gains. At eleven o'clock they went to bed, when his majesty came and drew the curtains, saying, 'Hey! St. George for England!'"

For a time both court and town seemed to forget the trouble and strife which beset them. Bonfires blazed in the streets, bells rang from church towers, the populace cheered lustily; whilst at Whitehall there were many brilliant entertainments. These terminated with a magnificent ball, held on the 15th instant, the queen's birthday; at the conclusion of this festivity the bride and bridegroom were to embark in their yacht, which was to set sail next morning for Holland. For this ball the princess had "attired herself very richly with all her jewels;" but her whole appearance betrayed a sadness she could not suppress in the present, and which the future did not promise to dispel. For already the bridegroom, whom the maids of honour had dubbed the "Dutch monster" and "Caliban," had commenced to reveal glimpses of his unhandsome character; "and the court began to whisper of his sullennesse or clownishnesse, that he took no notice of his princess at the playe and balle, nor came to see her at St. James', the day preceding that designed for their departure."

The wind being easterly, they were detained in England until the 19th, when, accompanied by the king, the Duke of York, and several persons of quality, they went in barges from Whitehall to Greenwich. The princess was sorely grieved, and wept unceasingly. When her tutor "kneeled down and kissed her gown" at parting, she could not find words to speak, but turned her back that she might hide her tears; and, later on, when the queen "would have comforted her with the consideration of her own condition when she came into England, and had never till then seen the king, her highness replied, 'But, madam, you came into England; but I am going out of England.'"

CHAPTER XVII.

The threatened storm bursts.--History of Titus Oates and Dr. Tonge.--A dark scheme concocted.--The king is warned of danger.--The narrative of a horrid plot laid before the treasurer.--Forged letters.--Titus Oates before the council.--His blunders.--A mysterious murder.--Terror of the citizens.--Lord Shaftesbury's schemes.--Papists are banished from the capital.--Catholic peers committed to the Tower.--Oates is encouraged.

The marriage of the Lady Mary, though agreeable to the public mind, by no means served to distract it from the turmoil by which it was beset. Hatred of catholicism, fear of the Duke of York, and distrust of the king, disturbed the nation to its core. Rumours were now noised abroad, which were not without foundation, that the monarch and his brother had renewed the treaty with France, by which Louis engaged to send troops into England to support Charles, when the latter saw fit to lay aside duplicity, and proclaim himself a catholic. And, notwithstanding the rigorous Test Acts, it was believed many high positions at court were held by those who were papists at heart. Occasion was therefore ripe for the invention of a monstrous fraud, the history of which has been transmitted under the title of the Popish Plot.

The chief contrivers of this imposture were Titus Oates and Dr. Tonge. The first of these was son of a ribbon-weaver, who, catching the fanatical spirit of the Cromwellian period, had ranted as an Anabaptist preacher. Dissent, however, losing favour under the restoration, Oates, floating with the current of the times, resolved to become a clergyman of the Church of England, He therefore took orders at Cambridge, officiated as curate in various parishes, and served as chaplain on board a man-of-war. The time he laboured as spiritual shepherd to his respective flocks was necessarily brief; for his grossly immoral practices becoming notable, he was in every case ousted from his charge. The odium attached to his name was moreover increased by the fact, that his evidence in two cases of malicious prosecution had been proved false; for which he had been tried as a perjurer. Deprived of his chaplaincy for a revolting act of profligacy, driven from congregations he had scandalized, homeless and destitute, he in an evil hour betook himself to Dr. Ezrael Tonge, to whom he had long been known, and besought compassion and relief.

The Rev, Dr. Tonge, rector of St. Michael's, Wood Street, was a confirmed fanatic and political alarmist. For some years previous to this time, he had published quarterly treatises dealing with such wicked designs of the Jesuits as his heated brain devised. These he had printed and freely circulated, in order, as he acknowledged, "to arouse and awaken his majesty and the parliament" to a sense of danger. He had begun life as a gardener, but left that honest occupation that he might cultivate flowers of rhetoric for the benefit of Cromwell's soldiers. Like Titus Oates, he had become suddenly converted to orthodox principles on return of the king, and had, through interest, obtained the rectorship of St. Michael's. Bishop Burnet considered him "a very mean divine, (who) seemed credulous and simple, and was full of projects and notions."

Another historian who lived in those days, the Rev. Laurence Eachard, Archdeacon of Stowe, states Dr. Tonge was "a man of letters, and had a prolific head filled with all the Romish plots and conspiracies since the reformation." According to this author, Tonge took Oates into his house, provided him with lodging, diet, and clothes; and when the latter complained he knew not where to get bread, the rector told him "he would put him in a way." After this, finding Oates a man of great ingenuity and cunning, "he persuaded him," says Archdeacon Eachard, "to insinuate himself among the papists, and get particular acquaintance with them; which being effected, he let him understand that there had been several plots in England to bring in popery, and that if he would go beyond sea among the Jesuits, and strictly observe their ways, it was possible there might be one at present; and if he could make that out, it would be his preferment for ever; but, however, if he could get their names, and some information from the papists, it would be very easy to rouse people with the fears of popery."

Hungering for gold, and thirsting for notoriety, Oates quickly agreed to the scheme laid before him. Accordingly he became acquainted with, and was received into the Catholic Church by, Father Berry, a Jesuit, and in May, 1677, was sent by the Jesuits to study in one of their seminaries, situated in Valladolid, in Spain. Oates, however, though he had proved himself an excellent actor, could not overcome his evil propensities, and before seven months had passed, he was expelled from the monastery.

Returning to England, he sought out Dr. Tonge, to whom he was unable to recount the secret of a single plot. Confident, however, that wicked schemes against the lives and properties of innocent protestants were being concocted by wily Jesuits, the fanatical divine urged Oates to present himself once more before them, bewail his misconduct, promise amendment, and seek readmission to their midst. Following his advice, Oates was again received by the Jesuits, and sent to their famous seminary at St. Omer's; where, though he had reached the age of thirty years, he was entered among the junior students. For six months he remained here, until his vices becoming noted, he was turned away in disgrace. Again he presented himself before the rector of St. Michael's, knowing as little of popish plots as he did on his previous return. But Tonge, though disappointed, was not disheartened; if no scheme existed, he would invent one which should startle the public, and save the nation. Such proposals as he made towards the accomplishment of this end were readily assented to by Oates, in whose breast wounded pride and bitter hate rankled deep. Therefore, after many consultations they resolved to draw up a "Narrative of a Horrid Plot." This was repeatedly changed and enlarged, until eventually it assumed the definite shape of a deposition, consisting of forty-three distinct articles, written with great formality and care, and embodying many shocking and criminal charges.

The narrative declared that in April, 1677, the deponent was employed to carry letters from the Jesuits in London to members of their order in Spain; these he broke open on the journey, and discovered that certain Jesuits had been sent into Scotland to encourage the presbyterians to rebel. Arrived in Valladolid, he heard one Armstrong, in a sermon delivered to students, charge his majesty with most foul and black-mouthed scandals, and use such irreverent, base expressions as no good subjects could repeat without horror. He then returned to England, and was soon after sent to St. Omer with fresh letters, in which was mentioned a design to stab or poison his majesty--Pere la Chaise, the French king's confessor, having placed ten thousand pounds at the disposal of the Jesuits that they might, by laying out such a sum, the more successfully accomplish this deed. While abroad the deponent had read many letters, relating to the execution of Charles II., the subverting of the present government, and the establishment of the Romish religion. Returning again to England, he became privy to a treaty with Sir George Wakeham, the queen's physician, to poison the king; and likewise with an agreement to shoot him, made between the Jesuits and two men, named Honest William and Pickering. He had heard a Jesuit preach a sermon to twelve persons of quality in disguise, in which he asserted "that protestants and other heretical princes were IPSO FACTO deposed because such; and that it was as lawful to destroy them as Oliver Cromwell or any other usurper." He also became aware that the dreadful fire had been managed by Strange, the provincial of the Jesuits, who employed eighty-six men in distributing seven hundred fire-balls to destroy the city; and that notwithstanding his vast expenses, he gained fourteen thousand pounds by plunder carried on during the general confusion, a box of jewels, consisting of a thousand carat weight of diamonds, being included in the robbery.

The document containing these remarkable statements was finished in August, 1678. It now remained to have it brought before the king or the council. Tonge was resolved this should be done in a manner best calculated to heighten the effect of their narrative; at the same time he was careful to guard the fact that he and Oates had an intimate knowledge of each other. Not knowing any one of interest at court, he sought out Christopher Kirby, a man employed in the king's laboratory, of whom he had some slight knowledge, and, pledging him to the strictest secrecy, showed him the "Narrative of the Horrid Plot," and besought his help in bringing it under the notice of his majesty in as private a manner as possible.

This aid was freely promised; and next day, the date being the 13th of August, when the monarch was about to take his usual airing in the park, Kirby drew near, and in a mysterious tone bade his majesty take care, for his enemies had a design against his life, which might be put into execution at any moment. Startled by such words, the king asked him in what manner was it intended his life should be taken; to which he replied, "It might be by pistol; but that to give a more particular account of the matter, required greater privacy." The monarch, who quickly recovered his first surprise, resolved to take his usual exercise; and, subduing his curiosity, he bade Kirby attend him on his return from the park, and tell him what he knew of the subject.

When the time arrived, Kirby saw his majesty alone, and related to him in brief that two men waited but an opportunity to shoot him; and Sir George Wakeham had been hired to poison him; which news, he concluded, had been imparted to him by a worthy man living close at hand, who would attend his majesty's pleasure when that was manifested.

Bewildered by such intelligence, yet suspicious of its veracity, the king ordered Kirby to summon his informant that evening by eight o'clock. When that hour came his majesty repaired to the Red Room, and there met Dr. Tonge, who delivered his narrative into his hands. The rector was convinced the great moment he had so long awaited, in which he would behold the monarch aroused to a sense of his danger, had arrived. He was doomed to bitter disappointment. His majesty coolly took the narrative, and without opening it, said it should be examined into. On this Tonge begged it might be kept safe and secret, "lest the full discovery should otherwise be prevented and his life endangered." The monarch replied that, before starting with the court to-morrow for Windsor, he would place it in the hands of one he could trust, and who would answer for its safety. He then bade him attend on the Lord Treasurer Danby next morning.

In obedience to this command, Tonge waited on his lordship at the appointed time, and by the character of his replies helped to develop his story of the plot. When asked if the document he had given his majesty was the original of the deponent, Tonge admitted it was in his own handwriting. On this, Lord Danby expressed a desire to see the original, and likewise become acquainted with its author. Nothing abashed, the rector replied the manuscript was in his house, and accounted for its possession by stating that, singularly enough, it had been thrust under his door--he did not know by whom, but fancied it must be by one who, some time before, had discussed with him on the subject of this conspiracy. Whereon his lordship asked him if he knew the man, and was answered he did not, but he had seen him lately two or three times in the streets, and it was likely he should see him soon again.

Being next questioned as to whether he had any knowledge of Honest William, or Pickering, the villains who sought the king's life, he answered he had not. Immediately, however, he remembered it was their habit to walk in St. James's Park, and said, if any man was appointed to keep him company, he was almost certain he would have opportunities of letting that person see these abominable wretches. Finally, Lord Danby asked him if he knew where they dwelt, for it was his duty to have them arrested at once; but of their abode Tonge was completely ignorant, though he was hopeful he should speedily be able to obtain the required information.

He was therefore dismissed, somewhat to his satisfaction, being unprepared for such particular examination; but in a couple of days he returned to the charge, determined his tale should not be discredited for lack of effrontery, On this occasion he said he had met the man he suspected of being author of the document, who owned himself as such, and stated that his name was Titus Oates, but requested Tonge would keep it a strict secret, "because the papists would murder him if they knew what he was doing." Moreover, Oates had given him a second paper full of fresh horrors concerning this most foul plot. Taking this with him, the lord treasurer hastened to Windsor, that he might consult the king, having first left a servant with Tonge, in hopes the latter might catch sight of Honest William and Pickering in their daily walk through the park, and have them arrested. On Danby recounting Tonge's statements to the king, his majesty was more convinced than before the narrative was wholly without foundation, and refused to make it known to his council or the Duke of York. Therefore the lord-treasurer, on conclusion of a brief visit, left Windsor for his country residence, situated at Wimbledon.

For some days no fresh disclosure was made concerning this horrid plot, until late one night, when Dr. Tonge arrived in great haste at Lord Danby's house, and informed him some of the intended regicides had resolved on journeying to Windsor next morning, determined to assassinate the king. He added, it was in his power to arrange that the earl's servant should ride with them in their coach, or at least accompany them on horseback, and so give due notice of their arrival, in order that they might be timely arrested. Alarmed by this intelligence, Danby at once hastened to Windsor, and informed the king of what had come to his knowledge. Both endured great suspense that night, and next day their excitement was raised to an inordinate pitch by seeing the earl's servant ride towards the castle with all possible speed. When, however, the man was brought into his majesty's presence, he merely delivered a message from Dr. Tonge, stating the villains "had been prevented from taking their intended journey that day, but they proposed riding to Windsor next day, or within two days at farthest." Before that time had arrived, another message came to say, "one of their horses being slipped in the shoulder, their trip to Windsor was postponed."

Taking these foolish excuses, as well as Dr. Tonge's prevaricating answers and mysterious statements, into consideration, the king was now convinced the "Narrative of a Horrid Plot" was an invention of a fanatic or a rogue. He was, therefore; desirous of letting the subject drop into obscurity; but Lord Danby, foreseeing in the sensation which its avowal would create, a welcome cloud to screen the defects of his policy, which parliament intended to denounce, urged his majesty to lay the matter before his privy council. This advice the king refused to accept, saying, "he should alarm all England, and put thoughts of killing him into people's heads, who had no such ideas before." Somewhat disappointed, the lord treasurer returned once more to Wimbledon, the king remaining at Windsor, and no further news of the plot disturbed the even tenour of their lives for three days.

At the end of that time Dr. Tonge, now conscious of the false steps he had taken, conceived a fresh scheme by which his story might obtain credence, and he gain wealth and fame. Accordingly he wrote to Danby, informing him a packet of letters, written by the Jesuits and concerning the plot, would, on a certain date, be sent to Mr. Bedingfield, chaplain to the Duchess of York. Such information was most acceptable to Danby at the moment; he at once started for Windsor, and laid this fresh information before the king. To his lordship's intense surprise, his majesty handed him the letters. These, five in number, containing treasonable expressions and references to the plot, had been some hours before handed by Mr. Bedingfield to the Duke of York, saying, he "feared some ill was intended him by the same packet, because the letters therein seemed to be of a dangerous nature, and that he was sure they were not the handwriting of the persons whose names were subscribed to the letters." On examination, they were proved to be most flagrant forgeries. Written in a feigned hand, and signed by different names, they were evidently the production of one man; the same want of punctuation, style of expression, and peculiarities of spelling being notable in all. The Duke of York, foreseeing malice was meant by them, forcibly persuaded the king to place the epistles before the privy council. Accordingly, they were handed to Sir William Jones, attorney general, and Sir Robert Southwell, who stated, upon comparing them with Dr. Tonge's narrative, they were convinced both were written by the same hand.

Meanwhile, Tonge and Oates, aware of the coldness and doubt with which his majesty had received the "Narrative of the Horrid Plot," and ignorant of the fact he had placed the letters before his privy council, resolved to make their story public to the world. It therefore happened on the 6th of September they presented themselves before Sir Edmondbury Godfrey, a justice of the peace, in the parish of St. Martin's, who, not without considerable persuasion, consented to receive a sworn testimony from Titus Oates regarding the truth of his narrative, which had now grown from forty-three to eighty-one articles. This action prevented further secrecy concerning the so-called plot.

A few days later the court returned to town for the winter, when the Duke of York besought the privy council to investigate the strange charges made in the declaration. Accordingly, on the 28th of the month, Tonge and Oates were summoned before it, when the latter, making many additions to his narrative, solemnly affirmed its truth. Aghast at so horrible a relation, the council knew not what to credit. The evil reputation Oates had borne, the baseness of character he revealed in detailing his actions as a spy, the mysterious manner in which the fanatical Tonge accounted for his possession of the document, tended to make many doubt; whilst others, believing no man would have the hardihood to bring forward such charges without being able to sustain them by proof, contended it was their duty to sift them to the end. Believing if he had been entrusted with secret letters and documents of importance, he would naturally retain some of them in order to prove his intended charges, the council asked Oates to produce them; but of these he had not one to show. Nor, he confessed, could he then furnish proof of his words, but promised if he were provided with a guard, and given officers and warrants, he would arrest certain persons concerned in the plot, and seize secret documents such as none could dispute. These being granted him, he immediately caused eight Jesuits to be apprehended and imprisoned. Then he commenced a search for treasonable letters, not only in their houses, but in the homes of such catholics as were noted for their zeal. His investigations were awaited with impatience; nor were they without furnishing some pretext for his accusations.

One of the first dwellings which Titus Oates investigated was that of Edward

Coleman. This gentleman, the son of an English divine, had early in life embraced catholicity, for the propagation of which he thenceforth became most zealous. Coming under notice of the court, he became the confidant of the Duke of York, and by him was made secretary to the duchess. A man of great mental activity, religious fervour, and considerable ambition, he had, about four years previous to this time, entered into a correspondence with the confessor of the French king and other Jesuits, regarding the hopes he entertained of Charles II. professing catholicity. Knowing him to be bold in his designs and incautious in his actions, the duke had discharged him from his post as secretary to the duchess, but had retained him in his dependence. This latter circumstance, together with a suspicion of the confidence which had existed between him and his royal highness, prompted Oates to have him arrested, and his house searched. Coleman, having received notice of this design, fled from his home, incautiously leaving behind him some old letters and copies of communications which had passed between him and the Jesuits. These were at once seized, and though not containing one expression which could be construed as treasonable, were, from expectations they set forth of seeing catholicity re-established in England, considered by undiscerning judges, proofs of the statements made by Oates.

On the strength of his discovery, Oates hastened to Sir Edmondbury Godfrey, and swore false informations; becoming aware of which, Coleman, conscious of his innocence, delivered himself up, in hopes of meeting a justice never vouchsafed him.

The Privy council now sat morning and evening, in order to examine Oates, whose evidence proved untrustworthy and contradictory to a bewildering degree. When it was pointed out to him the five letters, supposed to come from men of education, contained ill-spelling, bad grammar, and other faults, he, with much effrontery, declared it was a common artifice among the Jesuits to write in that manner, in order to avoid recognition; but inasmuch as real names were attached to the epistles, that argument was not considered just. The subject was not mentioned again. When an agent for these wicked men in Spain, he related, he had been admitted into the presence of Don John, and had seen him counting out large sums of money, with which he intended to reward Sir George Wakeham when he had poisoned the king. Hearing this, his majesty inquired what kind of person Don

John was. Oates said he was tall, lean, and black; whereas the monarch knew him to be small, stout, and fair. And on another occasion, when asked where he had heard the French king's confessor hire an assassin to shoot Charles, he replied, "At the Jesuits' monastery close by the Louvre;" at which the king, losing patience with the impostor, cried out, "Tush, man! the Jesuits have no house within a mile of the Louvre!" Presently Oates named two catholic peers, Lord Arundel of Wardour and Lord Bellasis, as being concerned in the plot, when the king again spoke to him, saying these lords had served his father faithfully, and fought his wars bravely, and unless proof were clear against them, he would not credit they sought him ill. Then Oates, seeing he had gone too far, said they did not know of the conspiracy, but it had been intended to acquaint them with it in good time. Later on he swore falsely against them.

Meanwhile the wildest sensation was caused by the revelations of this "hellish plot and attempt to murder the king." The public mind, long filled with hatred of papacy, was now inflamed to a degree of fury which could only be quenched by the blood of many victims. To the general sensation which obtained, a new terror was promptly added by the occurrence of a supposed horrible and mysterious murder.

On the evening of Saturday, the 12th of October, Sir Edmondbury Godfrey was missing from his home in the parish of St. Martin's. The worthy magistrate was an easy going bachelor of portly appearance, much given to quote legal opinions in his discourse, and to assert the majesty of the law as represented in his person. He was alike respected for his zeal by the protestants, and esteemed for his lenity by the catholics. Bishop Burnet records the worthy knight "was not apt to search for priests or mass-houses;" and Archdeacon Eachard affirms "he was well known to be a favourer rather than a prosecutor of the papists." Accordingly, his disappearance at first begot no evil suspicions; but as he did not return on Monday, his servants became alarmed at the absence of a master whose regularity was proverbial. His brothers were of opinion he was in debt, and sought escape from his creditors; whilst his friends, after their kind, were ready to name certain houses of doubtful repute in which they were certain he had taken temporary lodgings. On his papers being examined, it was found he had set his affairs in order, paid all his debts, and destroyed a quantity of his letters and documents. It was then remembered he had been occasionally susceptible to melancholia--a disease he inherited from his father, who had perished by his own hand. It was noted some days before that on which he was missed, he had appeared listless and depressed. It was known the imprisonment of his friend Coleman had weighed heavily on his spirits. A terrible fear now taking possession of his relatives and friends, thorough search was made for him, which proved vain until the Thursday following his disappearance, when he was accidentally discovered lying in a ditch, a cloth knotted round his neck, and a sword passed through his body, "at or near a place called Primrose Hill, in the midway between London and Hampstead."

If he had been murdered, no motive appeared to account for the deed; neither robbery nor revenge could have prompted it. His rings and money, gloves and cane, were found on and near his body; and it was known he had lived in peace with all men. Nor did an inquest lasting two days throw any light upon the mystery. If it were proved he had died by his own hand, the law of that day would not permit his brothers to inherit his property, which was found to be considerable. It was therefore their interest to ignore the fact that strangulation pointed to FELO DE SE, and to assume he had been murdered. Accordingly they prohibited the surgeons from opening the body, lest examination should falsify conclusions at which they desired to arrive. A verdict was ultimately returned "that he was murdered by certain persons unknown to the jurors, and that his death proceeded from suffocation and strangling by a certain piece of linen cloth of no value."

Occurring at such a moment, his death was at once attributed to the papists, who, it was said, being incensed that the magistrate had received the sworn testimonies of Oates, had sought this bloody revenge. Fear now succeeded bewilderment; desires of vengeance sprang from depths of horror. For two days the mangled remains of the poor knight were exposed to public view, "and all that saw them went away inflamed." They were then interred with all the pomp and state befitting one who had fallen a victim to catholicism, a martyr to protestantism. The funeral procession, which took its sad way through the principal thoroughfares from Bridewell to St. Martin's-in-the-Fields, numbered seventy-two divines, and over twelve hundred persons of quality and consideration. Arriving at the church, Dr. Lloyd, a clergyman remarkable for his fine abhorrence of papists, ascended the pulpit, where, protected by two men of great height and strength, he delivered a discourse, pointing to the conclusion that Sir Edmondbury Godfrey had been sacrificed to the catholic conspiracy, and instigating his hearers to seek revenge. Sir Roger North tells us the crowd in and about the church was prodigious, "and so heated, that anything called papist, were it cat or dog, had probably gone to pieces in a moment. The catholics all kept close in their houses and lodgings, thinking it a good composition to be safe there."

The whole city was terror-stricken. "Men's spirits were so sharpened," says Burnet, "that it was looked on as a very great happiness that the people did not vent their fury upon the papists about the town." Tonge and Oates went abroad protected by body guards, arresting hundreds of catholics; cannon were mounted around Whitehall and St. James's; patrols paraded the streets by day and night; the trained bands were ready to fall in at a moment's notice; preparations were made for barricading the principal thoroughfares; the city gates were kept closed so that admission could be only had through the wickets; and the Houses of Parliament demanded a guard should keep watch on the vaults over which they sat, lest imitators of Guy Fawkes might blow them to pieces. Moreover, it was not alone the safety of the multitude, but the protection of the individual which was sought to be secured. In the dark confusion which general terror produced, each man felt he might be singled out as the next victim of this diabolical plot, and therefore devised means to guard his life from the hands of murderous papists. North, in his "Examen," speaking of this period, tells us: "There was much recommendation of silk armour, and the prudence of being provided with it against the time the Protestants were to be massacred. And, accordingly, there were abundance of those silken back, breast, and headpots made and sold, that were pretended to be pistol proof; in which any man dressed up was as safe as in a house, for it was impossible anyone could go to strike him for laughing; so ridiculous was the figure, as they say, of hogs in armour. This was the armour of defence; but our sparks were not altogether so tame as to carry their provision no further, for truly they intended to be assailants upon fair occasion, and had for that end recommended also to them a certain pocket weapon, which for its design and efficacy had the honour to be called a protestant flail. It was for street and crowd work; and the engine lurking perdue in a coat pocket, might readily sally out to execution, and so, by clearing a great hall, or piazza or so, carry an election by a choice of polling called knocking down. The handle resembled a farrier's blood stick, and the fall was joined to the end by a strong nervous ligature, that in its swing fell just short of the hand, and was made of LIGNUM VITAE, or rather, as the poet termed it, MORTIS."

One day, whilst the town was in this state of consternation, Tonge sent for Dr. Burnet, who hastened to visit him in the apartments allotted him and Oates at Whitehall. The historian says he found Tonge "so lifted up that he seemed to have lost the little sense he had. Oates came in," he continues, "and made me a compliment that I was one that was marked out to be killed. He had before said the same to Stillingfleet of him. But he had made that honour which he did us too cheap, when he said Tonge was to be served in the same manner, because he had translated 'The Jesuits' Morals' into English. He broke out into great fury against the Jesuits, and said he would have their blood. But I, to divert him from that strain, asked him what were the arguments that prevailed on him to change his religion and to go over to the Church of Rome? He upon that stood up, and laid his hands on his breast, and said, 'God and His holy angels knew that he had never changed, but that he had gone among them on purpose to betray them.' This gave me such a character of him, that I could have no regard to anything he said or swore after that."

The agitation now besetting the public mind had been adroitly fanned into flame by the evil genius of Lord Shaftesbury. Eachard states that if he was not the original contriver of this disturbance, "he was at least the grand refiner and improver of all the materials. And so much he seemed to acknowledge to a nobleman of his acquaintance, when he said, 'I will not say who started the game, but I am sure I had the full hunting of it.'" In the general consternation which spread over the land he beheld a means that might help the fulfilment of his strong desires. Chief among these were the exclusion of the Duke of York from the throne, and the realization of his own inordinate ambition. A deist in belief, he abhorred catholicism; a worshipper of self, he longed for power. He had boasted Cromwell had wanted to crown him king, and he narrated to Burnet that a Dutch astrologer had predicted he would yet fill a lofty position. He had long schemed and dreamed, and now it seemed the result of the one and fulfilment of the other were at hand. The pretended discovery of this plot threatened to upheave the established form of government, for the king was one at heart with those about to be brought to trial and death. A quarter of a century had not passed since a bold and determined man had risen up and governed Great Britain. Why should not history repeat itself in this respect? the prospect was alluring. Possessing strong influence, great vanity, and an unscrupulous character, Shaftesbury resolved to stir the nation to its centre, at the expense of peace, honour, and bloodshed.

On the 21st of October, Parliament assembled, when Lord Danby, much against his majesty's inclination, brought the subject of the plot before the Commons. This was a movement much appreciated by the House, which, fired by the general indignation, resolved to deal out vengeance with a strong hand. As befitted such intention, they began by requesting his majesty would order a day of general fasting and prayer, to implore the mercy of Almighty God. The king complying with this desire, they next, "in consideration of the bloody and traitorous designs," besought him to issue a proclamation "commanding all persons being popish recusants, or so reputed," to depart ten miles from the city. Accordingly, upwards of thirty thousand citizens left London before the 7th of the following month, "with great lamentations leaving their trades and habitations." Many of them in a little while secretly returned again. A few days before this latest petition was presented to the monarch, Oates had been examined before the House for over six hours; and so delighted was he by the unprejudiced manner in which his statements were received, that he added several items to them. These were not only interesting in themselves, but implicated peers and persons of quality to the number of twenty-six. The former, including Lords Stafford, Powis, Petre, Bellasis, and Arundel of Wardour, were committed to the Tower, the latter to Newgate prison.

At the end of his examination he was several times asked if he knew more of the plot, or of those concerned with it, to which he emphatically replied he did not. Three days later he remembered a further incident which involved many persons not previously mentioned by him.

Both Houses now sat in the forenoon and afternoon of each day; excitement was not allowed to flag. Oates seldom appeared before the Commons without having fresh revelations to make; but the fertility of his imagination by no means weakened the strength of his evidence in the opinions of his hearers. "Oates was encouraged," writes John Evelyn, "and everything he affirmed taken for gospel." Indignation against the papists daily increasing in height, the decrees issued regarding them became more rigorous in severity.

On the 2nd of November the king, in obedience to his Parliament, offered a reward of twenty pounds for the discovery of any officer or soldier who, since the passing of the Test Act, "hath been perverted to the Romish religion, or hears mass." Two days later a bill was framed "for more effectually preserving the king's person and government, by disabling papists from sitting in either House of Parliament." As it was feared a clause would be inserted in this, excluding the Duke of York, the enemies of his royal highness more plainly avowed their object by moving that an address be presented to the king, praying his brother should "withdraw himself from his majesty's person and counsels." This was the first step towards the Bill of Exclusion from Succession which they hoped subsequently to obtain. The monarch, however, determined to check such designs whilst there was yet time; and accordingly made a speech to the peers, in which he said to them, "Whatever reasonable bills you shall present to be passed into laws, to make you safe in the reign of my successor, so they tend not to impeach the right of succession, nor the descent of the crown in the true line, shall find from me a ready concurrence."

The intended address was therefore abandoned for the present; but the bill for disabling catholics from sitting in either House of Parliament, having a clause which excepted the Duke of York from that indignity, passed on the 30th of November.

CHAPTER XVIII.

Reward for the discovery of murderers.--Bedlow's character and evidence.--His strange story.--Development of the "horrid plot."--William Staley is made a victim.--Three Jesuits hung.--Titus Oates pronounced the saviour of his country.--Striving to ruin the queen.--Monstrous story of Bedlow and Oates.--The king protects her majesty.--Five Jesuits executed.--Fresh rumours concerning the papists.--Bill to exclude the Duke of York.--Lord Stafford is tried.--Scene at Tower Hill.--Fate of the conspirators.

Before the remains of Sir Edmondbury Godfrey were laid to rest, a proclamation was issued by the king, offering a reward of five hundred pounds for discovery of the murderers. If one of the assassins betrayed those who helped him in the deed, he should receive, not only the sum mentioned, but likewise a free pardon, and such protection for his security as he could in reason propose. Two days after this had been made public, a man named William Bedlow put himself in communication with Sir William Coventry, Secretary of State, declaring he had a certain knowledge of the murder in question.

Archdeacon Eachard tells us this man "was one of a base birth and worse manners, who from a poor foot-boy and runner of errands, for a while got into a livery in the Lord Bellasis's family; and having for his villainies suffered hardships and want in many prisons in England, he afterwards turned a kind of post or letter carrier for those who thought fit to employ him beyond sea. By these means he got the names and habitations of men of quality, their relations, correspondents, and interests; and upon this bottom, with a daring boldness, and a dexterous turn of fancy and address, he put himself into the world. He was skilful in all the arts and methods of cheating; but his masterpiece was his personating men of quality, getting credit for watches, coats, and horses; borrowing money, bilking vintners and tradesmen, lying and romancing to the degree of imposing upon any man of good nature. He lived like a wild Arab upon prey, and whether he was in Flanders, France, Spain, or England, he never failed in leaving the name of a notorious cheat and impostor behind him."

On the 7th of November, Bedlow was brought before the king, and examined by two Secretaries of State. Here he made the extraordinary declaration that he had seen the body of the murdered magistrate lying at Somerset House--then the residence of the queen; that two Jesuits, named La Faire and Walsh, told him they, with the assistance of an attendant in the queen's chapel, had smothered Sir Edmondbury Godfrey between two pillows; that he had been offered two thousand guineas if he would safely remove the body, which on his refusal was carried away, a couple of nights after the murder, by three persons unknown to him, who were servants of the queen's household. Hearing this statement, Sir William Coventry asked him if he knew anything of the popish plot, when he affirmed on oath he was entirely ignorant regarding it; he likewise swore he knew no such man as Titus Oates.

That night he was lodged in Whitehall, in company with Tonge and Oates; and next morning appeared before the House of Lords, when it was evident his memory had wonderfully improved since the previous day. His story now assumed a more concise form. In the beginning of October, he stated, he had been offered the sum of four thousand pounds, to be paid by Lord Bellasis, provided he murdered a man whose name was withheld from him, This he refused. He was then asked to make the acquaintance and watch the movements of Sir Edmondbury Godfrey. With this he complied. Soon after dusk on the 12th of October, the magistrate had been dragged into the court of Somerset House by the Jesuits, and asked if he would send for the documents to which Oates had sworn. On his refusal he had been smothered with a piece of linen cloth; the story of suffocation by pillows, being at variance with the medical evidence, was now abandoned. One of the Jesuits, La Faire, had asked Bedlow to call at Somerset House that night at nine o'clock; and on presenting himself, he was conducted through a gloomy passage into a spacious and sombre room, where a group of figures stood round a body lying on the floor. Advancing to these, La Faire turned the light of a lantern he carried on the face of the prostrate man, when Bedlow recognised Sir Edmondbury Godfrey. He was then offered two thousand guineas if he would remove the body, which was allowed to remain there three days. This he promised to accomplish, but afterwards, his conscience reproving him, he resolved to avoid the assassins; and rather than accept the sum proffered, he had preferred discovering the villainy to the Government.

This improbable story obtained no credit with the king, nor indeed with those whose minds were free from prejudice. "His majesty," writes Sir John Reresby, "told me Bedlow was a rogue, and that he was satisfied he had given false evidence concerning the death of Sir Edmondbury Godfrey." Many circumstances regarding the narrator and his story showed the viciousness of the one and the falsity of the other. The authority just mentioned states, when Bedlow "was taxed with having cheated a great many merchants abroad, and gentlemen at home, by personating my Lord Gerard and other men of quality, and by divers other cheats, he made it an argument to be more credited in this matter, saying nobody but a rogue could be employed in such designs." Concerning the murder, it chanced the king had been at Somerset House visiting the queen, at the time when, according to Bedlow, the deed had been committed. His majesty had been attended by a company of guards, and sentries had been placed at every door; yet not one of them had witnessed a scuffle, or heard a noise. Moreover, on the king sending Bedlow to Somerset House, that he might indicate the apartment in which the magistrate's remains had lain three days, he pointed out a room where the footman waited, and through which the queen's meals were daily carried.

But the dishonesty of his character and falsity of his statements by no means prevented the majority of his hearers from believing, or pretending to believe, his statements; and therefore, encouraged by the ready reception they met, he ventured to make fresh and startling revelations. Heedless of the oath he had taken on the first day of his examination, regarding his ignorance of the popish plot, he now asserted he was well acquainted with all its details. For some four years he had been in the secret employment of the wicked Jesuits, and knew they intended to stab and poison his majesty, establish catholicity in England, and make the pope king. So far, indeed, had their evil machinations been planned, that several popish peers already held commissions for posts they expected to fill in the future. Lord Bellasis and Lord Powis were appointed commanders of the forces in the north and south; whilst Lord Arundel of Wardour had permission to grant such positions as he pleased. Then the Dukes of Buckingham, Ormond, and Monmouth, with Lords Shaftesbury and Ossory, together with many others, were to be murdered by forty thousand papists, who were ready to rise up all over the country at a moment's notice. "Nor was there," he added, "a Roman Catholic of any quality or credit but was acquainted with these designs and had received the sacrament from their father confessors to be secret in carrying it out."

It by no means pleased Oates that Bedlow should surpass him in his knowledge of this hellish plot. Therefore, that he might not lose in repute as an informer, he now declared he was also aware of the commissions held by popish peers. He, however, assigned them in a different order. Arundel was to be made chancellor; Powis, treasurer; Bellasis general of the army; Petre, lieutenant-general; Ratcliffe, major-general; Stafford, paymaster-general; and Langhorn, advocate-general. Nay, his information far outstripped Bedlow's, for he swore that to his knowledge Coleman had given four ruffians eighty guineas to stab the king, and Sir George Wakeham had undertaken to poison his majesty for ten thousand pounds. When, however, he was brought face to face with these men, he was unable to recognise them, a fact he accounted for by stating he was exhausted by prolonged examination.

All England was scared by revelations so horrible; "the business of life," writes Macpherson, "was interrupted by confusion, panic, clamour, and dreadful rumours." In London, two thousand catholics were cast into prison; houses were daily searched for arms and treasonable documents; and in good time merciless executions filled up the sum of bitter persecutions.

One of the first victims of this so-called plot was William Staley, a catholic banker of fair renown. The manner in which his life was sacrificed will serve as an example of the injustice meted to those accused. One day, William Staley happened to enter a pastrycook's shop in Covent Garden, opposite his bank, where there chanced to stand at the time a fellow named Carstairs; one of the infamous creatures who, envious of the honours and riches heaped on Oates and Bedlow, resolved to make new discoveries and enjoy like rewards. At this time he was, as Bishop Burnet states, "looking about where he could find a lucky piece of villainy." Unfortunately the banker came under his notice, and Bedlow and an associate pretended to have heard Staley say the king was a rogue and a persecutor of the people whom he would stab if no other man was found to do the deed. These words Carstairs wrote down, and next morning called on the banker, showed him the treasonable sentence, and said he would swear it had been uttered by him, unless he, Staley, would purchase his silence. Though fully aware of his danger, he refused to do this; whereon Carstairs had him instantly arrested and committed for trial. Hearing of his situation, and knowing the infamous character of his accusers, Dr. Burnet thought it his duty to let the lord chancellor and the attorney-general know "What profligate wretches these witnesses were." His interference was received with hostility. The attorney-general took it ill that he should disparage the king's evidence; Lord Shaftesbury avowed those who sought to undermine the credit of witnesses were to be looked on as public enemies; whilst the Duke of Lauderdale said Burnet desired to save Staley because of the regard he had for anyone who would murder his majesty. Frightened by such remarks at a time when no man's life or credit was safe, Burnet shrank from further action; but rumour of his interference having got noised abroad, it was resented by the public to such an extent, that he was advised not to stir abroad for fear of public affronts.

Within five days of his arrest, William Staley was condemned to death. In vain he protested his innocence, pointed out the improbability of his using such words in a public room, and referred to his character as a loyal man and worthy citizen. He was condemned and executed as a traitor.

The next victim was Coleman. He denied having hired assassins to murder his majesty, or entertained desires for his death; but honestly stated he had striven to advance his religion, not by bloodshed, but by tolerance. Whilst lying in chains at Newgate prison under sentence of death members of both Houses of Parliament visited him, and offered him pardon if he confessed a knowledge of the plot; but, in answer to all persuasions and promises, he avowed his innocence; protesting which, he died at Tyburn.

A little later, three Jesuits, named Ireland, Whitehead, and Fenwick, and two attendants of the queen's chapel, named Grove and Pickering, were executed on a charge of conspiracy to kill the king. Oates and Bedlow swore these Jesuits had promised Grove fifteen hundred pounds as price of the murder; Pickering chose as his reward to have thirty thousand masses, at a shilling a mass, said for him. Three times they had attempted this deed with a pistol; but once the flint was loose, another time there was no powder in the pan, and again the pistol was charged only with bullets. These five men died denying their guilt to the last.

Meanwhile, Dr. Tonge, the ingenious inventor of the plot, had sunk into insignificance by comparison with his audacious pupil. Not only did the latter have apartments at Whitehall allotted him, and receive a pension of twelve hundred a year, but he was lauded as the saviour of his country, complimented with the title of doctor of divinity, honoured in public, and entertained in private. Eachard mentions "a great supper in the city," given in compliment to Oates by "twenty eminent rich citizens;" and Sir John Reresby writes of meeting him at the dinner-table of Dr. Gunning, Bishop of Ely. Nothing could exceed the insolence and arrogance of the impostor. He appeared in a silk gown and cassock, a long scarf, a broad hat with satin band and rose, and called himself a doctor of divinity. No man dared contradict or oppose him, lest he should be denounced as a conniver of the plot, and arrested as a traitor. "Whoever he pointed at was taken up and committed," says North. "So that many people got out of his way as from a blast, and glad they could prove their last two years' conversation. The very breath of him was pestilential, and if it brought not imprisonment, it surely poisoned reputation." Sir John, speaking of him at the bishop's dinner-table, says "he was blown up with the hopes of running down the Duke of York, and spoke of him and his family after a manner which showed himself both a fool and a knave. He reflected not only on him personally, but upon her majesty; nobody daring to contradict him, for fear of being made a party to the plot. I at least did not undertake to do it, when he left the room in some heat. The bishop told me this was his usual discourse, and that he had checked him formerly for taking so indecent a liberty, but he found it was to no purpose."

The impostor's conversation on this occasion furnishes the key-note of a vile plot now contrived to intercept the lawful succession, either by effectually removing the queen, and thereby enabling the king to marry again; or otherwise excluding the Duke of York by act of parliament from lawful right to the crown. Though Shaftesbury's hand was not plainly seen, there can be no doubt it was busily employed in working out his favourite design.

The blow was first aimed at her majesty by Bedlow, who, on the 25th of November, accused her of conspiring to kill her husband. About eighteen months previously, he said, there had been a consultation in the chapel gallery at Somerset House, which had been attended by Lord Bellasis, Mr. Coleman, La Faire, Pritchard, Latham, and Sheldon, four Jesuits, and two Frenchmen whom he took to be abbots, two persons of quality whose faces he did not see, and lastly by her majesty. The Jesuits afterwards confided in him as a person of trust, that the queen wept at a proposal to murder the king which had been made, but subsequently yielding to arguments of the French abbots, had consented to the design. Indeed, Bedlow, who was in the sacristy when her majesty passed through at the termination of this meeting, noticed her face had much changed. Here his story ended; but, as was now usual, it was taken up and concluded by Oates.

Appearing at the Bar of the House of Commons, this vile impostor cried out, "Aye, Taitus Oates, accauce Caatharine, Quean of England, of haigh traison." Then followed his audacious evidence. In the previous July, Sir George Wakeham, in writing to a Jesuit named Ashby, stated her majesty would aid in poisoning the king. A few days afterwards, Harcourt and four other Jesuits having been sent for, attended the queen at Somerset House. On that occasion Oates waited on them; they went into a chamber, he stayed without. Whilst there he heard a woman's voice say she would endure her wrongs no longer, but should assist Sir George Wakeham in poisoning the king. He was afterwards admitted to the chamber, and saw no woman there but her majesty; and he heard the same voice ask Harcourt, whilst he was within, if he had received the last ten thousand pounds.

The appetite of public credulity seeming to increase by that on which it fed, this avowal was readily believed. That the accusation had not been previously made; that Oates had months before sworn he knew no others implicated in the plot beyond those he named; that the queen had never interfered in religious matters; that she loved her husband exceeding well, were facts completely overlooked in the general agitation. Parliament "was in a rage and flame;" and next day the Commons drew up an address to the king, stating that "having received information of a most desperate and traitorous design against the life of his sacred majesty, wherein the queen is particularly charged and accused" they besought him that "she and all her family, and all papists and reputed papists, be forthwith removed from his court." Furthermore, the House sent a message to the Peers, desiring their concurrence in this request; but the Lords made answer, before doing so they would examine the witnesses against her majesty. This resolution was loudly and indecently protested against by Lord Shaftesbury and two of his friends.

The king had discredited the story of the plot from the first; but remembering the unhappy consequences which had resulted upon the disagreement of the monarch and his parliament in the previous reign, he weakly resolved to let himself be carried away by the storm, other than offer it resistance. On the condemnation of the Jesuits, he had appeared unhappy and dissatisfied; "but," says Lord Romney, "after he had had a little advice he kept his displeasure to himself." The Duke of York states, in the Stuart Papers, that "the seeming necessity of his affairs made his majesty think he could not be safe but by consenting every day to the execution of those he knew in his heart to be most innocent." Now, however, when foul charges were made against the queen, calculated not merely to ruin her honour but destroy her life, he resolved to interfere. He therefore requested she would return to Whitehall, where she should be safe under his protection; and feeling assured Oates had received instructions from others more villainous than their tool, he ordered a strict guard to be kept upon him. This he was, however, obliged to remove next day at request of the Commons.

On the examination before the House of Lords of Oates and Bedlow, their evidence proved so vague and contradictory that it was rejected even by the most credulous. When Bedlow was asked "why he had not disclosed such a perilous matter in conjunction with his previous information touching the murder of Sir Edmondbury Godfrey," he coolly replied, "it had escaped his memory." On Oates being sent to point out the apartment in which he had seen her majesty and the Jesuits, he first selected the guard-room, and afterwards the privy chamber, places in which it would have been impossible to have held secret consultation. Aware that the king was resolved to protect her majesty, and conscious the evidence of her accusers was more wildly improbable than usual, the Lords refused to second the address of the Commons, when the charge against this hapless woman was abandoned, to the great vexation of my Lord Shaftesbury.

Though the queen happily escaped the toils of her enemies, the reign of terror was by no means at an end. At request of the king, the Duke of York left England and took refuge in Brussels; the catholic peers imprisoned in the Tower were impeached with high treason; Hill, Green, and Berry, servants of her majesty, charged with the murder of Sir Edmondbury Godfrey, were, without a shadow of evidence, hurried to the scaffold, as were soon after Whitebread, Fenwick, Harcourt, Gavan and Turner, Jesuits all, and Langhorn, a catholic lawyer, for conspiring to murder the king. On the morning when these unfortunate men stood ignominiously bound to the gallows at Tyburn, the instruments of death before their eyes, the angry murmurs of the surging mob ringing in their ears, suddenly the sound of a voice crying aloud, "A pardon! a pardon!" was heard afar off, and presently a horseman appeared riding at full speed. The soldiers with some difficulty making way for him through a line of excited people, he advanced to the foot of the scaffold, and handed a roll of paper bearing the king's seal to the sheriff, who, opening it, read a promise of pardon to those now standing face to face with death, provided "they should acknowledge the conspiracy, and lay open what they knew thereof." To this they replied they knew of no plot, and had never desired harm to the king; and, praying for those who had sought their lives, they died.

The firmness and patience with which the victims of judicial murder had one and all met death, refusing bribes, and resisting persuasions to own themselves guilty, could not fail in producing some effect upon the public mind; and towards the middle of the year 1679 the first signs of reaction became visible, when three Benedictine monks and the queen's physician were tried for conspiracy "to poison the king, subvert the government, and introduce popery." During the examination, Evelyn tells us, "the bench was crowded with the judges, lord mayor, justices, and innumerable spectators." After a tedious trial of nine hours, the jury brought the prisoners in not guilty, "without," says Evelyn, "sufficient disadvantage and reflection on witnesses, especially on Oates and Bedlow."

As my Lord Shaftesbury had not yet succeeded in his desired project of excluding the Duke of York from succession, the symptoms of change in public opinion were thoroughly distasteful to him. He therefore resolved to check them immediately, and stimulate the agitation and fear that had for many months reigned paramount through out the nation. For this purpose he had recourse to his former method of circulating wild and baseless reports. Accordingly a rumour was soon brought before the House of Commons of a horrible plot hatched by the papists to burn London to the ground. This, it was alleged, would be effected by a servant-maid setting a clothes-press on fire in the house of her master, situated in Fetter Lane. Two vile Irishmen were to feed the flames, and meanwhile the catholics would rise in rebellion, and, assisted by an army of sixty thousand French soldiers, kill the king, and put all protestants to the sword. Though this tale was in due time discredited, yet it served its purpose in the present. The violent alarm it caused had not subsided when another terrible story, started on the excellent authority of Lord Shaftesbury's cook, added a new terror. This stated the Duke of York had placed himself at the head of the French troops, with intention of landing in England, murdering the king and forcing papacy on his subjects. The scare was sufficiently effectual to cause Parliament to petition his majesty that he might revoke all licenses recently granted catholic householders to reside in the capital; and order the execution of all priests who administered sacraments or celebrated mass within the kingdom. Soon after this address, Lord Russell was sent by the Commons to the Peers, requesting their concurrence in the statement that "the Duke of York's being a papist, the hope of his coming to the crown had given the greatest countenance and encouragement to the conspiracies and designs of the papists." And now, in May, 1679, the condition of popular feeling promising well for its success, the Bill of Exclusion was introduced, ordaining that "James, Duke of York should be incapable of inheriting the crowns of England and Ireland; that on the demise of his majesty without heirs of his body, his dominions should devolve, as if the Duke of York were also dead, on that person next in succession who had always professed the protestant religion established by law." This passed the House of Commons by a majority of seventy-nine votes.

Alarmed by this bill, Charles resolved to show signs of resentment, and at the same time check the increasing power of the Commons, by a sudden and decisive movement. Therefore, without previously hinting at his intentions, he prorogued parliament before the bill was sent to the House of Lords. This was a keen surprise to all, and a bitter disappointment to Shaftesbury, who vowed those who advised the king to this measure should answer for it with their heads. Owing to various delays, the Bill of Exclusion was not brought before the Peers until eighteen months later. Its introduction was followed by a debate lasting six hours, in which Shaftesbury distinguished himself by his force and bitterness. At nine o'clock at night the House divided, when the measure was rejected by a majority of thirty-three votes, amongst which were those of the fourteen bishops present.

Mortified by this unexpected decision, the violent passions of the defeated party hurried them on to seek the blood of those peers lodged in the Tower. Of the five, William Howard, Viscount Stafford--youngest son of the Earl of Arran, and nephew of the Duke of Norfolk--was selected to be first put upon his trial; inasmuch as, being over sixty years, and a sufferer from many infirmities, it was judged he would be the least capable of making a vigorous defence. Three perjured witnesses swore he had plotted against the king's life, but no proof was forthcoming to support their evidence. Notwithstanding this was "bespattered and falsified in almost every point," it was received as authentic by the judges, who made a national cause of his prosecution, and considered no punishment too severe for a papist. After a trial of five days sentence of death was pronounced upon him, and on the 29th of December, 1680, he was beheaded on Tower Hill.

Like those who had suffered from similar charges, he protested his innocence to the last; but his words met with a reception different from theirs. Their dying speeches had been greeted by groans, hisses, and signs of insatiable fury; but his declarations fell upon silent and sympathizing hearts. When he had made denial of the crimes of which he was accused, a great cry rose from the mob, "We believe you--we believe you, my lord;" and then a single voice calling out "God bless you!" the words were taken up and repeated by a vast throng, so that the last sounds he heard on earth were those of prayer. He died with a firmness worthy of his caste. Having laid his head upon the block, the executioner brandished his axe in the air, and then set it quietly down at his feet. Raising his head, Lord Stafford inquired the cause of delay; the executioner replied he awaited a sign. "Take your time," said he who stood at the verge of eternity; "I shall make no sign." He who held the axe in his hand hesitated a second, and then said in a low and troubled voice, "Do you forgive me, sir?" To which Lord Stafford made brief answer, "I do." Then he laid his head again upon the blood-stained block. Once more the glitter of steel flashed through the air, a groan arose from the crowd, and Lord Stafford's head was severed from his body.

A reaction now set in, and gained strength daily. The remaining peers were in due time liberated; the blood of innocent victims was no longer shed; and the Duke of York was recalled. Such was the end of the popish plot, which, says Archdeacon Eachard, "after the strictest and coolest examinations, and after a full length of time, the government could find very little foundation to support so vast a fabrick, besides downright swearing and assurance; not a gun, sword, nor dagger, not a flask of powder or dark lanthorn, to effect this strange villainy, and with the exception of Coleman's writings, not one slip of an original letter of commission among those great numbers alledged to uphold the reputation of the discoveries."

Concerning those through whose malice such disturbance was wrought, and so much blood shed, a few words may be added. Within twelve months of Lord Stafford's execution, Shaftesbury was charged with high treason, but escaping condemnation, fled from further molestation to Holland, where, after a residence of six weeks, he died. Tonge departed this life in 1680, unbenefited by the monstrous plot he had so skilfully devised; and in the same year Bedlow was carried to the grave after an illness of four days. Oates survived to meet a share of the ignominy and punishment due to his crimes. After a residence of three years in Whitehall, he was driven out of the palace on account of "certain misdemeanors laid to his charge," and deprived of his salary. Two years later, in May, 1683, he was accused of calling the Duke of York a traitor, and using scandalous words towards his royal highness. Upon hearing of the case the jury fined him one hundred thousand pounds. Unable to pay the sum, he was cast into prison, where he remained six years, until liberated in the reign of William and Mary, His punishment was not, however, at an end. At the Michaelmas term of 1684 he was accused of having wilfully perjured himself at the late trials. As he pleaded not guilty, his case was appointed to be heard at the King's Bench Court. His trial did not take place until May, 1685, on which occasion the lord chief justice, in summing up the evidence, declared, "There does not remain the slightest doubt that Oates is the blackest and most perjured villain on the face of the earth."

After a quarter of an hour's absence from court, the jury returned a verdict of guilty, and sentence was pronounced against him. He was stripped of his canonical habit; forced to walk through all the courts of Westminster Hall proclaiming his crimes; to stand an hour on the pillory opposite Westminster Hall gate on Monday; an hour on the pillory at the Royal Exchange on Tuesday; and on Wednesday he was tied to a cart and whipt at the hands of the common hangman from Aldgate to Newgate, in the presence, says Eachard, "of innumerable spectators, who had a more than ordinary curiosity to see the sight."

CHAPTER XIX.

London under Charles II.--Condition and appearance of the thoroughfares.--Coffee is first drunk in the capital.--Taverns and their frequenters.--The city by night.--Wicked people do creep about.--Companies of young gentlemen.--The Duke of Monmouth kills a beadle.--Sir Charles Sedley's frolic.--Stately houses of the nobility.--St. James's Park.--Amusement of the town.--At Bartholomew Fair.--Bull, bear, and dog fights.--Some quaint sports.

During the first six years of the merry monarch's reign, London town, east of Temple Bar, consisted of narrow and tortuous streets of quaintly gabled houses, pitched roofed and plaster fronted. Scarce four years had passed after the devastating fire which laid this portion of the capital in ashes, when a new and stately city rose upon the ruins of the old. Thoroughfares lying close by the Thames, which were wont to suffer from inundations, were raised; those which from limited breadth had caused inconvenience and bred pestilence were made wide; warehouses and dwellings of solid brick and carved stone, with doors, window-frames, and breastsummers of stout oak, replaced irregular though not unpicturesque habitations; whilst the halls of companies, eminent taverns, and abodes of great merchants, were now built "with fair courtyards before them, and pleasant gardens behind them, and fair spacious rooms and galleries in them, little inferior to some princes' palaces." Moreover, churches designed by the genius of Christopher Wren, adorned with spires, steeples, and minarets, intersected the capital at all points.

This new, handsome, and populous city presented an animated, ever changing, and merry scene. From "the high street which is called the Strand," far eastwards, great painted signs, emblazoned with heraldic arms, or ornamented with pictures of grotesque birds and animals, swung above shop-doors and taverns. Stalls laden with wares of every description, "set out with decorations as valuable as those of the stage," extended into the thoroughfares. In the new Exchange, built by the worshipful company of mercers at a cost of eight thousand pounds, and adorned by a fair statue of King Charles II. in the habit of a Roman emperor, were galleries containing rows of very rich shops, displaying manufactures and ornaments of rare description, served by young men known as apprentices, and likewise by comely wenches.

At corners and nooks of streets, under eaves of churches and great buildings, and other places of shelter, sat followers of various trades and vendors of divers commodities, each in the place which had become his from daily association and long habit. These good people, together with keepers of stalls and shops, extolled their wares in deafening shouts; snatches of song, shouts of laughter, and the clang of pewter vessels came in bursts of discord from open tavern doors; women discoursed with or abused each other, according to their temper and inclination as they leaned from the jutting small-paned windows and open balconies of their homesteads; hackney coaches or "hell carts," as they drove by, cast filth and refuse lying in kennels upon the clothes of passengers; the carriers of sedan-chairs deposited their burthens to fight for right of way in narrow passages and round crowded corners.

Through the busy concourse flowing up and down the thoroughfares from dawn to dusk, street-criers took their way, bearing wares upon their heads in wicker baskets, before them on broad trays, or slung upon their backs in goodly packs. And as they passed, their voices rose above the general din, calling "Fair lemons and oranges, oranges and citrons!" "Cherries, sweet cherries, ripe and red!" "New flounders and great plaice; buy my dish of great eels!" "Rosemary and sweet briar; who'll buy my lavender?" "Fresh cheese and cream!" "Lily-white vinegar!" "Dainty sausages!" which calls, being frequently intoned to staves of melody, fell with pleasant sounds upon the ear. [These hawkers so seriously interfered with legitimate traders, that in 1694 they were forbidden to sell any goods or merchandise in any public place within the city or liberties, except in open markets and fairs, on penalty of forty shillings for each offence, both to buyers and sellers.] Moreover, to these divers sights and sounds were added ballad singers, who piped ditties upon topics of the day; quacks who sold nostrums and magic potions; dancers who performed on tight-ropes; wandering musicians; fire-eaters of great renown; exhibitors of dancing dolls, and such like itinerants "as make show of motions and strange sights," all of whom were obliged to have and to hold "a license in red and black letters, under the hand and seal of Thomas Killigrew, Esq., master of the revels to his sacred majesty Charles II."

Adown the Strand, Fleet Street, and in that part of the city adjoining the Exchange, coffee-houses abounded in great numbers. Coffee, which in this reign became a favourite beverage, was introduced into London a couple of years before the restoration. It had, however, been brought into England at a much earlier period. John Evelyn, in the year 1638, speaks of it being drunk at Oxford, where there came to his college "one Nathaniel Conoposis out of Greece, from Cyrill the patriarch of Constantinople, who, returning many years after, was made Bishop of Smyrna." Twelve good years later, a coffee-house was opened at Oxford by one Jacobs, a Jew, where this beverage was imbibed "by some who delighted in novelty." It was, however, according to Oldys the antiquarian, untasted in the capital till a Turkey merchant named Edwards brought to London a Ragusan youth named Pasqua Rosee, who prepared this drink for him daily. The eagerness to taste the strange beverage drawing too much company to his board, Edwards allowed the lad, together with a servant of his son-in-law, to sell it publicly; whence coffee was first sold in St. Michael's Alley in Cornhill by Pasqua Rosee, "at the sign of his own head," about the year 1658.

Though coffee-drinkers first met with much ridicule from wits about town, and writers of broadsheet ballads, the beverage became gradually popular, and houses for its sale quickly multiplied. Famous amongst these, in the reign of the merry monarch, besides that already mentioned, was Garraway's in Exchange Alley; the Rainbow, by the Inner Temple Gate; Dick's, situated at No. 8, Fleet Street; Jacobs', the proprietor of which moved in 1671 from Oxford to Southampton Buildings, Holborn; the Grecian in the Strand, "conducted without ostentation or noise;" the Westminster, noted as a resort of peers and members of parliament; and Will's, in Russell Street, frequented by the poet Dryden.

These houses, the forerunners of clubs, were, according to their situation and convenience, frequented by noblemen and men of quality, courtiers, foreign ministers, politicians, members of learned professions, wits, citizens of various grades, and all who loved to exchange greetings and gossip with their neighbours and friends. Within these low-ceilinged comfortable coffee-house rooms, fitted with strong benches and oak chairs, where the black beverage was drunk from handless wide brimmed cups, Pepys passed many cheerful hours, hearing much of the news he so happily narrates, and holding pleasant discourse with many notable men. It was in a coffee-house he encountered Major Waters, "a deaf and most amorous melancholy gentleman, who is under a despayer in love, which makes him bad company, though a most good-natured man." And in such a place he listened to "some simple discourse about quakers being charmed by a string about their wrists;" and saw a certain merchant named Hill "that is a master of most sorts of musique and other things, the universal character, art of memory, counterfeiting of hands, and other most excellent discourses."

In days before newspapers came into universal circulation, and general meetings were known, coffee-houses became recognised centres for exchange of thought and advocacy of political action. Aware of this, the government, under leadership of Danby, not desiring to have its motives too freely canvassed, in 1675 issued an order that such "places of resort for idle and disaffected persons" should be closed. Alarmed by this command, the keepers of such houses petitioned for its withdrawal, at the same time faithfully promising libels should not be read under their roofs. They were therefore permitted to carry on their business by license.

Next in point of interest to coffee-houses were taverns where men came to make merry, in an age when simplicity and good fellowship largely obtained. As in coffee-houses, gossip was the order of the day in such places, each tavern being in itself "a broacher of more news than hogsheads, and more jests than news." Those of good standing and fair renown could boast rows of bright flagons ranged on shelves round panelled walls; of hosts, rotund in person and genial in manner; and of civil drawers, who could claim good breeding. The Bear, at the bridge-foot, situated at the Southwark side, was well known to men of gallantry and women of pleasure; and was, moreover, famous as the spot where the Duke of Richmond awaited Mistress Stuart on her escape from Whitehall. The Boar's Head, in Eastcheap, which gained pleasant mention in the plays of William Shakespeare, when rebuilt, after the great fire, became a famous resort. The Three Cranes, in the Vintry, was sacred to the shade of rare Ben Jonson. The White Bear's Head, in Abchurch Lane, where French dinners were served from five shillings a head "to a guinea, or what sum you pleased," was the resort of cavaliers, The Rose Tavern, in the Poultry, was famous for its excellent ale, and no less for its mighty pretty hostess, to whom the king had kissed hands as he rode by on his entry. The Rummer was likewise of some note, inasmuch as it was kept by one Samuel Prior, uncle to Matthew Prior, the ingenious poet. On the balcony of the Cock, near Covent Garden, Sir Charles Sedley had stood naked in a drunken frolic; and at the King's Head, over against the Inner Temple Gate, Shaftesbury and his friends laid their plots, coming out afterwards on the double balcony in front, as North describes them, "with hats and no peruques, pipes in their mouths, merry faces and dilated throats, for vocal encouragement of the canaglia below."

All day long the streets were crowded by those whom business or diversion carried abroad; but when night fell apace, the keepers of stalls and shops speedily secured their wares and fastened their doors, whilst the honest citizen and his family kept within house. For the streets being unlighted, darkness fell upon them, relieved only as some person of wealth rode homewards from visiting a friend, or a band of late revellers returned from a feast, when the glare of flambeaux, carried by their attendants, for a moment brought the outlines of houses into relief, or flashed red light upon their diamond panes, leaving all in profound gloom on disappearing.

The condition of the thoroughfares favouring the inclination of many loose persons, they wandered at large, dealing mischief to those whose duty took them abroad. From the year 1556, in the reign of Queen Mary, "fit persons with suitable strength" had been appointed to walk the streets and watch the city by night; to protect those in danger, arrest suspected persons, warn householders of danger by fire and candle, help the poor, pray for the dead, and preserve the peace. These burly individuals were known as watch or bell men; one was appointed for each ward, whose duty it was to pass through the district he guarded ringing his bell, "and when that ceaseth," says Stow, "he salutes his masters and mistresses with his rhymes, suitable to the seasons and festivals of the year, and bids them look to their lights."

In the third year of the reign of King Charles II., whilst Sir John Robinson was mayor of London town, divers good orders were made by him and his common council for the better service of these watches. The principal of these set forth that each should be accompanied by a constable and a beadle selected from the inhabitants of their respective wards, who should be required in turn to render voluntary service in guarding the city, from nine of the clock at night till seven in the morning, from Michaelmas to the 1st of April; and from that date until the 31st of March, from ten at night till five in the morning.

These rules were not, however, vigorously carried out; the volunteers were frequently unwilling to do duty, or when, fearful of fine, they went abroad, they usually spent their time in tippling in ale-houses, so that, as Delaune remarks, "a great many wicked persons capable of the blackest villainies do creep about, as daily and sad experience shows." It was not only those who, with drawn swords, darted from some deep porch or sheltering buttress, in hopes of enriching themselves at their neighbour's expense, that were to be dreaded. It was a fashion of the time for companies of young gentlemen to saunter forth in numbers after route or supper, when, being merry with wine and eager for adventure, they were brave enough to waylay the honest citizen and abduct his wife, beat the watch and smash his lantern, bedaub signboards and wrench knockers, overturn a sedan-chair and vanquish the carriers, sing roystering songs under the casements of peaceful sleepers, and play strange pranks to which they were prompted by young blood and high spirits.

Among those who made prominent figures in such unholy sports was the king's eldest son, my Lord Duke of Monmouth. He and his young grace of Albemarle--son to that gallant soldier now deceased, who was instrumental in restoring his majesty--together with some seven or eight young gentlemen, whilst on their rounds one Sunday morning encountered a beadle, whose quaint and ponderous figure presented itself to their blithe minds as a fit object for diversion in lieu of better. Accordingly they accosted him with rough words and unceremonious usage, the which he resenting, they came to boisterous threats and many blows, that ended only when the poor fellow lay with outstretched limbs stark dead upon the pavement. Sir Charles Sedley and Lord Brockhurst were also notable as having been engaged in another piece of what has been called "frolick and debauchery," when "they ran up and down all night almost naked through the streets, at last fighting and being beaten by the watch, and clapped up all night."

It was not until the last years of the merry monarch's reign that there was introduced "an ingenious and useful invention for the good of this great city, calculated to secure one's goods, estates, and person; to prevent fires, robberies and housebreakings, and several accidents and casualties by falls to which man is liable by walking in the dark" This was a scheme for lighting the streets, by placing an oil-lamp in front of every tenth house on each side of the way, from Michaelmas to Lady-day, every night from six of the clock till twelve, beginning the third night after every full moon, and ending on the sixth night after every new moon; one hundred and twenty nights in all. The originator of this plan was one Edward Hemming, of London, gentleman. His project was at first ridiculed and opposed by "narrow-souled and self-interested people," who were no doubt children of darkness and doers of evil deeds; but was eventually hailed with delight by all honest men, one of whom, gifted with considerable imagination, declared these poor oil-lamps "seemed but one great solar light that turned nocturnal shades to noonday."

In this reign the city proper was confined eastward of Temple Bar; to the west lay the palaces of Somerset House and Whitehall, the stately parks, and great houses of the nobility surrounded by wide gardens and wooded grounds. Monsieur Sorbiere, who in this reign made a journey into England, an account of which he subsequently published "to divert a person of quality who loved him extremely," resided close by Covent Garden during his stay. It was usual, he writes, for people in the district to say, "I go to London," for "indeed 'tis a journey for those who live near Westminster. 'Tis true," he adds, "they may sometimes get thither in a quarter of an hour by water, which they cannot do in less than two hours by land, for I am persuaded no less time will be necessary to go from one end of its suburb to the other." For a crown a week this ingenious and travelled gentleman had lodgings in Covent Garden, not far removed from Salisbury House, a vicinity which he avows was "certainly the finest place in the suburbs." Covent Garden itself has been described by John Strype, native of the city of London, as "a curious large and airy square enclosed by rails, between which railes and houses runs a fair street." The square, or, as it was commonly called, garden, was well gravelled for greater accommodation of those who wished to take the air; and that its surface might more quickly dry after rain, it was raised by an easy ascent to the centre, where stood a sundial fixed on a black marble pillar, at the base of which were stone steps, "whereon the weary' might rest."

The west side of the square was flanked by the handsome portico of St. Paul's Church, erected at the expense of Francis, Earl of Bedford, from designs by Mr. Inigo Jones; the south side opened to Bedford Gardens, "where there is a small grotto of trees, most pleasant in the summer season." Here, on Tuesdays, Thursdays, and Saturdays, a market was held, well stocked with roots, fruits, herbs, and flowers. On the north and east sides stood large and stately houses of persons of quality and consideration, the fronts of which, being supported by strong pillars, afforded broad walks, known as the Piazza, and found convenient in wet and sultry weather.

Here amongst other houses was that of my Lord Brouncker, where Mr. Pepys enjoyed a most noble French dinner and much good discourse, in return for which he gave much satisfaction by the singing of a new ballad, to wit, Lord Dorset's famous song, "To all ye ladies now on land." Not far distant, its face turned to the Strand, was the stately residence of the Duke of Bedford, a large dark building, fronted by a great courtyard, and backed by spacious gardens enclosed by red-brick walls. Likewise in the Strand stood Arundel House, the residence of Henry Frederick Howard, Earl of Arundel and Surrey, and Earl Marshal of England; Hatfield House, built by Thomas Hatfield, Bishop of Durham, as a town residence for himself and his heirs lawfully begotten; York House, richly adorned with the arms of Villiers and Manners--one gloomy chamber of which was shown as that wherein its late noble owner, George, first Duke of Buckingham, was stabbed by Felton; Worcester House, at one time occupied by Lord Chancellor Clarendon; and Essex House, situated near St. Clement Danes, the town residence of Arthur Capel, Earl of Essex, "a sober, wise, judicious, and pondering person, not illiterate beyond the rate of most noblemen of this age."

There were also many other noble mansions lying westward, amongst them being those of the Dukes of Ormond and Norfolk in St. James's Square, which was built at this time; Berkeley House, which stood on the site now occupied by Berkeley Square, a magnificent structure containing a staircase of cedar wood, and great suites of lofty rooms; Leicester House, situated in Leicester Fields, subsequently known as Leicester Square, behind which stretched a goodly common; Goring House, "a very pretty villa furnished with silver jars, vases, cabinets, and other rich furniture, even to wantonnesse and profusion," on the site of which Burlington Street now stands;

Clarendon House, a princely residence, combining "state, use, solidity, and beauty," surrounded by fair gardens, that presently gave place to Bond Street; Southampton House, standing, as Evelyn says, in "a noble piazza--a little town," now known as Bloomsbury Square, whose pleasant grounds commanded a full view of the rising hills of Hampstead and Highgate; and Montagu House, described as a palace built in the French fashion, standing on the ground now occupied by the British Museum, which in this reign was backed by lonely fields, the dread scenes of "robbery, murder, and every species of depravity and wickedness of which the heart can think."

Besides the grounds and gardens surrounding these stately mansions, a further aspect of space and freshness was added to the capital by public parks. Foremost amongst these was St. James's, to which the merry monarch added several fields, and for its greater advantage employed Monsieur La Notre, the famous French landscape-gardener. Amongst the improvements this ingenious man effected were planting trees of stately height, contriving a canal one hundred feet broad and two hundred and eighty feet long, with a decoy and duck island, [The goodnatured Charles made Monsieur St. Evremond governor of Duck Island, to which position he attached a salary much appreciated by the exile. The island was removed in 1790 to make room for fresh improvements.] and making a pleasant pathway bordered by an aviary on either side, usually called Bird Cage Walk. An enclosure for deer was formed in the centre of the park; not far removed was the famous Physic Garden, where oranges were first seen in England; and at the western end, where Buckingham Palace has been erected, stood Arlington House, described as "a most neat box, and sweetly seated amongst gardens, enjoying the prospect of the park and the adjoining fields."

The great attraction of St. James's Park was the Mall, which Monsieur Sorbiere tells us was a walk "eight hundred and fifty paces in length, beset with rows of large trees, and near a small wood, from whence you may see a fine mead, a long canal, Westminster Abbey, and the suburbs, which afford an admirable prospect." This path was skirted by a wooded border, and at the extreme end was set with iron hoops, "for the purpose of playing a game with a ball called the mall." ["Our Pall Mall is, I believe, derived from paille maille, a game somewhat analogous to cricket, and imported from France in the reign of the second Charles. It was formerly played in St. James's Park, and in the exercise of the sport a small hammer or mallet was used to strike the ball. I think it worth noting that the Malhe crest is a mailed arm and hand, the latter grasping a mallet."--NOTES AND QUERIES, 1st series, vol. iii. p. 351.]

In St. James's Park Samuel Pepys first saw the Duke of York playing at "pele-mele"; and likewise in 1662 witnessed with astonishment people skate upon the ice there, skates having been just introduced from Holland; on another occasion he enjoyed the spectacle of Lords Castlehaven and Arran running down and killing a stout buck for a wager before the king. And one sultry July day, meeting an acquaintance here, the merry soul took him to the farther end, where, seating himself under a tree in a corner, he sung him some blithesome songs. It was likewise in St. James's Park the Duke of York, meeting John Milton one day, asked him if his blindness was not to be regarded as a just punishment from heaven, due to his having written against the martyred king. "If so, sir," replied the great poet and staunch republican, "what must we think of his majesty's execution upon a scaffold?" To which question his royal highness vouchsafed no reply.

It was a favourite custom of his majesty, who invariably rose betimes, to saunter in the park whilst the day was young and pass an hour or two in stroking the heads of his feathered favourites in the aviary, feeding the fowls in the pond with biscuits, and playing with the crowd of spaniels ever attending his walks. For his greater amusement he had brought together in the park a rare and valuable collection of birds and beasts; amongst which were, according to a quaint authority, "an onocratylus, or pelican, a fowl between a stork and a swan--a melancholy waterfowl brought from Astracan by the Russian ambassador." This writer tells us, "It was diverting to see how the pelican would toss up and turn a flat fish, plaice or flounder, to get it right into its gullet at its lower beak, which being filmy stretches to a prodigious wideness when it devours a great fish. Here was also a small waterfowl, not bigger than a more-hen, that went almost quite erect like the penguin of America. It would eate as much fish as its whole body weighed, yet ye body did not appear to swell the bigger. The Solan geese here are also great devourers, and are said soon to exhaust all ye fish in a pond. Here was a curious sort of poultry not much exceeding the size of a tame pidgeon, with legs so short as their crops seemed to touch ye earth; a milk-white raven; a stork which was a rarity at this season, seeing he was loose and could fly loftily; two Balearian cranes, one of which having had one of his leggs broken, and cut off above the knee, had a wooden or boxen leg and thigh, with a joint so accurately made that ye creature could walke and use it as well as if it had ben natural; it was made by a souldier. The park was at this time stored with numerous flocks of severall sorts of ordinary and extraordinary wild fowle breeding about the decoy, which, looking neere so greate a citty, and among such a concourse of souldiers and people, is a singular and diverting thing. There are also deere of several countries, white, spotted like leopards; antelopes, an elk, red deere, roebucks, staggs, Guinea goates, Arabian sheepe, etc. There are withy-potts or nests for the wild fowle to lay their eggs in, a little above ye surface of ye water."

Hyde Park, lying close by, likewise afforded a pleasant and convenient spot for recreation. Here, in a large circle railed off and known as the Ring, the world of quality and fashion took the air in coaches. The king and queen, surrounded by a goodly throng of maids of honour and gentlemen in waiting, were wont to ride here on summer evenings, whilst courtiers and citizens looked on the brilliant cavalcade with loyal delight. Horse and foot races were occasionally held in the park, as were reviews likewise, Cosmo, Grand Duke of Tuscany, "a very jolly and good comely man," whilst visiting England in 1669, was entertained by his majesty with a military parade held here one Sunday in May.

On arriving at Hyde Park, he found a great concourse of people and carriages waiting the coming of his majesty, who presently appeared with the Duke of York and many lords and gentlemen of the court. Having acknowledged an enthusiastic greeting, Charles retired under shade of some trees, in order to protect himself from the sun, and then gave orders for the troops to march past. "The whole corps," says the Grand Duke, "consisted of two regiments of infantry, and one of cavalry, and of three companies of the body-guard, which was granted to the king by parliament since his return, and was formed of six hundred horsemen, each armed with carabines and pistols, all well mounted and dressed, which are uniform in every thing but colour. When they had marched by, without firing either a volley or a salve, his majesty dismounted from his horse, and entering his carriage, retired to Whitehall."

Besides such diversions as were enjoyed in the parks, the people had various other sources of public amusement; amongst these puppet-shows, exhibitions of strength and agility, bear-baiting, cock-fighting, and dancing obtained. Until the restoration, puppet-shows had not been seen for years; for these droll dolls, being regarded as direct agents of Satan, were discountenanced by the puritans. With the coming of his majesty they returned in vast numbers, and were hailed with great delight by the people. One of these exhibitions which found special favour with the town, and speedily drew great audiences of gallants and ladies of quality, was situated within the rails of Covent Garden. And so perfect were the marionettes of this booth in the performance of divers sad tragedies and gay comedies, that they had the honour of receiving a royal command to play before their majesties at Whitehall. Amongst the most famous tumblers, or, as they were then styled, posturemakers, of this reign were Jacob Hall the friend of my Lady Castlemaine, and Joseph Clarke, beloved by the citizens. Though the latter was "a well-made man and rather gross than thin," we are told he "exhibited in the most natural manner almost every species of deformity and dislocation; he could dislocate his vertebrae so as to render himself a shocking spectacle; he could also assume all the uncouth faces he had seen at a quaker's meeting, at the theatre, or any public place. He was likewise the plague of all the tailors about town. He would send for one of them to take measure of him, but would so contrive it as to have a most immoderate rising in one of his shoulders; when his clothes were brought home and tried upon him, the deformity was removed into the other shoulder, upon which the tailor begged pardon for the mistake, and mended it as fast as he could; but on another trial found him as straight-shouldered a man as one would desire to see, but a little unfortunate in a hump back. In fact, this wandering tumour puzzled all the workmen about town, who found it impossible to accommodate so changeable a customer."

Florian Marchand, "the water-spouter," was another performer who enjoyed considerable fame. Such was the dexterity of this conjurer that, "drinking only fountaine-water, he rendered out of his mouth in severall glasses all sorts of wine and sweete waters." A Turk, who walked up an almost perpendicular line by means of his toes, danced blindfold on a tight rope with a boy dangling from his feet, and stood on his head on the top of a high mast, shared an equal popularity with Barbara Vanbeck, the bearded woman, and "a monstrous beast, called a dromedary." These wondrous sights, together with various others of a like kind, which were scattered throughout the town and suburbs during the greater part of the year, assembled in full strength at the fairs of St. Margaret, Southwark, and St. Bartholomew, in Smithfield. These gatherings, which usually lasted a fortnight, were looked forward to with considerable pleasure, and frequented not only by citizens bent on sport, but by courtiers in search of adventure.

Nay, even her majesty was tempted on one occasion to go a-fairing, as we gather from a letter addressed to Sir Robert Paston, contained in Ives's select papers. "Last week," says the writer thereof, "the queen, the Duchess of Richmond, and the Duchess of Buckingham had a frolick to disguise themselves like country lasses, in red petticoates, waistcoates, etc., and so goe see the faire. Sir Bernard Gascoign, on a cart jade, rode before the queen; another stranger before the Duchess of Buckingham, and Mr. Roper before Richmond. They had all so overdone it in their disguise, and look'd so much more like antiques than country volk, that as soon as they came to the faire, the people began to goe after them; but the queen going to a booth to buy a pair of yellow stockins for her sweethart, and Sir Bernard asking for a pair of gloves, sticht with blew, for his sweethart, they were soon, by their gebrish, found to be strangers, which drew a bigger flock about them. One amongst them [who] had seen the queen at dinner, knew her, and was proud of her knowledge. This soon brought all the faire into a crowd to stare at the queen. Being thus discovered, they as soon as they could got to their horses; but as many of the faire as had horses, got up with their wives, children, sweethearts, or neighbours behind them, to get as much gape as they could till they brought them to the court gate. Thus by ill conduct was a merry frolick turned into a penance."

On another occasion my Lady Castlemaine went to Bartholomew fair to see the puppets play "Patient Grissel;" and there was the street "full of people expecting her coming out," who, when she appeared, "suffered her with great respect to take the coach." Not only the king's mistress, but likewise the whole court went to St. Margaret's fair to see "an Italian wench daunce and performe all the tricks on the high rope to admiration; and monkies and apes do other feates of activity." "They," says a quaint author, "were gallantly clad A LA MODE, went upright, saluted the company, bowing and pulling off their hats, with as good a grace as if instructed by a dancing master. They turned heels over head with a basket having eggs in it, without breaking any; also with lighted candles on their heads, without extinguishing them; and with vessels of water without spilling a drop."

The cruel sport of bull and bear baiting was also commonly practised. Seated round an amphitheatre, the people witnessed these unfortunate animals being torn to pieces by dogs, the owners of which frequently jumped into the arena to urge them to their sanguinary work, on the result of which great wagers depended. Indignation arising against those who witnessed such sights may be somewhat appeased by the knowledge that infuriated bulls occasionally tossed the torn and bleeding carcases of their tormentors into the faces and laps of spectators. Pepys frequently speaks of dense crowds which assembled to witness this form of cruelty, which he designates as good sport; and Evelyn speaks of a gallant steed that, under the pretence that he had killed a man, was baited by dogs, but fought so hard for his life "the fiercest of them could not fasten on him till he was run through with swords." Not only bull and bear baiting, cock and dog fighting were encouraged, but prize combats between man and man were regarded as sources of great diversion. Pepys gives a vivid picture of a furious encounter he, in common with a great and excited crowd, witnessed at the bear-garden stairs, at Bankside, between a butcher and a waterman. "The former," says he, "had the better all along, till by-and-by the latter dropped his sword out of his hand; and the butcher, whether not seeing his sword dropped I know not, but did give him a cut over the wrist, so as he was disabled to fight any longer. But Lord! to see how in a minute the whole stage was full of watermen to revenge the foul play, and the butchers to defend their fellow, though most blamed him; and then they all fell to it to knocking down and cutting many on each side. It was pleasant to see, but that I stood in the pit, and feared that in the tumult I might get some hurt."

Among the more healthy sports which obtained during the reign were horse-racing, tennis, and bowling. The monarch had, at vast expense, built a house and stables at Newmarket, where he and his court regularly repaired, to witness racing. Here likewise the king and "ye jolly blades enjoyed dauncing, feasting, and revelling, more resembling a luxurious and abandoned route than a Christian court." He had likewise a tennis-court and bowling green at Whitehall, where at noonday and towards eve, blithe lords, and ladies in brave apparel, might be seen at play. Bowling was a game to which the people were much devoted, every suburban tavern having its green, where good friends and honest neighbours challenged each other's strength and skill. And amongst other pleasant sports and customs were those practised on May-day, when maids rose betimes to bathe their faces in dew, that they might become sweet-complexioned to men's sight; and milk-maids with garlands of spring flowers upon their pails, and posies in their breasts, danced to the merry music of fiddles adown the streets.

CHAPTER XX.

Court customs in the days of the merry monarch.--Dining in public.--The Duke of Tuscany's supper to the king.--Entertainment of guests by mountebanks.--Gaming at court.--Lady Castlemaine's losses.--A fatal duel.--Dress of the period.--Riding-habits first seen.--His majesty invents a national costume.--Introduction of the penny post.--Divorce suits are known.--Society of Antiquaries.--Lord Worcester's inventions.--The Duchess of Newcastle.

Few courts have been more brilliant than that of the merry monarch. All the beauty of fair women, the gallantry of brave men, and the gaiety of well-approved wits could compass, perpetually surrounded his majesty, making the royal palace a lordly pleasure house. Noble banquets, magnificent balls, and brilliant suppers followed each other in quick succession. Three times a week--on Wednesdays, Fridays, and Sundays--the king and queen dined publicly in ancient state, whilst rare music was discoursed, and many ceremonies observed, amongst these being that each servitor of the royal table should eat some bread dipped in sauce of the dish he bore. On these occasions meats for the king's table were brought from the kitchen by yeomen of the guard, or beef-eaters. These men, selected as being amongst the handsomest, strongest, and tallest in England, were dressed in liveries of red cloth, faced with black velvet, having the king's cipher on the back, and on the breast the emblems of the Houses of York and Lancaster. By them the dishes were handed to the gentlemen in waiting, who served royalty upon their knees. "You see," said Charles one day to the Chevalier de Grammont, "how I am waited on." "I thank your majesty for the explanation," said the saucy Frenchman; "I thought they were begging pardon for offering you so bad a dinner." [This mode of serving the sovereign continued unto the coming of George I.]

The costliness and splendour of some royal entertainments require the description of an eye-witness to be fully realized. Evelyn, speaking of a great feast given to the Knights of the Garter in the banqueting-hall, tells us "the king sat on an elevated throne, at the upper end of the table alone, the knights at a table on the right hand, reaching all the length of the roome; over against them a cupboard of rich gilded plate; at the lower end the musick; on the balusters above, wind musick, trumpets, and kettle-drums. The king was served by the lords and pensioners who brought up the dishes. About the middle of the dinner the knights drank the king's health, then the king theirs, when the trumpets and musick plaid and sounded, the guns going off at the Tower. At the banquet came in the queene and stood by the king's left hand hand, but did not sit. Then was the banquetting stuff flung about the roome profusely. In truth the crowd was so great that I now staied no longer than this sport began for fear of disorder. The cheere was extraordinary, each knight having forty dishes to his messe, piled up five or six high."

Concerning the habit mentioned by Evelyn, of mobs rushing into banquet-halls, in order to possess themselves of all on which they could lay hands, many instances are mentioned. The Duke of Tuscany, amongst other authorities, narrates the inconvenience it caused at a supper he gave the king. When his majesty drove to the duke's residence he was preceded by trumpeters and torch-bearers, attended by the horse-guards and a retinue of courtiers, and accompanied by a vast crowd. On alighting from the coach the Duke of Tuscany, together with the noblemen and gentlemen of his household, received and conducted him through passages lighted by torches to the banquet-hall. From the ceiling of this saloon was suspended a chandelier of rock crystal, blazing with tapers; beneath it stood a circular table, at the upper end of which was placed a chair of state for the king. The whole entertainment was costly and magnificent. As many as eighty dishes were set upon the table; foreign wines, famous for great age and delicate flavour, sparkled in goblets of chased gold; and finally, a dessert of Italian fruits and Portuguese sweetmeats was served. But scarce had this been laid upon the board, when the impatient crowd which had gathered round the house and forced its way inside to witness the banquet, now violently burst into the saloon and carried away all that lay before them. Neither the presence of the king nor the appearance of his soldiers guarding the entrance with carbines was sufficient to prevent entrance or hinder pillage. Charles, used to such scenes, left the table and retired into the duke's private apartments.

A quaint and curious account of a less ceremonious and more convivial feast, also graced by the king's presence, was narrated by Sir Hugh Cholmely to a friend and gossip. This supper was given by Sir George Carteret, a man of pleasant humour, and moreover treasurer of the navy. By the time the meats were removed, the king and his courtiers waxed exceedingly merry, when Sir William Armorer, equerry to his majesty, came to him and swore, "'By God, sir,' says he, 'you are not so kind to the Duke of York of late as you used to be.' 'Not I?' says the king. 'Why so?' 'Why,' says he, 'if you are, let us drink his health.' 'Why, let us,' says the king. Then he fell on his knees and drank it; and having done, the king began to drink it. 'Nay, sir,' says Armorer; 'by God, you must do it on your knees!' So he did, and then all the company; and having done it, all fell acrying for joy, being all maudlin and kissing one another, the king the Duke of York, the Duke of York the king; and in such a maudlin pickle as never people were."

Throughout this reign the uttermost hospitality and good-fellowship abounded. Scarce a day passed that some noble house did not throw open its doors to a brilliant throng of guests; few nights grew to dawn that the vicinities of St. James's and Covent Garden were not made brilliant by the torches of those accompanying revellers to their homes. The fashionable hour for dinner was three of the clock, and for greater satisfaction of guests it now became the mode to entertain them after that meal with performances of mountebanks and musicians, Various diaries inform us of this custom. When my Lord Arlington had bidden his friends to a feast, he subsequently diverted them by the tricks of a fellow who swallowed a knife in a horn sheath, together with several pebbles, which he made rattle in his stomach, and produced again, to the wonder and amusement of all who beheld him. [At a great dinner given by this nobleman, Evelyn, who was present, tells us that Lord Stafford, the unfortunate nobleman afterwards executed on Tower Hill, "rose from the table in some disorder, because there were roses stuck about the fruite when the descert was set on the table; such an antipathie it seems he had to them, as once Lady St. Leger also had, and to that degree, that, as Sirr Kenelm Digby tell us, laying but a rose upon her cheeke when she was asleepe, it raised a blister; but Sir Kenelm was a teller of strange things."] The master of the mint, worthy Mr. Slingsby, a man of finer taste, delighted his guests with the performances of renowned good masters of music, one of whom, a German, played to great perfection on an instrument with five wire strings called the VOIL D'AMORE; whilst my Lord Sunderland treated his visitors to a sight of Richardson, the renowned fire eater, who was wont to devour brimstone on glowing coals; melt a beer-glass and eat it up; take a live coal on his tongue, on which he put a raw oyster, and let it remain there till it gaped and was quite broiled; take wax, pitch and sulphur, and drink them down flaming; hold a fiery hot iron between his teeth, and throw it about like a stone from hand to hand, and perform various other prodigious feats.

Other means of indoor amusement were practised in those days, which seem wholly incompatible with the gravity of the nation in these latter times. Pepys tells us that going to the court one day he found the Duke and Duchess of York, with all the great ladies, sitting upon a carpet on the ground playing "I love my love with an A, because he is so-and-so; and I hate him with an A, because of this and that;" and some of the ladies were mighty witty, and all of them very merry. Grown persons likewise indulged in games of blind man's buff, and amusements of a like character; whilst at one time, the king, queen, and the whole court falling into much extravagance, as Burnet says, "went about masked, and came into houses unknown, and danced there with a great deal of wild frolic. In all this they were so disguised, that without being in the secret, none could distinguish them. They were carried about in hackney chairs. Once the queen's chairmen, not knowing who she was, went from her; so she was alone and was much disturbed, and came to Whitehall in a hackney coach; some say it was in a cart."

Dancing was also a favourite and common amusement amongst all classes. Scarce a week went by that Whitehall was not lighted up for a ball, at which the king, queen, and courtiers danced bransles, corants, and French figures; [The bransle, or brawl, had all the characteristics of a country-dance; several persons taking part in it, and all at various times joining hands. The corant was a swift lively dance, in which two persons only took part, and was not unlike our modern galop.] and no night passed but such entertainments were likewise held in the city. Billiards and chess were also played, whilst gambling became a ruling passion. The queen, Duchess of York, and Duchess of Cleveland had each her card-table, around which courtiers thronged to win and lose prodigious sums. The latter being a thorough rake at heart, delighted in the excitement which hazard afforded; and the sums changing owners at her hoard were sometimes enormous. Occasionally she played for a thousand, or fifteen hundred pounds at a cast, and in a single night lost as much as twenty-five hundred guineas. It is related that once when playing basset she lost all her money; but, being unwilling to retire, and hopeful of regaining her losses, she asked young Churchill, on whom she had bestowed many favours, to lend her twenty pieces. Though the wily youth had a thousand before him on the table, he coolly refused her request, on the plea that the bank--which he was then keeping--never lent. "Not a person in the place," says the narrator of this anecdote, "but blamed him; as to the duchess, her resentment burst out into a bleeding at her nose, and breaking of her lace, without which aid it is believed her vexation had killed her on the spot."

The courtly Evelyn speaks of a certain Twelfth-night, when the king opened the revels in his privy chamber by throwing dice, and losing one hundred pounds; and Pepys describes the groom-porters' rooms where gambling greatly obtained, and "where persons of the best quality do sit down with people of any, though meaner." Cursing and swearing, grumbling and rejoicing, were heard here to an accompanying rattle of guineas; the whole causing dense confusion. And amongst the figures crouching round the tables of this hell, that of my Lord St. Albans was conspicuous. So great, indeed, was his passion for gambling, that when approaching his eightieth year, and quite blind, he was unable to renounce his love for cards, but with the help of a servant who named them to him, indulged himself in this way as of yore.

As may be expected, disputes, frequently ending in duels, continually arose betwixt those who gambled. Although the king had, on his restoration, issued a proclamation against this common practice, threatening such as engaged in it with displeasure, declaring them incapable of holding any office in his service, and forbidding them to appear at court, yet but little attention was paid his words, and duels continually took place, Though most frequently resorted to as a means of avenging outraged honour, they were occasionally the result of misunderstanding. A pathetic story is told of a fatal encounter, caused by a trifle light as air, which took place in the year 1667 at Covent Garden, between Sir Henry Bellasis and Tom Porter--the same witty soul who wrote a play called "The Villain," which was performed at the Duke's Theatre, and described as "a pleasant tragedy."

These worthy gentlemen and loyal friends loved each other exceedingly. One fatal day, both were bidden to dine with Sir Robert Carr, at whose table it was known all men drank freely; and having feasted, they two talked apart, when bluff Sir Henry, giving words of counsel to honest Tom, from force of earnestness spoke louder than his wont. Marvelling at this, some of those standing apart said to each other, "Are they quarrelling, that they talk so high?" overhearing which the baronet replied in a merry tone, "No, I would have you know I never quarrel but I strike; and take that as a rule of mine." At these words Tom Porter, being anxious, after the manner of those who have drunk deep, to apprehend offence in speech of friend or foe, cried out he would like to see the man in England that durst give him a blow. Accepting this as a challenge, Sir Henry dealt him a stroke on the ear, which the other would have returned in anger but that they were speedily parted.

And presently Tom Porter, leaving the house full of resentment for the injury he had received, and of resolution to avenge it, met Mr. Dryden the poet, to whom he recounted the story. He concluded by requesting he might have his boy to bring him word which way Sir Henry Bellasis would drive, for fight he would that night, otherwise he felt sure they should be friends in the morning, and the blow would rest upon him. Dryden complying with his request, Tom Porter, still inflamed by fury, went to a neighbouring coffee-house, when presently word arrived Sir Harry's coach was coming that way. On this Tom Porter rushed out, stopped the horses, and bade the baronet alight. "Why," said the man, who but an hour before had been his best friend, "you will not hurt me in coming out, will you?" "No," answered the other shortly. Sir Henry then descended, and both drew their swords. Tom Porter asked him if he were ready, and hearing he was, they fought desperately, till of a sudden a sharp cry was heard; Sir Henry's weapon fell upon the ground, and he placed one hand to his side, from which blood flowed freely. Then calling his opponent to him, he looked in his face reproachfully, kissed him lovingly, and bade him seek safety. "For, Tom," said he, struggling hard to speak, "thou hast hurt me; but I will make shift to stand upon my legs till thou mayest withdraw, and the world not take notice of you, for," continued he, with much tenderness, "I would not have thee troubled for what thou hast done." And the little crowd who had gathered around carried him to his coach and twenty days later they followed him to his grave.

Throughout this merry reign, many fantastic changes took place in the costumes of courtiers and their followers. At the restoration, the dress most common to women of all ranks consisted of a gown with a laced stomacher and starched neckerchief, a sad-coloured cloak with a French hood, and a high-crowned hat. Such habiliments, admitting of little variety and less ornament, found no favour in the eyes of those who returned from foreign courts with the king, and therefore a change was gradually effected. The simple gown of wool and cotton gave place to loose and flowing draperies of silk and satin; the stiff neckerchief was removed to display fair shoulders and voluptuous breasts; the hat was bedecked by feathers of rare plumage and rich colour; the cloaks changed hues from sad to gay; the hoods being of "yellow bird's eye," and other bright tints. Indeed, the prodigal manner in which ladies of quality now exposed their bosoms, though pleasing to the court, became a matter of grave censure to worthy men. One of these in a pamphlet, entitled "A Just and Seasonable Reprehension of Naked Breasts and Shoulders," charges women of fashion with "overlacing their gown bodies, and so thrusting up their breasts in order that they might show them half-naked." It was not only at balls and in chambers of entertainment, he avowed, they appeared in this manner, but likewise at church, where their dress was "not only immodest, but sometimes impudent and lascivious;" for they braved all dangers to have the satisfaction of being seen, and the consolation of giving pleasure.

The riding-habit, first introduced in 1664 caused considerable notice, and no small amount of mirth. The garb, as it was called, consisted of a doublet buttoned up the breast, a coat with long skirts, a periwig and tall hat, so that women clad in this fashion might be mistaken for men, if it were not for the petticoat which dragged under the coat. At the commencement of the reign, ladies of the court wore their hair after the French fashion, cut short in front and frizzed upon the forehead. When the queen arrived, her hair was arranged A LA NEGLIGENCE, a mode declared mighty pretty; but presently a fashion came in vogue of wearing "false locks set on wyres to make them stand at a distance from the head; as fardingales made the clothes stand out in Queen Elizabeth's reign." Painting the face, which had been practised during the Commonwealth, became fashionable; as did likewise the use of patches and vizards or masks; which from the convenience they afforded wearers whilst witnessing an immoral play, or conducting a delicate intrigue, came greatly into use.

According to Randal Holmes's notes on dress, in the Harleian Library, the male costume at the restoration consisted of "a short-waisted doublet, and petticoat breeches--the lining, being lower than the breeches, is tied above the knees. The breeches are ornamented with ribands up to the pocket, and half their breadth upon the thigh; the waistband is set about with ribands, and the shirt hanging out over them." This dress gradually increased in richness and ornamentation: the doublet and breeches being changed from cloth to velvet and satin, the hat trimmed with plumes of gay feathers, and the neck adorned with bands of cambric, trimmed with Flanders and Brussels lace. The perfection and costliness to which the costume eventually reached is best shown by a description of Sir Richard Fanshaw ambassador of the king, as presented in the diary of his spouse. "Sir Richard was dressed," she writes, "in a very rich suit of clothes of a dark FILLEMONTE brocade, laced with silver and gold lace--nine laces--every one as broad as my hand, and a little silver and gold lace laid between them, both of very curious workmanship; his suit was trimmed with scarlet taffety ribbon; his stockings of white silk upon long scarlet silk ones; his shoes black, with scarlet shoestrings and gaiters; his linen very fine, laced with rich Flanders lace; a black beaver buttoned on the left side with a jewel of twelve hundred pounds' value, a rich curious wrought gold chain, made in the Indies at which hung the king his master's picture, richly set with diamonds; on his fingers he wore two rich rings; his gloves trimmed with the same ribbon as his clothes."

The uttermost extravagance and luxury in dress now obtained; indeed, to such a passion and pride did it reach that the monarch resolved on giving it some check by inventing a suit of plainer pretensions, which should become the national costume, and admit no change.

This determination he solemnly declared to his council in October, 1666, and on the 14th of the month appeared clad in a long vest slashed with white silk, reaching the knee, having the sword girt over it, a loose coat, straight Spanish breeches ruffled with black ribbons, and buskins instead of shoes and stockings. Though the habit was pronounced decent and becoming to his majesty, and was quickly adopted by the courtiers, there were those amongst his friends who offered him a wager he would not persist in wearing it long. At this the king stated his resolution afresh of never changing; but before the month was out he had made an alteration, for inasmuch as the vest being slashed with white, was said by a wag to make the wearers look like magpies, his majesty changed the colour of the silk to black. This "manly and comely habit" might have become permanently the fashion, if the King of France, by way of ridiculing the merry monarch, had not caused his footmen to be clad in like manner. Therefore, in less than two years, this mode gave place to others more fantastical. The vest was retained, but the shape and material were altered; the surcoat of cloth was discarded for velvet and rich plush, adorned with buckles of precious stones and chains of gold; the Spanish leather boots were laid aside for high-heeled shoes with rosettes and silver buckles. Towards the close of the reign the costume became much plainer. Through all these varying fashions the periwig, introduced in 1663, held its own, increasing in length and luxuriance with time. On its first coming into general use, the clergy had cried out against it as ministering to the vanity and extravagance of the age; but in a while many of them adopted its use, for, as Granger remarks, "it was observed that a periwig procured many persons a respect and even veneration which they mere strangers to before, and to which they had not the least claim from their personal merit."

Amongst other strange innovations and various improvements known in this reign, the introduction of a penny post may be considered the most useful. King James I., of happy memory, had, in imitation of like regulations in other countries, established a general post for foreign parts; King Charles I. had given orders to Thomas Witherings, Esquire, his postmaster-general, to settle "a running post or two, to run night and day between Edinburgh, in Scotland, and the city of London, to go thither and back in six days;" but the organization of a penny post, for the conveyance of letters and parcels throughout the capital and suburbs, was reserved for the reign of the merry monarch. This beneficial scheme was originated by an upholsterer named Murray, who communicated it to one William Dockwra, a man who for over ten years had laboured with fidelity in the Custom House. Uniting their efforts, they, with great labour and vast expense, carried the plan into execution in the year 1680.

The principal office was stationed at the residence of William Dockwra, in Lime Street; seven sorting-houses and as many as four hundred receiving-houses were speedily established in the cities of London, Westminster, and the suburbs;

and a great number of clerks and messengers were employed to collect, enter, and deliver parcels and letters not exceeding one pound in weight nor ten pounds in value. Stamps were used as an acknowledgment that postage was paid, and likewise to mark the hours when letters were sent out from the offices, by which, in case of delay, its cause might be traced to the messengers; and deliveries took place ten times in the vicinity of the Exchange and Inns of Court, and four times in the suburbs daily. All persons were requested to post their communications before six o'clock in the winter, and seven in the summer, on Saturday nights, "that the many poor men employed may have a little time to provide for their families against the Lord's Day." And it was moreover intimated that upon three days at Christmas, and two at Easter and Whitsuntide, as likewise upon the 30th of January, the post would not be delivered.

From the first this scheme promised success, the manner in which it was carried out being wholly admirable; yet there were many who raised their voices against it persistently. Porters and messengers declared it took away their means of subsistence; whilst those of higher grade were confident it was a contrivance of the papists, which enabled them to carry out their wicked schemes with greater security. But these illusions vanished with time; and the penny post became such a success that Government laid claim to it as a branch of the General Post Office, and annexed its revenues to the Crown. [In the year 1703 Queen Anne bestowed a grant on Elizabeth, Dowager countess of Thanet, to erect a penny post-office in Dublin, similar to that in existence in London.]

Another innovation in this interesting reign were stage-coaches, described as affording "admirable commodiousness both for men and women of better rank, to travel from London and to almost all the villages near this great city, that the like hath not been known in the world, wherein one may be transported to any place, sheltered from foul weather and foul ways, free from endamaging one's health or body by hard jogging or over-violent emotion, and this not only at a low price, as about a shilling for every five miles in a day; for the stage-coaches called flying coaches make forty or fifty miles in a day, as from London to Cambridge or Oxford, and that in the space of twelve hours, not counting the time for dining, setting forth not too early, nor coming in too late."

Likewise were divorce suits introduced whilst Charles II. sat upon the throne for the first time--if the case of Henry VIII. be excepted--when my Lord Rosse, in consequence of the misconduct of his lady, had a bill brought into the House of Lords for dissolving his marriage and enabling him to wed again. There being at this period, 1669, a project for divorcing the king from the queen, it was considered Lord Rosse's suit, if successful, would facilitate a like bill in favour of his majesty. After many and stormy debates his lordship gained his case by a majority of two votes. It is worth noting that two of the lords spiritual, Dr. Cosin, Bishop of Durham, and Dr. Wilkins, Bishop of Chester, voted in favour of the bill.

The social history of this remarkable reign would be incomplete without mention of the grace and patronage which Charles II. extended towards the Society of Antiquaries. This learned body, according to Stow, had been in existence since the days of Elizabeth; but for lack of royal acknowledgment of its worth and lore, was permitted to languish in neglect and finally become extinct. However, under the commonwealth the society had revived, from the fact that numbers of the nobility being unemployed in affairs of state, and having no court to attend, applied themselves whilst in retirement to the study of chemistry, mathematics, mechanism, and natural philosophy. The Duke of Devonshire, Marquis of Worcester, Viscount Brouncker, Honourable Robert Boyle, and Sir Robert Murray, built laboratories, made machines, opened mines, and perfected inventions. When the temper of the times permitted, these men, with various others of like tastes, drew together, held weekly meetings at Gresham College in Bishopsgate Street, discoursed on abstruse subjects, and heard erudite lectures, from Dr. Petty on chemistry, from Dr. Wren on astronomy, from Mr. Laurence Rooke on geometry; so that the Society of Antiquaries may be said to have been founded in the last years of the republic.

Now Charles II., having some knowledge of chemistry and science, looked upon the society with favourable eyes; and in the first year of his restoration desired to become one of its members; expressed satisfaction it had been placed upon a proper basis in his reign; represented the difficulty of its labours; suggested certain investigations, and declared his interest in all its movements. Moreover, in the year 1662 he bestowed on the society a charter in which he styled himself its founder and patron; presented it with a silver mace to be borne before the president on meeting days; and gave it the use of the royal arms for a seal. Nor did his concern for its welfare cease here. He was frequently present at its meetings, and occasionally witnessed, and assisted "with his own hands," in the performance of experiments. Some of these were of a singularly interesting character; amongst which may be mentioned infusion of the blood of an animal into the veins of a man. This took place in the year 1667, the subject being one Arthur Coga, a minister poor in worldly substance, who, in exchange for a guinea, consented to have the operation performed on him. Accordingly two surgeons of great skill and learning, named Lower and King, on a certain day injected twelve ounces of sheep's blood into his veins. After which he smoked an honest pipe in peace, drank a glass of good canary with relish, and found himself no worse in mind or body. And in two days more fourteen ounces of sheep's blood were substituted for eight of his own without loss of virility to him.

Nor were experiments in vivisection unknown to the Royal Society, as it was called, for the "Philosophical Transactions" speak of a dog being tied through the back above the spinal artery, thereby depriving him of motion until the artery was loosened, when he recovered; and again, it is recorded that Dr. Charleton cut the spleen out of a living dog with good success.

The weighty discourses of the learned men who constituted the society frequently delighted his majesty; though it must be confessed he sometimes laughed at them, and once sorely puzzled them by asking the following question. "Supposing," said Charles, assuming a serious expression, and speaking in a solemn tone, "two pails of water were placed in two different scales and weighed alike, and that a live bream or small fish was put into one, now why should not the pail in which it was placed weigh heavier than the other?" Most members were troubled to find the king a fitting reply, and many strange theories were advanced by way of explaining why the pail should not be found heavier, none of them being thought satisfactory. But at last a man sitting far down the table was heard to express an opinion, when those surrounding him laughed; hearing which the king, who had not caught his words, asked him to repeat them. "Why, your majesty," said he boldly, "I do believe the pail would weigh heavier." "Odds-fish!" cried Charles, bursting out into laughter, "you are right, my honest fellow!" and so the merriment became general.

The Royal Society was composed of men of quality with a genius for investigation, and men of learning eager for further knowledge. Persons of all nationalities, religions, and professions were admitted members; and it was continually enriched by the addition of curiosities, amongst which in particular were an herb which grew in the stomach of a thrush; the skin of a Moor tanned, with the beard and hair white; a clock, having movements directed by loadstone; an ostrich, whose young had been born alive; mummies; strange fish; and the hearts and livers of vipers. Likewise was the society endowed with gifts, amongst the most notable being the valuable library of Henry Howard, afterwards Duke of Norfolk.

Fostered by this society, science received its first impulse towards the astounding progress it has since achieved. Nay, in this reign the germs of some inventions were sown, which, subsequently springing into existence, have startled the world by their novelty, utility, and power, Monsieur Sorbiere, when in England, was shown a journal kept by Montconis, concerning the transactions of the Royal Society, in which several new devices, "which scarce can be believed unless seen," were described. Amongst these were an instrument for showing alterations in the weather, whether from heat, cold, wind, or rain; a method for blowing up ships; a process for purifying salt water, so that it could be drunk; and an instrument by which those ignorant of drawing could sketch and design any object. He also states Dr. Wallis had taught one born deaf and dumb to read.

In 1663, "the right honourable (and deservedly to be praised and admired) Edward Somerset, Marquis of Worcester," published a quaint volume entitled "A Century of the Names and Scantlings of such Inventions as at present I can call to mind to have tried and perfected, which (my former notes being lost) I have, at the instance of a powerful friend, endeavoured to set down in such a way as may sufficiently instruct me to put any of them in practice." Amongst these are enumerated false decks, such as in a moment should kill and take prisoners as many as should board the ship, without blowing her up, and in a quarter of an hour's time should recover their former shape without discovering the secret; a portable fortification, able to contain five hundred men, which in the space of six hours might be set up, and made cannon-proof; a dexterous tinder-box which served as a pistol, and was yet capable of lighting a fire or candle at any hour of the night without giving its possessor the trouble of stretching his hand from bed; a lock, the ways of opening which might be varied ten millions of times, but which on a stranger touching it would cause an alarm that could not be stopped, and would register what moneys had been taken from its keeping; a boat which would work against wind and tide; with various other discoveries to the number of one hundred, all arrived at from mathematical studies.

The means of propelling a boat against such disadvantages, to which the Marquis of Worcester alludes, was in all probability by steam-power. This he described as "an admirable and most forcible way to drive up water by fire," the secret of which he is believed to have first discovered. [Before the century was concluded, Captain Savery contrived a steam-engine which was certainly the first put to practical uses. It has been stated that he owed the knowledge of this invention to hints conveyed in Lord Worcester's little volume.] In the preface to his little book, the marquis states he had sacrificed from six to seven hundred thousand pounds in bringing his various inventions to perfection; after which it is satisfactory to find he derived some profit from one of them, conceived, as he says, "by heavenly inspiration." This was a water-engine for drying marsh-lands and mines, requiring neither pump, suckers, barrels, bellows, nor external nor additional help, save that afforded from its own operations. This engine Sorbiere describes as one of the most curious things he had a mind to see, and says one man by the help of this machine raised four large buckets full of water in an instant forty feet high, through a pipe eight inches long. An act of parliament was passed enabling the marquis to reap the benefit and profit from this invention, subject to a tenth part which was reserved for the king and his heirs.

The Royal Society soon became one of the foremost objects of interest in the city. Foreigners of distinction were conducted to its rooms that they might behold the visible signs of knowledge it could proudly boast; and women of culture were admitted to hear the lectures its members delivered.

Amongst these latter may be mentioned the eccentric Duchess of Newcastle; a lady who dressed her footmen in velvet coats, habited herself in antique gowns, wrote volumes of plays and poetry, desired the reputation of learning, and indulged in circumstances of pomp and state. Having expressed her desire to be present at one of the meetings of the Royal Society, the council prepared to receive her, not, it must be admitted, without some fear her extravagance would expose them to the ridicule of the town, and place them fit the mercy of ballad-mongers. So it happened one fair May-day, in the year 1667 a vast concourse of people had assembled to witness her arrival at Arundel House in the Strand, where the society held its meetings for some years after the burning of Gresham College. And she in good time reaching there, surrounded by her maids of honour, gentlemen in waiting, and lackeys, was met by the president, Viscount Brouncker, having his mace carried before him, and was conducted to the great room. When the meeting was over, various experiments were tried for her satisfaction; amongst others a piece of roasted mutton was turned into pure blood. The while she witnessed these sights, crowds of gallants gathered round her that they might catch and retain such fine things as fell from her lips; but she only cried out her wonder and admiration at all she saw; and at the end of her visit was conducted in state to her coach by several noble lords, notable amongst whom was a vastly pretty young man, Francis Seymour, fifth Duke of Somerset.

CHAPTER XXI.

A period rich in literature.--John Milton's early life.--Writing "Paradise Lost."--Its publication and success.--His later works and death.--John Dryden gossips with wits and players.--Lord Rochester's revenge.--Elkanah Settle.--John Crowne.--Thomas Otway rich in miseries.--Dryden assailed by villains.--The ingenious Abraham Cowley.--The author of "Hudibras."--Young Will Wycherley and Lady Castlemaine--The story of his marriage.--Andrew Marvell, poet and politician.--John Bunyan.

The men of genius who lived in the days of the merry monarch have rendered his reign, like that of Elizabeth, illustrious in the annals of literature. The fact of "Paradise Lost," the "Pilgrim's Progress," "Hudibras," and "Alexander's Feast" being given to the world whilst Charles II. occupied the throne, would have sufficiently marked the epoch as one exceeding in intellectual brilliancy; but besides these works, an abundance of plays, poems, satires, treatises, and histories added fresh lustre to this remarkable age.

At the period of the restoration, John Milton had reached his fifty-second year. He had studied in the University of Cambridge; published the "Masque of Comus;" likewise a treatise against the Established Church; taught school at Aldersgate Street; married a wife and advocated divorce; printed a pamphlet to compose the minds of those disturbed by the murder of Charles I.; as also a defence of his murderers, justifying the monarch's execution, for which the author was awarded a thousand pounds; had become secretary to Cromwell, whom he stooped to flatter; and had even, on the advent of his majesty's return, written and set forth "A Ready and Easy Way to establish a Free Commonwealth." ["To your virtue," writes John Milton to Oliver Cromwell, "overpowering and resistless, every man gives way, except some who, without equal qualifications, aspire to equal honours, who envy the distinctions of merit greater than their own, and who have yet to learn that, in the coalition of human society, nothing is more pleasing to God, or more agreeable to reason, than that the highest mind should have the sovereign power. Such, sir, are you, by general confession: such are the things achieved by you, the greatest and most glorious of our countrymen, the director of our public councils, the leader of unconquered armies the father of your country; for by that title does every good man hail you with sincere and voluntary praise."]

On the landing of Charles II. Milton withdrew to the privacy afforded by a residence in Bartholomew Close, near West Smithfield. For a time he was apprehensive of punishment. His pamphlet justifying the late king's execution was, with others of a like kind, burned by the common hangman; but though parliament ordered the attorney-general would prosecute the authors of these works, Milton was neither seized nor brought to trial. Soon after his arrival, Charles published an act of grace promising free pardon to those instrumental in overthrowing his father's government, with the exception of such as had contrived his death; and inasmuch as Milton had but justified that monstrous act after it had taken place, he escaped condemnation. Moreover, he received a special pardon, which passed the privy seal in December, 1660. His escape has been attributed to his friend Davenant. This loyal soldier had, when taken by Cromwell's troopers in the civil war, been condemned to speedy death; from which, by Milton's intercession, he escaped; an act of mercy Davenant now repaid in kind, by appealing to his friends in behalf of the republican's safety.

Having secured his freedom, Milton lived in peace and obscurity in Jewin Street, near Aldersgate Street. During the commonwealth his first wife, the mother of his three children, had died; on which he sought solace and companionship in a union with Catherine Woodcock, who survived her marriage but twelve months; and being left free once more, he, in the year of grace 1661, entered into the bonds of holy matrimony for a third time, with Elizabeth Minshul, a lady of excellent family and shrewish temper, who rendered his daughters miserable in their father's lifetime, and defrauded them after his death.

In order to support his family he continued to keep a school, and likewise employed himself in writing "Paradise Lost" the composition of which he had begun five years previously. From his youth upwards he had been ambitious to furnish the world with some important work; and prevision of resulting fame had given him strength and fortitude in periods of difficulty and depression. And now the time had arrived for realization of his dream, though stricken by blindness, harassed by an unquiet wife, and threatened by poverty, he laboured sore for fame. The more fully to enjoy quiet necessary to his mental condition, he removed to a house in Artillery Walk, Bunhill Fields. His life was one of simplicity. He rose as early as four o'clock in summer and five in winter, and being "smit with the love of sacred song," had a chapter of the Bible read to him; studied until twelve, dined frugally at one, and afterwards held discourse with such friends as came to visit him.

One of these was Thomas Elwood, a quaker much esteemed amongst good men, who, in order that he might enjoy the advantages of the poet's conversation, read Latin to him every afternoon save Sunday. The whilst his voice rose and fell in regular monotony, the blind man drank his words with thirsty ears; and so acute were the senses remaining to him, that when Elwood read what he did not understand, Milton perceived it by the inflection of his voice, and stopped him to explain the passage. In fair weather the poet wandered abroad, enjoying the fragrance of sweet pasture land, and the warmth of glad sunlight he might not behold. And anon, seated in a high-backed chair without his door, his straight pale face full of repose and dignity, his light brown hair falling in curls upon his shoulders, his large grey eyes, "clear to outward view of blemish or of spot," fixed on vacancy, his figure clad in coarse cloth--he received those who sought his society.

In their absence the poet spent solitary hours conning over as many lines of the great poem as his memory could store, until one of his friends arrived, and relieved him by taking the staazas down. Frequently his nephew, Edward Philips, performed this task for him. To him Milton was in the habit of showing his work as it advanced, and Philips states he found it frequently required correction in orthography and punctuation, by reason of the various hands which had written it. As summer advanced, he was no longer favoured by a sight of the poem; inquiring the reason of which, Milton told him "his vein never happily flowed but from the autumnal equinox to the vernal; and that whatever he attempted at other times was never to his satisfaction, though he courted his fancy never so much."

In the year 1665 "Paradise Lost" was completed, but no steps were taken towards its publication, as the author, in company with his neighbours, fled from the dreaded plague. The following year the citizens were harassed by losses sustained from the great fire, so that Milton did not seek to dispose of his poem until 1667; when, on the 27th of April, it was sold to Samuel Simmons, a publisher residing in Aldersgate Street. The agreement entered into stated Milton should receive an immediate payment of five pounds, with the stipulation that he should be given an equal sum on sale of thirteen hundred copies of the first edition, and five pounds on disposal of the same number of the second edition, and yet five pounds more after another such sale of the third edition. Each edition was to number fifteen hundred books. Two years after the publication of "Paradise Lost," its author received the second payment of five pounds; five years later a third payment was made him; before the fourth fell due his life had been set free from care.

From the first his poem had come in contact with a few receptive minds, and borne the blessed fruit of appreciation. Richardson recounts that Sir John Denham, a poet and man of culture, one morning brought a sheet of the great epic fresh from the press to his friend Sir George Hungerford. "Why, what have you there?" asked the latter. "Part of the noblest poem that was ever written in any, language or in any age," said Sir John, as he laid the pages before him. And a few weeks later my Lord Dorset, looking over a bookstall in Little Britain, found a copy of this work, which he opened carelessly at first, until he met some passages which struck him with surprise and filled him with admiration: observing which the honest bookseller besought him to speak in favour of the poem, for it lay upon his hands like so much waste-paper. My lord bought a copy, carried it home, read and sent it to Dryden, who, in due time returning the volume, expressed his opinion of its merits in flattering terms. "The author," said he, "cuts us all out--aye, even the ancients too."

Such instances as these were, however, few in number. That the work did not meet with wider appreciation and quicker sale is not surprising when it is called to mind that from 1623 to 1664 but two editions of Shakespeare's works, comprising in all about one thousand copies, had been printed. In an age when learning was by no means universal, and polite reading uncommon, it was indeed a scource of congratulation, rather than a topic for commiseration, that the work of a republican had in two years reached a sale of thirteen hundred copies.

Before a third edition was required his fame had spread. The house in which he had been born, in Bread Street, was shown with pride to foreign visitors; parents sent their sons to read to him, that they might reap the benefit of his remarks. The latter testimony to his genius was a tribute the blind poet appreciated. But it happened there were times and seasons when these obliging youths were not at hand, or when it was inconvenient for him to receive them. On such occasions he demanded that his daughters should read him the books he required, though these were frequently written in Hebrew, Greek, Latin, Italian, and Spanish--languages of which they were wholly ignorant. The torment this inflicted on those striving to pronounce unaccustomed words which had no meaning to their ears, and the torture endured by him, may readily be conceived. Expressions of complaint on the one side, and of pain on the other, continually interrupted the readings, which were eventually wholly abandoned; the poet sending his children, whose education was so limited that they were unable to write, to learn "ingenious sorts of manufacture proper for women, particularly embroideries in gold and Silver."

When in 1665 Milton had shown his poem to Elwood, the good quaker observed, "Thou hast said a great deal upon Paradise Lost: what hast thou to say upon Paradise Found?" This question resting in the poet's mind, in due time produced fruit; for no sooner had his first poem been published than he set about composing the latter, which, under the name of "Paradise Regained," was given to the world in 1670 "This," said he to Elwood, "is owing to you; for you put it into my head by the question which you put to me, which otherwise I had not thought of." This poem, he believed, had merits far superior to those of "Paradise Lost," which he could not bear to hear praised in preference to "Paradise Regained." In the same year he published "Samson Agonistes," and two years later a treatise on "Logic," and another on "True Religion, Heresy, Schism, Toleration, and the Best Methods to Prevent the Growth of Popery." In this, the mind which had soared to heaven and descended to hell in its boundless flight, argues that catholics should not be allowed the right of public or private worship. In the last year of his life he republished his "Juvenile Poems," together with "Familiar Epistles in Latin."

He had now reached his sixty-sixth year. His life had been saddened by blindness, his health enfeebled by illness, his domesticity troubled by his first marriage and his last, his desires disappointed by the result of political events. So that when, on the 10th of November, 1674, death summoned him, he departed without regret.

Amongst those who visited Milton was John Dryden, whom the author of "Paradise Lost" regarded as "a good rhymester, but no poet," an opinion with which posterity has not held. At the restoration, John Dryden was in his twenty-ninth year. The son of Sir Erasmus Dryden, Baronet, of Canons Ashby, he enjoyed an income of two hundred pounds a year, a sum then considered sufficient to defray the expenses of a young man of good breeding. He had passed through Westminster School, taken a degree at Cambridge, written a eulogistic stanza on the death of Cromwell, and a joyous poem on the happy restoration of the merry monarch.

Three years after the arrival of his majesty, Dryden's comedy entitled "The Wild Gallant" was produced, this being the first of twenty-eight plays which followed. In the year 1668 he had the honour to succeed Sir William Davenant as poet laureate, the salary attached to which office was one hundred pounds a year and a tierce of wine. His dignity was moreover enhanced, though his happiness was by no means increased, by his marriage with the Lady Elizabeth Howard, daughter of the Earl of Berkshire. For my lady's temper sorely marred the poet's peace, and left such impressions upon his mind, that to the end of his days his invectives against the bonds of matrimony were bitter and deep. In justice it must be mentioned the Lady Elizabeth's mental condition was supposed to be unsettled; a conjecture which was proved true by a madness which befell her, subsequent to her husband's death.

Dryden was now a well known figure in town, consorting with men of the highest quality and parts, and gossiping with wits and players who frequented Will's coffee-house. Here, indeed, a special chair was appropriated to his use; which being placed by the fire in winter, and on the balcony in summer, he was pleased to designate as his winter and his summer seat. At Will's he was wont to hold forth on the ingenuity of his plays, the perfection of his poems, and the truth of astrology. It was whilst leaving this coffee house one night a memorable occurrence befell the poet, of which more anon.

It happened at one time the brilliant, poetical, and mercurial Earl of Rochester extended his favour and friendship towards Dryden, gratified by which, the poet had, after the manner of those days, dedicated a play to him, "Marriage a la Mode." This favour his lordship received with graciousness, and no doubt repaid with liberality. After a while, Dryden, led by choice or interest, sought a new patron in the person of the Earl of Mulgrave. For this nobleman Rochester had long entertained a bitter animosity, which had arisen from rivalry, and had been intensified from the fact that Rochester, refusing to fight him, had been branded as a coward. Not daring to attack the peer, Rochester resolved to avenge himself upon the poet. In order to effect his humiliation, the earl at once bestowed his favour on Elkanah Settle, a playwright and poet of mean abilities. He had originally been master of a puppet-show, had written verses to order for city pageants, and produced a tragedy in heroic verse, entitled "Cambyses, King of Persia."

His patron being at this time in favour with the king, introduced Settle to the notice of the court, and induced the courtiers to play his second tragedy, "The Empress of Morocco," at Whitehall, before their majesties. This honour, which Dryden, though poet laureate, had never received, gave Elkanah Settle unmerited notoriety; the benefit of which was apparent by the applause his tragedy received when subsequently produced at the Duke's Theatre in Dorset Gardens. Nor did the honour and profit which "The Empress of Morocco" brought him end here; it was published by William Cademan, and had the distinction of being the first English play ever illustrated, or sold for the price of two shillings. It was scarce to be expected, in an age when men ventilated their merest grievances by the publication of pamphlets, Dryden could refrain from pointing out to the public the mistake into which they had fallen by honouring this man. Nor was he singular in his feelings of animosity. The poets Shadwell and Crowne, believing themselves ignored and neglected, whilst their rival was enriched and exalted, joined Dryden in writing a merciless criticism upon Settle's tragedy. This was entitled "The Empress of Morocco, or some few erratas to be printed instead of the sculptures [Illustrations.], with the second edition of the play." In this Settle was described as "an animal of a most deplored intellect, without reading and understanding;" whilst his play was characterized as "a tale told by an idiot, full of noise and fury signifying nothing." To these remarks and others of like quality, Settle replied in the same strain, so that the quarrel diverted the town and even disturbed the quiet of the universities. Time did ample justice to both men; lowering Settle to play the part of a dragon in a booth at Bartholomew Fair, and consecrating Dryden to immortality.

Before the clamour resulting from this dispute had ended, Rochester, fickle and eccentric, grew weary of his PROTEGE and consequently abandoned him. He had not, however, tired of humiliating the laureate, and to mortify him the more, introduced a new poet at court, This was John Crowne, a man then little known to the town, and now best remembered as author of "Sir Courtly Nice," a comedy of wit and entertainment. So well did he succeed in obtaining favour at court, through Rochester's influence, that the queen ordered him to write a masque. This command he immediately obeyed, producing "Calisto, or the Chaste Nymph," which was acted at Whitehall by the Duke of York's fair daughters, the Princesses Mary and Anne, together with many gracious ladies and noble lords. Dryden, probably the better to hide the mortification he felt at seeing his office as laureate unceremoniously usurped, offered to write an epilogue for the occasion; but this service was, through Rochester's interference, rejected. The masque proved a brilliant success; "the dancing, singing, and music, which were all in the highest perfection, and the graceful action, incomparable beauty, and splendid habits of those ladies who accompanied them, afforded the spectators extraordinary delight." "Calisto" was therefore performed thirty times.

The author's gratitude for his lordship's patronage was only equalled by his disappointment upon its hasty withdrawal. Growing weary of him, Rochester found a more worthy object for his favour in Thomas Otway, a poet rich in all the miseries which afflicted genius in those days. Son of the rector of Woolbeding, pupil at Winchester School, and commoner of Christchurch, Cambridge, he had on his arrival in town vainly sought employment as an actor, and barely earned bread as a play-writer. Before he became a PROTEGE of my Lord Rochester he had written "Alcibiades," a tragedy, he being then, in 1665, in his twenty-fifth year. His next play was "Don Carlos, Prince of Spain," which, through the earl's influence, gained great success. In the preface to this tragedy he acknowledges his unspeakable obligations to my lord, who he says made it his business to establish "Don Carlos" in the good opinion of the king and of his royal highness the Duke of York. Unwarned by the fate of his predecessors, and heedless of the fickleness of his patron, he basked in hope in the present, mercifully unconscious of the cruel death by starvation which awaited him in the future. Alas! Rochester not only forsook him, but loaded him with satire in a poem entitled "Session of the Poets."

In verses which he wrote soon after, entitled "An Allusion to the Tenth Satire," Rochester likewise attacked Dryden; who, in the preface of his "All for Love," replied in like manner. Then there appeared an "Essay on Satire," which ridiculed the king, dealt severely with his mistresses, said uncivil things of the courtiers in general, and of my Lord Rochester in particular. The noble earl was indeed described as being "lewd in every limb," affected in his wit, mean in his actions, and cowardly in his disposition. Now, though this was conceived and brought forth by my Lord Mulgrave, Rochester suspected Dryden of its authorship, and resolved to punish him forthwith. Accordingly on the night of the 18th of December, 1679, when Dryden was passing through Rose Street, Covent Garden, on his homeward way from Will's Coffee House, he was waylaid by some ruffians, and, before he could draw his sword, promptly surrounded and severely beaten.

This occurrence caused considerable sensation throughout the town, and though surmises arose in many minds as to who had hired the bravoes, it was found impossible to prove them. In hope of gaining some clue to the instigator of the attack, Dryden caused the following advertisement to be inserted in the LONDON GAZETTE AND DOMESTIC INTELLIGENCE for three consecutive days: "Whereas John Dryden, Esq., was on Monday, the 18th instant, at night, barbarously assaulted and wounded in Rose Street, in Covent Garden, by divers men unknown; if any person shall make discovery of the said offenders to the said Mr. Dryden, or to any justice of the peace, he shall not only receive fifty pounds, which is deposited in the hands of Mr. Blanchard Goldsmith, next door to Temple Bar, for the said purpose; but if he be a principal or an accessory in the said fact, his majesty is graciously pleased to promise him his pardon for the same."

Dryden sought no opportunity for revenge; for which restraint, outliving Rochester, and having a noble mind and generous disposition, he was no doubt glad at heart. Not only did he survive the earl, but likewise the king. To the company and conversation of that gracious sovereign the poet was frequently admitted, a privilege which resulted in satisfaction and pleasure to both. One pleasant day towards the end of his majesty's reign, whilst they walked in the Mall, Charles said to him, "If I were a poet, and indeed I think I am poor enough to be one, I would write a satire on sedition." Taking this hint, Dryden speedily set himself to work, and brought a poem on such a subject to his royal master, who rewarded him with a hundred broad pieces.

Amongst Dryden's friends was the excellent and ingenious Abraham Cowley, whose youth had given the promise of distinction his manhood fulfilled. It is related that when quite a lad, he found in the window recess of his mother's apartment a copy of Spencer's "Faerie Queene." Opening the book, he read it with delight, and his receptive mind reflecting the poet's fire, he resolved likewise to exercise the art of poesy. In 1628, when at the age of ten, he wrote "The Tragic History of Pyramus and Thisbe;" five years later he published a volume of poems; and whilst yet a schoolboy wrote his pastoral comedy, "Love's Riddle."

When at St. John's College, Oxford, he gave proof of his loyalty by writing a poem entitled the "Puritan and the Papist," which gained him the friendship of courtiers. On the Queen of Charles I. taking refuge in France, he soon followed her, and becoming secretary to the Earl of St. Albans, conducted the correspondence between her majesty and the king, ciphering and deciphering their letters, and such as were sent or received by those immediately concerned in the cause of royalty. In this situation he remained until four years previous to the restoration, when he was sent into England for the purpose of observing the condition of the nation, and reporting the same. Scarce had he set foot in London when he was seized, examined, and only liberated on a friend offering bail for him to the amount of one thousand pounds.

The better to disguise the object of his visit, and lull suspicions of republicans, he took out the degree of Doctor of Physic at Oxford; after which he retired into Kent, where he devoted a great portion of his time to the study of botany and the composition of poetry. On Cromwell's death he hastened to France, and remained there until the king's return; which he celebrated by a song of triumph. Like hundreds of others who had served Charles in his exile, he looked forward to gratitude and reward, but met disappointment and neglect. Amongst the numerous places and employments the change of government opened in court and state, not one was offered the loyal poet.

Nay, his hardships did not end here; for having, in 1663, produced his merry comedy, "Cutter of Coleman Street," it was treated with severity as a censure upon the king. Feeling over-nervous to witness the result of its first representation, the poet absented himself from the playhouse; but thither his friends Dryden and Sprat sped, hoping they might be able to bear him tidings of its triumph. When they returned to him at night and told him of its fate, "he received the news of its ill success," says Sprat, "not with so much firmness as might have been expected from so great a man." Of all intent to satirize the king he was entirely innocent--a fact he set before the public in the preface to his play on its publication. Having, he argues, followed the fallen fortunes of the royal family so long, it was unlikely he would select the time of their restoration to quarrel with them.

Feeling his grievances acutely, he now published a poem called "The Complaint," which met with but little success; whereon, depressed by ill-fortune and disgusted by ingratitude, he sought consolation in the peace of a country life. Through the influence of his old friend, Lord St. Albans, and the Duke of Buckingham, he obtained a lease of the queen's lands at Chertsey, which produced him an income of about three hundred pounds a year--a sum sufficient for his few wants and moderate desires. He resided here but two years, when he died, on the 28th of July, 1667. Milton, on hearing of his death, was troubled. The three greatest English poets, he declared, were Spenser, Shakespeare, and Cowley.

The ungrateful neglect with which he was treated in life was sought to be atoned for by useless honours paid him after death. His remains were first conveyed to Wallingford House, then a residence of the Duke of Buckingham, from whence they were carried in a coach drawn by six horses, and followed by all the men of letters and wits of the town, divers stately bishops, courtiers, and men of quality, whose carriages exceeded one hundred in number, to Westminster Abbey. Here the Poet was laid at rest beside Geoffrey Chaucer, and not far removed from gentle Spenser, whose words had first inspired his happy muse.

The literary wealth of this reign was furthermore enhanced by the genius of Butler, the inimitable author of "Hudibras," concerning whom little is known, save that he was born in 1612, and spent his life in poverty. He passed some years as clerk to a justice of the peace; he also served a great man's steward, and acted as secretary to Sir Samuel Luke, one of Cromwell's officers. With those of the commonwealth he held no part; that he was a royalist at heart his great satire indicates. The first part of this was published in the third year of the restoration, and was introduced to the notice of his majesty by my Lord Dorset. So delighted was the monarch by its wit that its lines were continually on his lips, an example speedily followed by the courtiers. It was considered certain a man possessing such brilliant genius and loyal nature would be rewarded with place or pension; but neither boon was bestowed upon him. Resting his hopes on future achievements, the second part of "Hudibras" appeared in 1664; but again his recompense was delayed. Clarendon made him promises of valuable employments, which were never fulfilled; and to soothe his disappointment the king sent him a present of three hundred guineas.

Indignant at the neglect from which he suffered, his friend Wycherley spoke to the Duke of Buckingham on his behalf, saying it was a shame to the court a man of Butler's parts should be allowed to suffer want. With this his grace readily agreed, and promised to use his influence towards remedying the poet's ill-fortune; but time went by, and his condition remained unaltered. Whereon Wycherley conceived the idea of bringing Butler and the duke together, that the latter might the more certainly remember him. He therefore succeeded in making his grace name an hour and place in which they might meet. So it came to pass they were together one day at the Roebuck Tavern; but scarce had Buckingham opened his lips when a pimp of his acquaintance--"the creature was likewise a knight"--passed by with a couple of ladies. To a man of Buckingham's character the temptation was too seductive to be neglected; accordingly, he darted after those who allured him, leaving the needy poet, whom he saw no more. Butler lived until 1680, dying in poverty. Longueville, having in vain solicited a subscription to defray the expenses of the poet's burial in Westminster Abbey, laid him to rest in the churchyard of Covent Garden.

Wycherley, the friend of Butler, though a child of the Muses, was superior to poverty. He was born in the year of grace 1640, and early in life sent for his better education into France. Returning to England soon after the king had come unto his own, young Wycherley entered Queen's College, Oxford, from whence he departed without obtaining a degree. He then betook himself to town, and became a law student. The Temple, however, had less attraction for him than the playhouse. Indeed, before leaving Oxford he had, written a couple of comedies--to wit, "Love in a Wood," and "The Gentleman Dancing Master," a fact entitling him to be considered a man of parts. Not satisfied with this distinction, he soon developed tastes for pleasures of the town, and became a man of fashion. His wit illuminated choice gatherings of congenial spirits at coffee-houses; his epigrams were repeated by boon companions in the precincts of the court.

In the year 1672 his comedy "Love in a Wood" was produced. It immediately gained universal favour, and, moreover, speedily attracted the attention of his majesty's mistress, the Duchess of Cleveland. Wycherley was a man well to look upon:

her grace was a lady eager for adventure. Desiring his acquaintance, and impatient of delay, she introduced herself to his notice in a manner eminently characteristic of the age. It happened when driving one day through Pall Mall, she encountered Wycherley riding in his coach in an opposite direction. Thrusting her head out of the window of her vehicle, she saluted the author with a title unknown to the conversations of polite society in the present day.

The fashionable playwright understanding the motive which prompted her remark, hastily ordered his coach to follow hers; and, overtaking her, uncovered and began a speech becoming so ardent a gallant.

"Madam," said he, "you have been pleased to bestow a title on me which belongs only to the fortunate. Will your ladyship be at the play to-night?"

"Well," replied her grace, well pleased at this beginning, "what if I am there?"

"Why, then," answered he, "I will be there to wait on your ladyship, though I disappoint a fine woman who has made me an assignation."

"So," said this frail daughter of Eve, greedily swallowing his flattery, "you are sure to disappoint a woman who has favoured you for one who has not?"

"Yes," quoth he, readily enough, "if the one who has not favoured me is the finer woman of the two. But he who can be constant to your ladyship till he can find a finer, is sure to die your captive."

That night her grace sat in the front row of the king's box at Drury Lane playhouse, and sure enough there was handsome Will Wycherley sitting in the pit underneath. The gentleman cast his eyes upwards and sighed; the lady looked down and played with her fan; after which preliminaries they fell into conversation which both found far more interesting than the comedy then being enacted before their eyes. This was the beginning of an intimacy concerning which the court made merry, and of which the town spoke scandal. My lady disguised herself as a country wench, and visited his chambers, Mr. Wycherley dedicated his play, "Love in a Wood," to her in elegant phraseology, He was of opinion that she stood as little in need of flattery as her beauty did of art; he was anxious to let the world know he was the greatest admirer she had; and he was desirous of returning her his grateful acknowledgment for the favours he had received from her.

The interest of this romance was presently intensified by the introduction of a rival in the person of the Duke of Buckingham. Probably from fear an intrigue with such a prominent figure would, if indulged in, quickly become known to the king, she refused to encourage Buckingham's love. His grace was not only a passionate lover, but likewise a revengeful man; accordingly, he resolved to punish my lady for her lack of good taste. It therefore became his habit to speak of her intrigues before the court, and to name the individuals who received her favours. Now Wycherley, being amongst these, grew fearful his amour with the duchess should become known to the king, from whom at this time he expected an appointment. Accordingly, he besought his good friends, Lord Rochester and Sir Charles Sedley, to remonstrate on his behalf with the duke. These gentlemen undertook that kindly office, and in order to make the rivals acquainted, besought his grace to sup with the playwright. The duke complying with their request, met Wycherley in a friendly spirit, and soon professed himself delighted with his wit; nay, before the feast was over he drank his health in a bumper of red wine, and declared himself Mr. Wycherley's very good friend and faithful servant henceforth.

Moreover, he was as good as his word; for, being master of the horse, he soon after appointed Wycherley an equerry, and subsequently gave him a commission as captain of a regiment of which he was colonel. Nor did the duke's services to the dramatist end here; for when occasion offered he introduced him to the merry monarch, and so pleased was the king with the author's conversational powers that he admitted him to his friendship. His majesty's regard for Wycherley gradually ripened, and once when he lay ill of fever at his lodgings in Bow Street, Covent Garden, the merry monarch visited him, cheered him with words of kindness, and promised he would send him to Montpelier when he was well enough to travel. For this good purpose Charles sent him five hundred pounds, and Wycherley spent the winter of 1679 abroad.

Previous to this date he had written, besides his first comedy, three others which had been received with great favour by the town, viz., "The Gentleman Dancing Master," "The Country Wife," and "The Plain Dealer." Soon after his return to England the crisis of his life arrived, and he married. His introduction to the lady whom fate ordained to become his wife is not the least singular episode in a remarkable biography. Being at Tunbridge Wells, then a place of fashion and liberty, he was one day walking with a friend named Fairbeard. And it happened as they were passing a book-stall they overheard a gentlewoman inquire for the "Plain

Dealer."

"Madam," says Mr. Fairbeard, uncovering, "since you are for the 'Plain Dealer,' there he is for you;" whereon he led Wycherley towards her.

"This lady," says that gentleman, making her a profound bow, "can bear plain speaking; for she appears to be so accomplished, that what would be compliment said to others, spoken to her would be plain dealing."

"No truly, sir," replied the lady; "I am not without my faults, like the rest of my sex; and yet, notwithstanding all my faults, I love plain dealing, and never am more fond of it than when it points out my errors."

"Then, madam," said Mr. Fairbeard, "you and the plain dealer seem designed by heaven for each other."

These pretty speeches having been delivered and received with every mark of civility, Mr. Wycherley made his exit with the lady, who was none other than the Countess of Drogheda, a young widow gifted with beauty and endowed by fortune. Day by day he waited on her at her lodging, accompanied her in her walks, and attended her to the assemblies. Finally, when she returned to town he married her. It is sad yet true the union did not result in perfect happiness. Mr. Wycherley had a reputation for gallantry, the Countess of Drogheda was the victim of suspicion. Knowing jealousy is beget by love, and mindful of sacrifices she had made in marrying him, Wycherley behaved towards her with much kindness. In compliance with her wishes he desisted visiting the court, a place she probably knew from experience was rife with temptation; and moreover when he cracked a bottle of wine with convivial friends at the Cock Tavern, opposite his lodgings in Bow Street, he, for the greater satisfaction of his wife, would leave the windows open of the room in which he sat, that she might from the vantage ground of her home see there were no hussies in the company.

As proof of her love, she, when dying, settled her fortune upon him; but unhappily his just right was disputed by her family. The case therefore went into litigation, for the expenses of which, together with other debts, Wycherley was cast into prison. Here the brilliant wit, clever writer, and boon companion, was allowed to remain seven long years. When released from this vile bondage, another king than the merry monarch occupied the English throne.

The name of Andrew Marvel is inseparably connected with this period. He was born in the year 1620 in the town of Kingston-upon-Hull; his father being a clever school-master, worthy minister, and "an excellent preacher, who never broached what he had never brewed, but that which he had studied some compitent time before." At the age of fifteen, Andrew Marvell was sent to Trinity College, Cambridge. But he had not long been there when he withdrew himself, lured, as some authorities state, by wiles of the wicked Jesuits; repulsed, as others say, by severities of the head of his college. Leaving the university, he set out for London, where his father, who hastened thither in search of him, found him examining some old volumes on a book-stall. He was prevailed to return to his college, where, in 1638, he took his degree as bachelor of arts.

On the completion of his studies and death of his father, he travelled through Holland, France, and Italy. Whilst abroad he began to produce those satirical verses such as were destined to render him famous. One of his earliest efforts in this direction was aimed at the Abbe de Maniban, a learned ecclesiastic, whose chief fault in Marvell's eyes lay in the fact of his professing to judge characters from handwriting.

Whilst in Italy, Andrew Marvell met John Milton, and they having many tastes and convictions in common, became fast friends. In 1653, the former returned to England, and for some time acted as tutor to Mistress Fairfax; he being an excellent scholar, and a great master of the Latin tongue. He now led a peaceful and obscure life until 1657. In that year, Milton, "laying aside," as he wrote, "those jealousies, and that emulation which mine own condition might suggest to me," introduced him to Bradshaw; soon after which he was made assistant-secretary to Milton, who was then in the service of Cromwell.

He had not been long engaged in this capacity, when the usurper died; and Marvell's occupation being gone, the goodly burgesses of the town of Hull, who loved him well, elected him as their representative in parliament, for which service, in accordance with a custom of the time, he was paid. The salary, it is true, was not large, amounting to two shillings a day for borough members; yet when kindly feeling and honest satisfaction mutually existed between elector and representative, as in Marvell's case, the wage was at times supplemented by such acceptable additions as home-cured pork and home-brewed ale, "We must first give you thanks," wrote Marvell on one occasion to his constituents, on the receipt of a cask of beer, "for the kind present you have pleased to send us, which will give occasion to us to remember you often; but the quantity is so great, that it might make sober men forgetful."

He now, in the warfare of political life, made free use of his keen wit and bitter sarcasm as serviceable weapons. These were chiefly employed in exposing measures he considered calculated to ruin the country, though they might gratify the king. However, he had no hatred of monarchy, but would occasionally divert Charles by the sharpness of his satire and brilliancy of his wit. Considering how valuable these would be if employed in service of the court, Charles resolved to tempt Marvell's integrity. For this purpose the Lord Treasurer Danby sought and found him in his chamber, situated in the second floor of a mean house standing in a court off the Strand. Groping his way up the dark and narrow staircase of the domicile, the great minister stumbled, and falling against a door, was precipitated into Marvell's apartment, head foremost. Surprised at his appearance, the satirist asked my Lord Danby if he had not mistaken his way. "No," said the courtier with a bow, "not since I have found Mr. Marvell." He then proceeded to tell him that the king, being impressed by a high sense of his abilities, was desirous of serving him. Apprehending what services were expected in return, Marvell answered that he who accepted favours from the court was bound to vote in its interests. "Nay," said my lord, "his majesty but desires to know if there is any place at court you would accept." On which Marvell replied he could receive nothing with honour, for either he must treat the king with ingratitude by refusing compliance with court measures, or be a traitor to his country by yielding to them. The only favour he therefore begged was, that his majesty would esteem him a loyal subject; the truer to his interests in refusing his offers than he would be by accepting them. It is stated that Lord Danby, surprised at so much purity in an age of corruption, furthermore tempted him with a bag of gold, which Marvell obstinately refused to accept.

He died suddenly in the year 1678, leaving behind him a reputation for humour and satire which has rarely been excelled.

Besides these poets and dramatists, there were other great men, who as prose writers, helped to render the literary history of the period remarkable for its brilliancy. Amongst these were Lord Clarendon, High Chancellor of England, concerning whom much has already been said; and Thomas Hobbs of Malmesbury, better known as author of "The History of the Causes of the Civil War," and of "Human Nature," than as a translator of the Iliad and the Odyssey. Dr. Gilbert Burnet, author of "The History of his Own Times;" and Dr. Ralph Cudworth, author of "The True Intellectual System of the Universe," were likewise men of note. But one whose name is far more familiar than any writer of his time is John Bunyan, author of "The Pilgrim's Progress."

He was the son of a tinker, and was born within a mile of Bedford town in the year 1628. He imbibed at an early age the spirit of Puritanism, fought in the civil wars, took to himself a wife, and turned preacher. Six months after the merry monarch landed, Bunyan was flung into Bedford gaol, where, rather than refrain from puritanical discourses, in the utterance of which he believed himself divinely inspired, he remained, with some short intervals of liberty, for twelve years. When offered freedom at the price of silence, he replied, "If you let me out to-day, I will preach to-morrow." Nay, even in his confinement he delivered sermons to his fellow-prisoners; and presently he commenced to write. His convictions leading him to attack the liturgy of the Church of England, and the religion of the Quakers, his productions became popular amongst dissenters. At length, by an act annulling the penal statutes against Protestant Nonconformists and Roman Catholics, passed in 1671, he was liberated. When he left prison he carried with him a portion of his "Pilgrim's Progress," which was soon after completed and published, though at what date remains uncertain. In 1678 a second edition was printed, and such was the growth of its popularity, that six editions were issued within the following four years.

Now he became famous, his lot was far different from what it had been; his sermons were heard by eager audiences, his counsel was sought by those in trouble, his prayers were regarded as the utterances of inspiration. Once a year he rode, attended by vast crowds, from Bedford Town to London City, that he might preach to those burdened by sin; and from the capital he made a circuit of the country, where he was hailed as a prophet. His life extended beyond the reign of King Charles; his influence lasted till his death.

CHAPTER XXII.

Time's flight leaves the king unchanged.--The Rye House conspiracy.--Profligacy of the court.--The three duchesses.--The king is taken ill.--The capital in consternation.--Dr. Ken questions his majesty.--A Benedictine monk sent for.--Charles professes catholicity and receives the Sacraments.--Farewell to all.--His last night on earth.--Daybreak and death.--He rests in peace.

His majesty's habits changed but little with the flight of time, To the end of his reign the court continued brilliant and profligate. Wits, courtezans, and adventurers crowded the royal drawing-rooms, and conversed without restraint; the monarch pursued his pleasures with unsatiated zest, taking to himself two new mistresses, Lady Shannon and Catherine Peg, who respectively bore him a daughter and a son, duly created Countess of Yarmouth and Earl of Plymouth. For a while, indeed, a shadow fell upon the life of the merry monarch, when, in 1683, he was roused to a sense of danger by discovery of the Rye House conspiracy.

This foul plot, entered into by the Whigs on failure of the Exclusion Bill, had for its object the murder of his majesty and of the Duke of York. Before arriving at maturity its existence and intentions were revealed by one of the conspirators, when William Lord Russell, the Earl of Essex, and Algernon Sidney, second son of the Earl of Leicester, were arrested and charged with high treason. My Lord Essex died in the Tower by his own hand; Lord Russell was condemned on testimony of one witness, and duly executed; as was likewise Algernon Sidney, whose writings on Republicanism were used as evidence against him. On the revelation of this wicked scheme the country became wildly excited, and the king grievously afflicted. A melancholy seized upon his majesty, who stirred not abroad without double guards; and the private doors of Whitehall and avenues of the park were closed.

From this condition, however, he gradually recovered, and resumed his usual habits. Accordingly, we find him engaged in "luxurious dalliance and prophaneness" with the Duchess of Mazarine, and visiting the Duchess of Portsmouth betimes in her chamber, where that bold and voluptuous woman, fresh risen from bed, sat in loose garments talking to the king and his gallants, the while her maids combed her beautiful hair.

"I can never forget," says John Evelyn, writing on the 4th of February, 1685, "the inexpressible luxury and prophaneness, gaming, and all dissoluteness, and as it were total forgetfullnesse of God (it being Sunday evening), which this day se'nnight I was witness of, the king sitting and toying with his concubines, Portsmouth, Cleveland, and Mazarine, etc., a French boy singing love songs in that glorious gallery, whilst about twenty of the greate courtiers and other dissolute persons were at basset round a large table, a bank of at least two thousand in gold before them, upon which two gentlemen who were with me made reflections with astonishment. Six days after was all in the dust."

For now the end of all things had come for Charles Stuart. It happened on the morning of the 2nd of February, 1685, the day being Monday, the king whilst in his bedroom was seized by an apoplectic fit, when crying out, he fell back in his chair, and lay as one dead. Wildly alarmed, his attendants summoned Dr. King, the physician in waiting, who immediately bled him, and had him carried to bed. Then tidings spread throughout the palace, that his majesty hovered betwixt life and death; which should claim him no man might say. Whereon the Duke of York hastened to his bedside, as did likewise the queen, her face blanched, her eyes wild with terror. His majesty after some time recovering consciousness, slowly realized his sad condition. Then he conceived a fear, the stronger as begotten by conviction, that the sands of his life had run their course. Throughout that day and the next he fainted frequently, and showed symptoms of epilepsy. On Wednesday he was cupped and bled in both jugulars; but on Thursday he was pronounced better, when the physicians, anxious to welcome hope, spoke of his probable recovery.

But, alas, the same evening he grew restless, and signs of fever became apparent. Jesuits' powders, then of great repute, were given him, but with no good result. Complaining of a pain in his side, the doctors drew twelve ounces more of blood from him. Exhaustion then set in; all hope of life was over.

Meanwhile, the capital was in a state of consternation. Prayers for his majesty's recovery were offered up in all churches throughout the city; likewise in the royal chapels, where the clergy relieved each other every quarter of an hour. Crowds gathered by day and night without the palace gates, eager to learn the latest change in the king's condition from those who passed to and fro. Inside Whitehall all was confusion. Members of the Privy Council assembled in the room adjoining that where the monarch lay; politicians and ambassadors conversed in whispers in the disordered apartments; courtiers of all degrees flocked through the corridors bearing signs of deep concern upon their countenances.

And amongst others who sought his majesty's presence was the Archbishop of Canterbury, together with the Bishops of London, Durham, Ely, and Bath and Wells; all being anxious to render spiritual services to the king. Of these good men, Charles liked best Dr. Ken, Bishop of Bath and Wells, having most faith in his honesty. For, when his lordship was a prebend of Winchester, it had happened Charles passed through that city, accompanied by Nell Gwynn, when Dr. Ken refused to receive her beneath his roof even at the king's request. This proof of integrity so pleased his majesty, that he gave him the next vacant bishopric by way of reward. And now, his lordship being at hand, he read prayers for the Sick from out the Common Prayer Book for his benefit, until coming to that part where the dying are exhorted to make confession of their sins, when the bishop paused and said such was not obligatory. He then asked his majesty if he were sorry for the iniquities of his life? when the sick man, whose heart was exceeding heavy, replied he was; whereon the bishop pronounced absolution, and asked him if he would receive the Sacrament. To this Charles made no reply, until the same question had been repeated several times, when his majesty answered he would think of it.

The Duke of York, who stood by the while, noting the king's answer, and aware of his tendencies towards Catholicism, bade those who had gathered round stand aside; and then, bending over him, asked in a low tone if he might send for a priest. A look of unspeakable relief came into the king's face, and he answered, "For God's sake do, brother, and lose no time." Then another thought flashing across his mind, he said, "But will not this expose you to much danger?" James made answer, "Though it cost me my life I will bring you a priest." He then hurried into the next room, where, among all the courtiers, he could find no man he could trust, save a foreigner, one Count Castelmachlor. Calling him aside, he secretly despatched him in search of a priest.

Between seven and eight o'clock that evening, Father Huddleston, the Benedictine friar who had aided the king's escape after the battle of Worcester, awaited at the queen's back stairs the signal to appear in his majesty's presence. The duke being made aware of the fact, announced it to the king, who thereon ordered all in his room to withdraw; but James, mindful that slander might afterwards charge him with killing his brother, begged the Earl of Bath, the lord of the bedchamber then in waiting, and the Earl of Feversham, captain of the guard, might stay--saying to the king it was not fitting he should be unattended in his weak condition. These gentlemen therefore remained. And no sooner had all others departed than the monk was admitted by a private entrance to the chamber. The king received him with great joy and satisfaction, stating he was anxious to die in the communion of the catholic church, and declaring he was sorry for the wrongs of his past life, which he yet hoped might be pardoned through the merits of Christ.

He then, as we read in the Stuart Papers, "with exceeding compunction and tenderness of heart," made an exact confession of his sins, after which he repeated an act of contrition, and received absolution. He next desired to have the other Sacraments of the church proper to his condition administered to him: on which the Benedictine asked if he desired to receive the Eucharist; eagerly he replied, "If I am worthy pray fail not to let me have it." Then Father Huddleston, after some exhortation, prepared to give him the Sacrament; when the dying man, struggling to raise himself, exclaimed, "Let me meet my heavenly Lord in a better posture than lying in bed." But the priest begged he would not move, and then gave him the Communion, which he received with every sign of fervour. And for some time he prayed earnestly, the monk and the duke kneeling by the while, silence obtaining in the room. This was presently broken by the sad and solemn tones of the priest's voice, reading a commendation of the soul to its Maker: the which being ended, the Benedictine, with tears in his eyes, took leave of his majesty. "Ah," said Charles, "you once saved my body; you have now saved my soul." Then the monk gave him his benediction, and departed as quietly as he had come.

Then those waiting without were once more admitted to the room, when

Charles nerved himself to take a sad farewell of those around him. He first publicly thanked his brother for the services and affection he had ever rendered him through life, and extolled his obedience and submission to his commands. Giving him his keys, he said he had left him all he possessed, and prayed God would bless him with a happy and prosperous reign. Finally, he recommended all his children to him by name, excepting only the Duke of Monmouth then in Holland, and suffering from the king's displeasure; and besought him to extend his kindness towards the Duchesses of Portsmouth and Cleveland; "and do not," said he, "let poor Nelly starve." Whilst these commands were addressed him, the duke had flung himself on his knees by the bedside, and, bursting into tears, kissed his brother's hand.

The queen, who had scarce left his majesty since the beginning of his illness, was at this time absent, her love and grief not permitting her to endure this afflicting scene. He spoke most tenderly of her; and when presently she sent a message praying he would pardon her absence in regard to her excessive grief, and forgive her withal if at any time she had offended him, he replied, "Alas, poor woman! She beg my pardon?--I beg hers, with all my heart." He next summoned his children to him, one by one, and addressing them with words of advice, embraced them heartily and blessed them fervently. And he being the Lord's anointed, the bishops present besought he would give them his benediction likewise, and all that were present, and in them the whole body of his subjects; in compliance with which request he, with some difficulty, raised himself, and all falling on their knees, he blessed them fervently. Then they arose and departed.

Silence fell upon the palace; night wore slowly away. Charles tossed upon his bed racked with pain, but no complaint escaped his lips. Those who watched him in the semi-darkened room heard him ask God to accept his sufferings in atonement for his sins. Then, speaking aloud, he declared himself weary of life, and hoped soon to reach a better world. Courteous to the last, he begged pardon for the trouble he gave, inasmuch as he was long in dying. And anon he slumbered, and quickly woke again in agony and prayed with zeal. Never had time moved with slower passage for him; not hours, but weeks, seemed to elapse between each stroke of the clock; and yet around him was darkness and tardy night. But after much weary waiting, morning was at hand, the time-piece struck six. "Draw the curtains," said the dying man, "that I may once more see day." The grey light of a February dawn, scarce brightened to eastward a cheerless sky; but he hailed this herald of sunrise with infinite relief and terrible regret; relief that he had lived to see another day; regret that no more morns should break for him.

His soul tore itself from his body with fierce struggles and bitter pain. It was hard for him to die, but he composed himself to enter eternity "with the piety becoming a Christian, and the resolution becoming a king;" as his brother narrates. About ten o'clock on Friday morning, February 6th, 1685, he found relief in unconsciousness; before midday chimed he was dead. He had reached the fifty-fifth year of his life, and the twenty-fifth year of his reign.

His illegitimate progeny was numerous, numbering fifteen, besides those who died in infancy. These were the Duke of Monmouth and a daughter married to William Sarsfield, children of Lucy Walters; the Dukes of Southampton, Grafton, and Northumberland, the Countesses of Litchfield and of Sussex, and a daughter Barbara, who became a nun, children of the Duchess of Cleveland; the Duke of Richmond, son of the Duchess of Portsmouth; the Duke of St. Albans, and a son James, children of Nell Gwynn; Lady Derwentwater, daughter of Moll Davis; the Countess of Yarmouth, daughter of Lady Shannon; and the Earl of Plymouth, son of Catherine Peg.

For seven days the remains of the late king lay in state; on the eighth they were placed in Westminster Abbey. The ceremony was of necessity conducted in a semi-private manner for by reason of his majesty dying in the Catholic religion, his brother considered it desirable the ceremonies prescribed for the occasion by the English church should be dispensed with. Therefore, in order to avoid disputes or scandal, the king was laid in the tomb without ostentation. At night his remains were carried from the painted chamber in Westminster sanctuary to the abbey. The procession, headed by the servants of the nobility, of James II., and his queen, of the dowager queen, and of the late king, was followed by the barons, bishops, and, peers according to their rank; the officers of the household, and the Archbishop of Canterbury. Then came all that was mortal of his late majesty, borne under a canopy of velvet, supported by six gentlemen of the privy chamber, the pall being held by six earls. Prince George of Denmark--subsequently husband of Queen Anne--acted as chief mourner, attended by the Dukes of Somerset and Beaufort, and sixteen earls. One of the kings of Arms carried the crown and cushion, the train being closed by the king's band of gentlemen pensioners, and the yeomen of the guard.

At the abbey entrance the dean and prebendaries, attended by torch bearers, and followed by a surpliced choir, met the remains, and joined the procession, the slow pacing figures of which seemed spectral in this hour and place; then the sad cortege passed solemnly through the grey old abbey, the choir chanting sorrowfully the while, the yellow flare of torches marking the prevailing gloom. And being come to the chapel of Henry VII., the body of the merry monarch was suffered there to rest in peace.

www.bookjungle.com email: sales@bookjungle.com fax: 630-214-0564 mail: Book Jungle PO Box 2226 Champaign, IL 61825

The Codes Of Hammurabi And Moses
W. W. Davies

QTY

The discovery of the Hammurabi Code is one of the greatest achievements of archaeology, and is of paramount interest, not only to the student of the Bible, but also to all those interested in ancient history...

Religion   ISBN: *1-59462-338-4*   Pages:132   *MSRP $12.95*

The Theory of Moral Sentiments
Adam Smith

QTY

This work from 1749. contains original theories of conscience amd moral judgment and it is the foundation for systemof morals.

Philosophy ISBN: *1-59462-777-0*   Pages:536   *MSRP $19.95*

Jessica's First Prayer
Hesba Stretton

QTY

In a screened and secluded corner of one of the many railway-bridges which span the streets of London there could be seen a few years ago, from five o'clock every morning until half past eight, a tidily set-out coffee-stall, consisting of a trestle and board, upon which stood two large tin cans, with a small fire of charcoal burning under each so as to keep the coffee boiling during the early hours of the morning when the work-people were thronging into the city on their way to their daily toil...

Childrens   ISBN: *1-59462-373-2*   Pages:84   *MSRP $9.95*

My Life and Work
Henry Ford

QTY

Henry Ford revolutionized the world with his implementation of mass production for the Model T automobile. Gain valuable business insight into his life and work with his own auto-biography... "We have only started on our development of our country we have not as yet, with all our talk of wonderful progress, done more than scratch the surface. The progress has been wonderful enough but..."

Biographies/   ISBN: *1-59462-198-5*   Pages:300   *MSRP $21.95* www.bookjungle.com *email: sales@bookjungle.com fax: 630-214-0564 mail: Book Jungle PO Box 2226 Champaign, IL 61825*

The Art of Cross-Examination
Francis Wellman

QTY

I presume it is the experience of every author, after his first book is published upon an important subject, to be almost overwhelmed with a wealth of ideas and illustrations which could readily have been included in his book, and which to his own mind, at least, seem to make a second edition inevitable. Such certainly was the case with me; and when the first edition had reached its sixth impression in five months, I rejoiced to learn that it seemed to my publishers that the book had met with a sufficiently favorable reception to justify a second and considerably enlarged edition. ..

Reference ISBN: *1-59462-647-2*

Pages:412
MSRP *$19.95*

On the Duty of Civil Disobedience
Henry David Thoreau

QTY

Thoreau wrote his famous essay, On the Duty of Civil Disobedience, as a protest against an unjust but popular war and the immoral but popular institution of slave-owning. He did more than write—he declined to pay his taxes, and was hauled off to gaol in consequence. Who can say how much this refusal of his hastened the end of the war and of slavery ?

Law ISBN: *1-59462-747-9*

Pages:48
MSRP *$7.45*

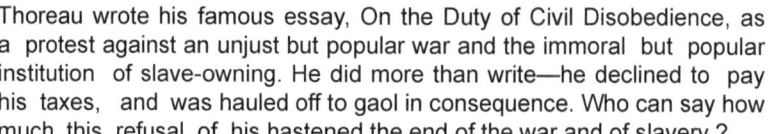

Dream Psychology Psychoanalysis for Beginners
Sigmund Freud

QTY

Sigmund Freud, born Sigismund Schlomo Freud (May 6, 1856 - September 23, 1939), was a Jewish-Austrian neurologist and psychiatrist who co-founded the psychoanalytic school of psychology. Freud is best known for his theories of the unconscious mind, especially involving the mechanism of repression; his redefinition of sexual desire as mobile and directed towards a wide variety of objects; and his therapeutic techniques, especially his understanding of transference in the therapeutic relationship and the presumed value of dreams as sources of insight into unconscious desires.

Psychology ISBN: *1-59462-905-6*

Pages:196
MSRP *$15.45*

The Miracle of Right Thought
Orison Swett Marden

QTY

Believe with all of your heart that you will do what you were made to do. When the mind has once formed the habit of holding cheerful, happy, prosperous pictures, it will not be easy to form the opposite habit. It does not matter how improbable or how far away this realization may see, or how dark the prospects may be, if we visualize them as best we can, as vividly as possible, hold tenaciously to them and vigorously struggle to attain them, they will gradually become actualized, realized in the life. But a desire, a longing without endeavor, a yearning abandoned or held indifferently will vanish without realization.

Self Help ISBN: *1-59462-644-8*

Pages:360
MSRP *$25.45*

www.bookjungle.com email: sales@bookjungle.com fax: 630-214-0564 mail: Book Jungle PO Box 2226 Champaign, IL 61825

QTY

| ☐ | **The Rosicrucian Cosmo-Conception Mystic Christianity** by *Max Heindel* | ISBN: *1-59462-188-8* | **$38.95** |

The Rosicrucian Cosmo-conception is not dogmatic, neither does it appeal to any other authority than the reason of the student. It is: not controversial, but is: sent forth in the, hope that it may help to clear...
New Age/Religion Pages 646

| ☐ | **Abandonment To Divine Providence** by *Jean-Pierre de Caussade* | ISBN: *1-59462-228-0* | **$25.95** |

"The Rev. Jean Pierre de Caussade was one of the most remarkable spiritual writers of the Society of Jesus in France in the 18th Century. His death took place at Toulouse in 1751. His works have gone through many editions and have been republished...
Inspirational/Religion Pages 400

| ☐ | **Mental Chemistry** by *Charles Haanel* | ISBN: *1-59462-192-6* | **$23.95** |

Mental Chemistry allows the change of material conditions by combining and appropriately utilizing the power of the mind. Much like applied chemistry creates something new and unique out of careful combinations of chemicals the mastery of mental chemistry...
New Age Pages 354

| ☐ | **The Letters of Robert Browning and Elizabeth Barret Barrett 1845-1846 vol II** | ISBN: *1-59462-193-4* | **$35.95** |

by *Robert Browning* and *Elizabeth Barrett*
Biographies Pages 596

| ☐ | **Gleanings In Genesis (volume I)** by *Arthur W. Pink* | ISBN: *1-59462-130-6* | **$27.45** |

Appropriately has Genesis been termed "the seed plot of the Bible" for in it we have, in germ form, almost all of the great doctrines which are afterwards fully developed in the books of Scripture which follow...
Religion/Inspirational Pages 420

| ☐ | **The Master Key** by *L. W. de Laurence* | ISBN: *1-59462-001-6* | **$30.95** |

In no branch of human knowledge has there been a more lively increase of the spirit of research during the past few years than in the study of Psychology, Concentration and Mental Discipline. The requests for authentic lessons in Thought Control, Mental Discipline and...
New Age/Business Pages 422

| ☐ | **The Lesser Key Of Solomon Goetia** by *L. W. de Laurence* | ISBN: *1-59462-092-X* | **$9.95** |

This translation of the first book of the "Lernegton" which is now for the first time made accessible to students of Talismanic Magic was done, after careful collation and edition, from numerous Ancient Manuscripts in Hebrew, Latin, and French...
New Age/Occult Pages 92

| ☐ | **Rubaiyat Of Omar Khayyam** by *Edward Fitzgerald* | ISBN: *1-59462-332-5* | **$13.95** |

Edward Fitzgerald, whom the world has already learned, in spite of his own efforts to remain within the shadow of anonymity, to look upon as one of the rarest poets of the century, was born at Bredfield, in Suffolk, on the 31st of March, 1809. He was the third son of John Purcell...
Music Pages 172

| ☐ | **Ancient Law** by *Henry Maine* | ISBN: *1-59462-128-4* | **$29.95** |

The chief object of the following pages is to indicate some of the earliest ideas of mankind, as they are reflected in Ancient Law, and to point out the relation of those ideas to modern thought.
Religion/History Pages 452

| ☐ | **Far-Away Stories** by *William J. Locke* | ISBN: *1-59462-129-2* | **$19.45** |

"Good wine needs no bush, but a collection of mixed vintages does. And this book is just such a collection. Some of the stories I do not want to remain buried for ever in the museum files of dead magazine-numbers an author's not unpardonable vanity..."
Fiction Pages 272

| ☐ | **Life of David Crockett** by *David Crockett* | ISBN: *1-59462-250-7* | **$27.45** |

"Colonel David Crockett was one of the most remarkable men of the times in which he lived. Born in humble life, but gifted with a strong will, an indomitable courage, and unremitting perseverance...
Biographies/New Age Pages 424

| ☐ | **Lip-Reading** by *Edward Nitchie* | ISBN: *1-59462-206-X* | **$25.95** |

Edward B. Nitchie, founder of the New York School for the Hard of Hearing, now the Nitchie School of Lip-Reading, Inc, wrote "LIP-READING Principles and Practice". The development and perfecting of this meritorious work on lip-reading was an undertaking...
How-to Pages 400

| ☐ | **A Handbook of Suggestive Therapeutics, Applied Hypnotism, Psychic Science** | ISBN: *1-59462-214-0* | **$24.95** |

by *Henry Munro*
Health/New Age/Health/Self-help Pages 376

| ☐ | **A Doll's House: and Two Other Plays** by *Henrik Ibsen* | ISBN: *1-59462-112-8* | **$19.95** |

Henrik Ibsen created this classic when in revolutionary 1848 Rome. Introducing some striking concepts in playwriting for the realist genre, this play has been studied the world over.
Fiction/Classics/Plays 308

| ☐ | **The Light of Asia** by *sir Edwin Arnold* | ISBN: *1-59462-204-3* | **$13.95** |

In this poetic masterpiece, Edwin Arnold describes the life and teachings of Buddha. The man who was to become known as Buddha to the world was born as Prince Gautama of India but he rejected the worldly riches and abandoned the reigns of power when...
Religion/History/Biographies Pages 170

| ☐ | **The Complete Works of Guy de Maupassant** by *Guy de Maupassant* | ISBN: *1-59462-157-8* | **$16.95** |

"For days and days, nights and nights, I had dreamed of that first kiss which was to consecrate our engagement, and I knew not on what spot I should put my lips..."
Fiction/Classics Pages 240

| ☐ | **The Art of Cross-Examination** by *Francis L. Wellman* | ISBN: *1-59462-309-0* | **$26.95** |

Written by a renowned trial lawyer, Wellman imparts his experience and uses case studies to explain how to use psychology to extract desired information through questioning.
How-to/Science/Reference Pages 408

| ☐ | **Answered or Unanswered?** by *Louisa Vaughan* | ISBN: *1-59462-248-5* | **$10.95** |

Miracles of Faith in China
Religion Pages 112

| ☐ | **The Edinburgh Lectures on Mental Science (1909)** by *Thomas* | ISBN: *1-59462-008-3* | **$11.95** |

This book contains the substance of a course of lectures recently given by the writer in the Queen Street Hall, Edinburgh. Its purpose is to indicate the Natural Principles governing the relation between Mental Action and Material Conditions...
New Age/Psychology Pages 148

| ☐ | **Ayesha** by *H. Rider Haggard* | ISBN: *1-59462-301-5* | **$24.95** |

Verily and indeed it is the unexpected that happens! Probably if there was one person upon the earth from whom the Editor of this, and of a certain previous history, did not expect to hear again...
Classics Pages 380

| ☐ | **Ayala's Angel** by *Anthony Trollope* | ISBN: *1-59462-352-X* | **$29.95** |

The two girls were both pretty, but Lucy who was twenty-one who supposed to be simple and comparatively unattractive, whereas Ayala was credited, as her Bombwhat romantic name might show, with poetic charm and a taste for romance. Ayala when her father died was nineteen...
Fiction Pages 484

| ☐ | **The American Commonwealth** by *James Bryce* | ISBN: *1-59462-286-8* | **$34.45** |

An interpretation of American democratic political theory. It examines political mechanics and society from the perspective of Scotsman James Bryce
Politics Pages 572

| ☐ | **Stories of the Pilgrims** by *Margaret P. Pumphrey* | ISBN: *1-59462-116-0* | **$17.95** |

This book explores pilgrims religious oppression in England as well as their escape to Holland and eventual crossing to America on the Mayflower, and their early days in New England...
History Pages 268

www.bookjungle.com *email: sales@bookjungle.com fax: 630-214-0564 mail: Book Jungle PO Box 2226 Champaign, IL 61825*

QTY

The Fasting Cure by *Sinclair Upton* ISBN: *1-59462-222-1* **$13.95**
In the Cosmopolitan Magazine for May, 1910, and in the Contemporary Review (London) for April, 1910, I published an article dealing with my experiences in fasting. I have written a great many magazine articles, but never one which attracted so much attention... *New Age/Self Help/Health Pages 164*

Hebrew Astrology by *Sepharial* ISBN: *1-59462-308-2* **$13.45**
In these days of advanced thinking it is a matter of common observation that we have left many of the old landmarks behind and that we are now pressing forward to greater heights and to a wider horizon than that which represented the mind-content of our progenitors... *Astrology Pages 144*

Thought Vibration or The Law of Attraction in the Thought World ISBN: *1-59462-127-6* **$12.95**
by *William Walker Atkinson* *Psychology/Religion Pages 144*

Optimism by *Helen Keller* ISBN: *1-59462-108-X* **$15.95**
Helen Keller was blind, deaf, and mute since 19 months old, yet famously learned how to overcome these handicaps, communicate with the world, and spread her lectures promoting optimism. An inspiring read for everyone... *Biographies/Inspirational Pages 84*

Sara Crewe by *Frances Burnett* ISBN: *1-59462-360-0* **$9.45**
In the first place, Miss Minchin lived in London. Her home was a large, dull, tall one, in a large, dull square, where all the houses were alike, and all the sparrows were alike, and where all the door-knockers made the same heavy sound... *Childrens/Classic Pages 88*

The Autobiography of Benjamin Franklin by *Benjamin Franklin* ISBN: *1-59462-135-7* **$24.95**
The Autobiography of Benjamin Franklin has probably been more extensively read than any other American historical work, and no other book of its kind has had such ups and downs of fortune. Franklin lived for many years in England, where he was agent... *Biographies/History Pages 332*

Name	
Email	
Telephone	
Address	
City, State ZIP	

☐ Credit Card   ☐ Check / Money Order

Credit Card Number	
Expiration Date	
Signature	

Please Mail to: Book Jungle
PO Box 2226
Champaign, IL 61825
or Fax to: 630-214-0564

ORDERING INFORMATION

web: *www.bookjungle.com*
email: *sales@bookjungle.com*
fax: *630-214-0564*
mail: *Book Jungle PO Box 2226 Champaign, IL 61825*
or PayPal *to sales@bookjungle.com*

Please contact us for bulk discounts

DIRECT-ORDER TERMS

**20% Discount if You Order
Two or More Books**
Free Domestic Shipping!
Accepted: Master Card, Visa,
Discover, American Express

www.ingramcontent.com/pod-product-compliance
Lightning Source LLC
Chambersburg PA
CBHW081210230426
43666CB00015B/2705